*A Short History of Electoral Systems
in Western Europe*

A Short History of Electoral Systems in Western Europe

ANDREW McLAREN CARSTAIRS

Formerly Senior Lecturer, Department of Modern History,
University of Dundee

London
GEORGE ALLEN & UNWIN
Boston   Sydney

First published in 1980

GEORGE ALLEN & UNWIN LTD
40 Museum Street, London WC1A 1LU

© Andrew McLaren Carstairs, 1980

British Library Cataloguing in Publication Data

Carstairs, Andrew McLaren
  A short history of electoral systems in Western
  Europe.
  1. Elections – Europe – History
  I. Title
  324'.21'094   JN94.A95   80-40547

  ISBN 0-04-324006-2

Set in 10 on 11 point Plantin by Trade Linotype Ltd, Birmingham
and printed in Great Britain
by Lowe & Brydone Limited, Thetford, Norfolk

Contents

List of Tables

Acknowledgements

The author wishes to express his thanks to the staffs of the University Library, Dundee, and of the British Library, for securing the literature necessary for this work, much of it from libraries abroad; and also to the staffs of the International Centre for Parliamentary Documentation, Inter-Parliamentary Union, Geneva, and of the Bibliothèque Royale Albert 1er, Brussels, for assistance given during visits to those institutions.

Introduction

The years 1864 and 1885 may be regarded as milestones in the history of electoral systems in the parliaments of Europe, because in each of these years there was held an international conference to consider and assess new ideas which had recently been put forward on the subject of electoral reform.

In September 1864, in Amsterdam, a conference of the Association Internationale pour le Progrès des Sciences Sociales devoted two days to the examination of the system of proportional representation which had recently been devised by the English barrister Thomas Hare. This system, which has come to be known as the 'single transferable vote', is the system which has been most widely advocated in English-speaking countries ever since. The conference was significant, however, not because of the specific recommendations which were examined and discussed, but because it marked the growth of a general movement in favour of proportional representation in place of the majority systems which had, to an increasingly notorious extent, resulted in some countries in the election of parliaments which did not fairly represent the opinions of electors, and in which minorities were often greatly under-represented.

Hare's publications (from 1857 onwards) were not the first occasion on which the principles of proportional representation, or representation of minorities, had been advocated. Origins of ideas are inevitably hard to trace, but reference was commonly made to two individuals in particular who seem to have been among the first to make an impact with their ideas on the subject. One of these was the 'Radical Duke' of Richmond who, in 1780, proposed in the British House of Lords that for elections to the House of Commons the country should be divided into constituencies as nearly equal in population as possible. This was not, of course, proportional representation of parties or of minorities, but ensured only that each member should represent an equal number of the population; but the duke's proposals sowed the idea of proportionality. Also, the method he advocated, which was to divide the total population by the number of seats in parliament, and arrive at a quota or quotient of population which each member should represent, was basically the same as the method used later in some systems of proportional representation, including the single transferable vote.

The other individual, more famous and more widely quoted than the 'Radical Duke', was the Marquis de Mirabeau who, in a speech made to the Assembly of Provence in 1789, put forward the argument that the composition of a parliament should reflect in accurate detail the will of the electorate. Just as a map reproduces on a small scale the various features of a landscape, so should a parliament reproduce on a small scale the desires of the electors. Parliament should be a mirror of the political opinions of the whole electorate.

Earlier than Mirabeau, two French mathematicians, Jean-Charles de Borda (in 1770) and the Marquis de Condorcet (in 1785), had been the first (effectively at least) to draw attention to some technical problems involved in securing fair and accurate results from elections. It was Mirabeau's imagery which fired the imagination, but it was largely the practical difficulties of putting such ideas into effect which were responsible for a delay of some generations before they were applied to elections for any parliamentary institutions in Europe.

Meanwhile, many varieties of electoral system were devised, and some experiments in proportional representation occasionally took place. Histories of these were later compiled by the electoral reformers Ernest Naville in Switzerland and Maurice Vernes in France. But it was with the publications of Thomas Hare and John Stuart Mill in England that the movement in favour of proportional representation may be regarded as having 'taken off into sustained growth'.

The Hare system, in its earlier versions, proposed that the whole nation should be a single constituency, and this novel suggestion deterred many potential supporters of proportional representation. Also, in its earlier forms, the results of the system were liable to be influenced by random factors and chance, and it was thus open to criticism by those who sought a system which would be consistent and accurate as well as fair. There was therefore much debate in the 1860s and 1870s about the relative merits of alternative electoral systems. A principal forum for this discussion was Switzerland, where the distorted representation of communities divided by race, language and religion created political difficulties which were particularly acute. In 1865 the Association Réformiste de Genève was founded, and from 1868 onwards its bulletins disseminated ideas on the subject derived from leading thinkers in many countries. In 1867 the association adopted as its recommended system of proportional representation a *list* system of election, devised (perhaps first) by Victor Considérant in France in 1834, and developed by Antoine Morin in Switzerland in 1862.

In Belgium, where communities were also deeply divided by language, an electoral reform society was formed in 1881, entitled the Association Réformiste pour l'Adoption de la Représentation Proportionnelle. One of its founders was Victor D'Hondt, whose system of proportional represen-tation of parties was formulated in the following year. One of the earliest acts of the new Belgian association was to convene an international conference on electoral reform, which was held in Antwerp on 7, 8 and 9 August 1885. Its proceedings were recorded in the monthly journal *La Représentation proportionnelle*, published by the Belgian association. It was expected, and perhaps intended, that this occasion would provide the platform for a debate between the supporters of the Hare and the D'Hondt systems, and a decision in favour of one or the other.

So far as the debate between the Hare and D'Hondt systems was concerned, the conference of 1885 was a disappointment. The most active delegates were those from Switzerland, France and Belgium, and although there were representatives also from Germany, Italy, Holland and Denmark there was none from the recently formed Proportional Representation Society in England. Sir John Lubbock, chairman of that society, wrote to express his regrets at not being able to attend, and the only British contribution was a paper written by Thomas Hare, which was read to the conference in the writer's absence.

As regards a choice between electoral systems, the conference came to a decision in favour of the D'Hondt system. At the end of the proceedings a motion was proposed by Maurice Vernes of France and seconded by Eduard Hagenbach-Bischoff of Switzerland, and was carried without dissent by members of the conference. The terms of the resolution, translated from the French, were as follows:

The international conference on proportional representation, convened by the Association Réformiste Belge, and assembled at Antwerp on 7, 8 and 9 August 1885, resolves:

1 that the system of elections by absolute majorities violates the liberty of the elector, provokes fraud and corruption, and can give a majority of seats to a minority of the electorate;

2 that proportional representation is the only means of assuring power to the real majority of the country, an effective voice to minorities, and exact representation to all significant groups of the electorate;

3 that while the particular needs of each country are recognised, the D'Hondt system of competing lists with divisors, adopted by the Belgian association, is a considerable advance on the systems previously proposed, and constitutes a practical and efficient means of achieving proportional representation.

The D'Hondt system, and variations of the party-list and divisor systems on which it is based, are those which have universally been adopted in those countries of Continental Europe which have discarded majority systems in favour of proportional representation, and the decisions of 1885 must have contributed to this outcome. Appropriately, it was in Belgium that the system devised by the Belgian, Victor D'Hondt, was first adopted, in 1899. By 1920 proportional representation had been adopted in most countries of Western Europe, and it is with the history of electoral systems in these countries that this work is mainly concerned.

A distinct feature of the electoral systems in Europe is the variety of devices which were adopted. Although their basic principles were largely similar, based on D'Hondt, each country adopted a system which in certain important respects was different from every system adopted anywhere else. The differences are due to the variety of circumstances which influenced the process of electoral reform in each country. No electoral system is adopted without reference to the framework of constitutional and political institutions within which it must operate; and these in turn have been shaped by history and custom, and by internal relations between communities which may differ in race, language and religion. These aspects of historical development must be taken into account when one seeks to understand the changes in the electoral systems in each country.

It is also generally the experience that changes in electoral systems were brought about as a result of practical compromises between divergent political interests, or in pursuit of the aims of a particular political party. It would not be correct to assume, however, that political idealism and the search for theoretical perfection in electoral systems did not play a significant part in the progress of electoral reform. It was, after all, some variation of systems devised by the theorists which was generally adopted, particularly those devised by Thomas Hare, Victor D'Hondt, Eduard Hagenbach-Bischoff and A. Sainte-Laguë.

In Part One of this book a brief analysis will be given of the principal types of electoral system which were used in Western Europe. It is not possible to adhere to any chronological scheme, since different countries were at any given time at different stages of development. Instead, the countries of Western Europe will thereafter be grouped in a manner suggested by some features which they have in common.

Part Two is devoted to Belgium and the Netherlands, starting with Belgium, which was the first country in Europe to establish proportional representation for its popular assembly. The historical evolution of these two countries was influenced by their unification at the Congress of Vienna in 1815, and the independence movement in Belgium thereafter. (Luxemburg is omitted, although it has an interesting electoral system which enables electors to exercise an effective choice between individual candidates as well as parties. Apart from a chapter by Dieter Nohlen in *Die Wahl der Parlamente*, the handbook referred to below, there is a shortage of literature on the history of this electoral system.)

Part Three includes the Scandinavian countries, and also their Nordic neighbour, Finland. The dynastic and constitutional relationships between the Scandinavian countries had a profound influence on their constitutional histories, and a bearing on the electoral systems which they adopted. The parliamentary histories of Norway and Finland were closely linked with the struggles for independence in those two countries. One feature which the Scandinavian countries had in common was that, unlike most other countries in Europe which adopted proportional representation, they were each largely homogeneous in race, language and religion, and were in this respect not faced with political problems arising out of differences between communities. In Finland there existed a Swedish or Swedish-speaking minority which was better educated and more affluent than the Finns, but this was a factor of diminishing importance. All the Scandinavian countries eventually adopted a version of the electoral system devised in 1910 by the Frenchman A.Sainte-Laguë, while Finland adopted a distinctive system unique in Europe.

Part Four refers to Austria and Switzerland, which are examples of states deeply divided between different races, languages and religions, and which carried the principles of proportional representation further than most other countries.

Part Five includes the Great Powers on the Continent, Italy, Germany and France, each of which had a quite distinct history of electoral systems and of electoral reforms.

Part Six relates to Ireland and the United Kingdom. The Republic of Ireland is the only independent nation in Western Europe, apart from Denmark and Malta, in which the single transferable vote has been adopted for parliamentary election. It was in the United Kingdom that the system was devised, and the history of the electoral reform movement in the United Kingdom is largely a history of unsuccessful attempts to have this system adopted for elections to the UK parliament.

During the long periods of dictatorship in modern Spain and Portugal electoral systems in those countries were incapable of representing the political views of the population, and they have therefore not been included in this study.

The focus throughout is on the popular or lower chamber of parliament, where more than one chamber exists. Upper chambers (in some countries called the second chamber, and in others the first) are rarely intended to be fairly representative of the whole population, and where elections for such chambers take place at all the precise nature of the electoral system is rarely of major importance. There are exceptions, and where the composition of the upper chamber, or elections to that chamber, have a bearing on proposals for electoral reform, these circumstances will be taken into account. Also excluded are elections to the European Parliament. It is intended that a common electoral system should be adopted for future elections to this parliament, and if this is achieved the elections held in 1979 may be the only ones using the systems then adopted separately in each country.

REFERENCES: INTRODUCTION

There is no work of reference in English which corresponds to the monumental series edited by Dolf Sternberger and Bernard Vogel, *Die Wahl der Parlamente und anderer Staatsorgane: Ein Handbuch* (Volume I, Europe). This has superseded the earlier standard work by Karl Braunias, *Das Parlamentarische Wahlrecht*. The handbook reviews the political theory of democracy, examines the various electoral systems which have been used, and gives a history of the electoral system in each country, accompanied by lists of documentary sources, historical statistics of election results and extensive bibliographies.

As a guide to the constitutional context within which parliamentary institutions have been developed and electoral systems introduced, there is the series edited by Albert B. Blaustein and Gisbert Flanz, *Constitutions of the Countries of the World*. This gives a chronological summary of past constitutional developments, and is continuously brought up to date.

For histories of election results reference may be made to Stein Rokkan and Jean Meyriat (eds), *International Guide to Electoral Statistics*, and to T. Mackie and R. Rose (eds), *The International Almanac of Electoral History*, the first of which indicates in tabular form the main changes which have taken place in the electoral systems used. For recent election results information is provided in *Keesings Contemporary Archives*. In these works only overall election results are given for each nation. If one wishes to examine in detail how an electoral system has operated and influenced the results it is necessary to have the figures for individual constituencies, and this information has to be sought in fuller reports or studies of particular elections.

PART ONE
Electoral Systems

1

The Earlier Electoral Systems

In the nations of Western Europe in the nineteenth century and in the earlier decades of the twentieth century there was a general movement in the direction of more democratic political institutions which took several different forms, each of which tended to reinforce the others. There was a movement for the establishment or strengthening of parliamentary institutions, with governments becoming responsible to parliaments, and parliaments increasingly able to influence or control the appointment of governments. Extensions of the franchise for parliamentary elections enabled an increasingly large proportion of the population to gain representation in parliament. The growth of political parties, sometimes at first in parliament itself and later in the electorate as a whole, made possible the more effective representation of particular sections of the population, the development of more coherent political policies and the exercise of greater influence on governments. With these developments it became a matter of increasing concern that the elected members of parliament and the parties they supported should fairly represent the various interests and opinions of the electorate. The struggle to attain any one of these objectives in particular might be achieved in a different order. The history of the electoral systems in each country will have to take into account the constitutional and political context within which it operated; but this section of the work is concerned in the first place with the various electoral systems by means of which it was possible for electors to gain representation in parliament.

In Western Europe systems of proportional representation were introduced for parliamentary elections between 1899 and 1920, and these have continued, with some modifications and interruptions, until the present day. Before the establishment of proportional representation (hereafter, in accordance with common practice, abbreviated to PR), there was a considerable variety of electoral systems in the different countries. Unlike the United Kingdom, most countries had systems which required that elections should be by an absolute majority in a first ballot, and if this did not result in the election of the required number of members one or more additional ballots were required, the rules for which varied considerably. In some countries which provided for two-ballot or multi-ballot elections these were held in single-member constituencies, as in Austria, Germany, Italy, the Netherlands and Norway. In others, which included Belgium, Luxemburg and Switzerland, they were held in multi-member constituencies. Only in Denmark and Sweden were elections held in single-member constituencies in a single ballot, with a simple or relative majority ('first past the post') sufficing in that ballot. In Finland, the remaining country in Western Europe which adopted PR, there was no period of transition between an Estates system and a single-chamber parliament elected by a system of proportional representation.

The requirement of two or more ballots was intended to avoid a situation in which a member is returned to parliament with the support of only a minority of electors in a constituency. The additional ballot or ballots were intended to give a further opportunity for the election of a member by an absolute majority, after some members had voluntarily withdrawn, or else had been eliminated in accordance with previously established rules. If there was still no absolute majority, then a relative majority would have to suffice.

However, it became increasingly evident in many countries that while such a system might lead to fairer representation in a particular constituency, it did not necessarily lead to fairer representation in parliament of the different political parties which existed in the nation as a whole. The geographical distribution of votes for parties, or more precisely their distribution between different constituencies, might be of such a kind that a party which had a large number of votes in the nation (or a region) as a whole, might not return a correspondingly large number of members to parliament; and indeed a party with more votes than another might return fewer members. Table 1.1 is intended to illustrate how the distribution of votes can distort the representation of parties, and why the requirement of absolute majorities in each constituency may fail to provide any remedy.

Suppose three parties, A, B and C, contest an election in which there are 6 million electors divided between 100 constituencies, with exactly 60,000 electors in each. For simplicity it is assumed that the nation can be divided into southern and northern constituencies, and that within each of these areas the votes of each party are evenly divided between the individual constituencies. Then party A, which has a substantial majority of votes in the fifty-one southern constituencies, wins every seat there; and party B, which has a substantial majority of votes in the forty-nine northern constituencies, wins every seat there. In this example party A

Table 1.1 *Absolute majorities and disproportionate representation*

	Party A	Party B	Party C	Total
51 southern constituencies				
Votes	1,560,600	275,400	1,224,000	3,060,000
% of votes	51	9	40	100
Seats	51	0	0	51
49 northern constituencies				
Votes	235,200	1,587,600	1,117,200	2,940,000
% of votes	8	54	38	100
Seats	0	49	0	49
All constituencies				
Votes	1,795,800	1,863,000	2,341,200	6,000,000
% of votes	30	31	39	100
Seats	51	49	0	100

Result:

	Percentage of Votes	Percentage of Seats
Party A	30	51
Party B	31	49
Party C	39	0

has the fewest votes but an absolute majority of seats, while party C has more votes than either of the other two parties, but has no representation at all. In every constituency one party has an absolute majority, but in the country as a whole there is a great discrepancy between votes and seats.

In practice, of course, it is likely that where elections are held in single-member constituencies support for each party in each area will be concentrated more heavily in some constituencies than in others, and that each party will succeed in gaining at least some representation. The more numerous the total members of parliament, and the more numerous (and smaller) the individual constituencies, the more likely will it be that each party, including minorities, will gain representation. Nevertheless, the representation which each party gains will be determined not simply by the number of votes it is given, but by how these votes are distributed. A disproportionately small number of seats will be gained by a party whose votes are widely dispersed among constituencies in which it is in a minority, or else are heavily concentrated in a small number of constituencies where they pile up much larger majorities than are needed for the election of members.

When elections are held in multi-member constituencies the discrepancies which arise between votes and seats in majority elections are not essentially different, but they tend to be exaggerated. In the Western European countries the 'block vote' was used in such constituencies, which meant that each elector had as many votes as there were seats in the constituency. It commonly happened that electors would cast all their votes for candidates of the same party, that all candidates of one party would have a majority of votes over all candidates of any other party, and that all seats would be gained by members of the same party. A slight 'swing' in votes from one election to another might suffice to displace every sitting member of one party by members elected by their opponents. It was the experience of anomalous results of this kind, depriving entire communities of representation, as it did on occasions in the canton of Geneva, which gave impetus in the nineteenth century to the movement for electoral reform.

One suggested remedy for such anomalies in multi-member constituencies was the adoption of the system of the 'limited vote'. Under this system, electors were not permitted to vote for as many candidates as there were seats, but only for fewer candidates. It was intended that this should limit the number of members any one party could elect, and therefore make it correspondingly easier for smaller parties to gain at least some representation. This system was adopted for elections in some constituencies in the United Kingdom between 1867 and 1885, but was not adopted for parliamentary elections in the Continental countries before the adoption of PR. The system was not, in fact, appropriate for the achievement of a fairer representation of parties, and the reasons for this may be demonstrated by a practical example.

Suppose there is a multi-member constituency in which three members are to be elected, but each elector may cast only two votes. There are 46,000 electors, and the total possible number of votes is therefore 92,000. The election is contested by two parties, of which party A is supported by 30,000 electors (and 60,000 votes), and party B by 16,000 electors (and 32,000 votes). Examples are given in Table 1.2 of three possible results of an election. These examples show that the device of the limited vote can only offer the possibility that seats may be more fairly distributed to minorities than otherwise, and cannot exclude the possibility that they will be just as unfairly distributed as under the 'block vote'. They also show that the system may not result in a proportional allocation of seats. In such an election a reasonably proportional result would be achieved if party A obtained two seats and party B obtained one, but it happens that this result was not achieved in any of the examples given.

Table 1.2 *Limited vote elections*

Election 1	Party A		Party B	
	Candidate	Votes	Candidate	Votes
	a	20,000*	d	16,000
	b	20,000*	e	16,000
	c	20,000*		
		60,000		32,000
Result	3 seats		no seat	
Election 2				
	a	30,000*	d	16,000*
	b	15,000	e	16,000*
	c	15,000		
		60,000		32,000
Result	1 seat		2 seats	
Election 3				
	a	30,000*	d	11,000
	b	15,000*	e	11,000
	c	15,000*	f	10,000
		60,000		32,000
Result	3 seats		no seat	

(Asterisks denote successful candidates.)

One of the defects of this system is that the results can depend on a deliberate and organised manipulation of votes. A party will seek to estimate accurately the total number of votes their candidates may expect to gain, and therefore the optimum number of candidates they should nominate – neither too many, so that the votes are too thinly spread between them, nor too few, so that large numbers of votes are wasted. Equally important, votes must be evenly spread between them, so that each receives the minimum number of votes required for election. In Election 1, party A secured a favourable distribution of votes and captured all three seats, while in Election 2 party B succeeded in gaining two seats out of three, in spite of having far fewer votes than party A.

When the limited vote was in operation in the United Kingdom, the Liberal Party 'caucus' in Birmingham acquired much skill in directing its supporters how to vote, so that too many votes were not given to one candidate and too few to another. Such manipulation discredited the limited vote system, and led to its discontinuance in 1885. This was perhaps one reason why no similar system was adopted on the Continent.

Another device intended, like the limited vote, to improve the chances of minorities in multi-member constituencies, is the 'cumulative vote', that is to say, a method which entitles an elector to cast two or more votes in favour of one candidate. For purposes of party elections this system has defects similar to the limited vote, since the results will depend on the number of each party's candidates and the manner in which votes are distributed between them. This device is, however, used in certain proportional systems to allocate seats between individual candidates.

2

Party-List Systems of Proportional Representation

The earliest types of proportional systems were based on the use of 'quotas'. When it had been ascertained, after an election, how many votes had been cast, a calculation was made of the number of votes required to gain a single seat, and any candidate who gained this number of votes was entitled to the allocation of one seat. In party-list systems of election, each party was entitled to one seat for every quota of votes which was cast in favour of the list of candidates nominated by that party.

The first problem was how to calculate the quota. The earliest type of quota was obtained simply by dividing the total number of votes by the total number of seats. In the United Kingdom this is called the 'Hare' quota, after Thomas Hare, who used it in conjunction with the system of the single transferable vote which he devised. On the Continent it is commonly called the 'simple' or the 'natural' quota. However, for some purposes this quota proved to be unsatisfactory. For the allocation of seats, it established not the *minimum* number of votes necessary to gain one seat, but the *maximum* number of votes which all successful candidates could possibly gain. If there were five seats and 60 votes, the Hare quota would be 12. This number of votes could be gained by five candidates, but only if each obtained exactly the same number of votes (i.e. 12 votes), and no other candidates obtained any.

In practice, therefore, this was a quota which could be gained only by fewer candidates than there were seats. It was to help to solve this problem that Henry Droop, an English barrister, devised another quota, which was obtained by dividing the total number of votes, not by the number of seats, but by the number of seats *plus one*, and either rounding to the next higher number or *adding one*. Thus, in the example given, 60 votes would be divided by 6 (number of seats plus one), and one would be added to the result, making a quota of 11 votes. Any candidate who obtained 11 votes was bound to be elected. If the votes had been divided by 6 *without* adding one, then the quota would have been 10, and it would be just possible for six candidates to obtain 10 votes each, so that no one candidate could be certain of the allocation of one of the five seats. Therefore, the minimum quota had to be more than 10. In the United Kingdom this is called the 'Droop' quota after its inventor. On the Continent it is called after Eduard Hagenbach-Bischoff, who became the chief advocate of its use in conjunction with the D'Hondt system of election.

It is an advantage of the Droop quota that in the first stage of an election it immediately allocates more seats to candidates than is possible with the Hare quota. The smaller the quota, the more easily is it attained, and the larger the number of candidates who can attain it at a first count of the votes. Even so, it commonly happens that when the Droop quota is used fewer candidates gain the requisite quota than there are seats to be allocated. How many do gain the quota depends on how many candidates there are, and how the votes are distributed between them. In order to allocate as many seats as possible at the first count some electoral systems therefore use quotas which are still smaller than the Droop quota. An example of this is what is called the Imperiali quota, which is obtained by dividing the total number of votes by the total number of seats *plus two*, instead of plus one. The drawback of this is that while the Droop quota is the minimum quota which is bound to win a seat, any smaller quota may result in more quotas being gained than there are seats to be allocated. In such a case the electoral count has to be carried out again, using a higher quota.

When fewer quotas are gained in a first count than there are seats to be allocated, some method must be used to allocate the remaining seats. The first solution to this problem was what is known as the method of the 'largest remainder'. If each party submits a list of candidates, and if after the first allocation of seats by means of a quota some seats remain unallocated, then each remaining seat is allocated to the party with the largest remainder of votes. This is illustrated in Table 2.1, which shows what happens when the Hare quota is used, but the same principle applies whatever the quota may be.

In the election illustrated by the table, three seats are to be allocated,

Table 2.1 *Proportional representation of parties:*
quota system and 'largest remainder'

Party	Votes	Quotas	Remainder of votes
A	80	1	30
B	36	0	36
C	34	0	34

150 votes are cast, and the Hare quota is therefore 150 votes divided by 3, or 50 votes. After each party's votes have been divided by the quota, A achieves one quota and therefore one seat, but the other two parties do not achieve a quota. Two seats remain to be allocated. Party B has the largest remainder, and is allocated the next seat. Party C has the next highest remainder, and is allocated the third seat.

Result:	Party A	1 seat
	Party B	1 seat
	Party C	1 seat

In this example the allocations are such that parties B and C, which jointly have fewer votes than party A (jointly 70 votes against 80), have twice as many seats. The number of votes party A has gained for each seat it has been allocated is more than twice as great as for either party B or party C.

It is to rectify this anomaly that instead of the 'largest remainder' system the allocation of remaining seats may take place on the basis of which party, after an additional seat has been allocated to it, will have the 'highest average' of votes for each seat it has gained. In Table 2.1 party A has one quota seat, and if it is allocated one more seat it will have two seats and an average of 40 votes for each seat. Party B has no quota seat, and if it is allocated one seat it will have an 'average' of 36 votes for each seat. Similarly, party C would have an 'average' of 34 votes. Party A would have the 'highest average' of votes per seat, and is therefore entitled to the first remaining seat to be allocated. Party B would have the second 'highest average', and is therefore entitled to the next remaining seat.

Result:	Party A	2 seats
	Party B	1 seat
	Party C	no seat

It may be noticed that the largest remainder system favours the smaller parties, and the highest average system favours the larger party. Since the way in which electoral systems favour parties of different sizes is very commonly the chief criterion by which they are compared, it will be as well to demonstrate further this important distinction between the two systems, this time using the Droop instead of the Hare quota.

Suppose there are six seats to be allocated; four parties, A, B, C and D are in contention; and there are 1,765 votes. The Droop quota is therefore 1,765 votes divided by 7 (number of seats *plus one*), which, when rounded to the next highest whole number, is 253. Possible elections which enable a comparison to be made of the largest remainder and

Table 2.2   *Quota system and 'largest remainder'*

Party	Votes	Quotas	Remainder of votes
A	1,000	3	241*
B	430	1	177
C	210	0	210*
D	125	0	125

highest average systems are described in the Tables 2.2 and 2.3. In Table 2.2 Party A has the largest remainder of votes, and party C the second largest. These two parties therefore receive the remaining two seats.

Result: Party A   4 seats
            Party B   1 seat
            Party C   1 seat
            Party D   no seat

Table 2.3   *Quota system and 'highest average'*

Party	Votes	Quotas	Next seat to be allocated	Average votes per seat with the additional seat
A	1,000	3	4th	250*
B	430	1	2nd	215*
C	210	0	1st	210
D	125	0	1st	125

In Table 2.3 Party A has the highest average of votes per seat after the addition of one seat beyond the quota, and therefore receives the first additional seat. Party B has the second-highest average, and receives the second additional seat.

Result: Party A   4 seats
            Party B   2 seats
            Party C   no seat
            Party D   no seat

Again, a smaller party does better under the 'largest remainder' system than under the 'highest average' system.

We have now, by this route, arrived at the D'Hondt system of election, named after the Belgian, Victor D'Hondt, who was not actually its first inventor but was mainly responsible for its adoption as the system of proportional representation most widely used in Europe. It is based on the same principle as the 'highest average' method, and it has the same results. The system can be demonstrated by setting out in a table the *average* number of votes per seat for each party, corresponding to the successive number of seats which the party may gain. In Table 2.4 the same set of party votes is used as before. Seats are allocated from the

Table 2.4   *D'Hondt as a 'highest average' system*

Party	Average votes per seat for					
	1 seat	*2 seats*	*3 seats*	*4 seats*	*5 seats*	*6 seats*
A	1,000*	500·0*	333·3*	250·0*	200·0	166·7
B	430*	215·0*	143·3	107·5	86·0	71·7
C	210	105·0	70·0	52·5	42·0	35·0
D	125	62·5	41·7	31·25	25·0	20·8

outset by the system of the 'highest average', without any use of a quota. Each successive seat, starting from the first, is allocated to the party which, after the allocation of an additional seat, will have the highest average of votes per seat. At first, of course, no party will have any seat, and if one seat is allocated party A will have the highest 'average' with 1,000 votes per seat. After the allocation of an additional seat, party A will still, with an average of 500 votes per seat, have the highest average, and will therefore obtain a second seat before any other party gains any. Party B will gain the third seat, party A the fourth, and so on. The asterisks show how the first six seats will be allocated, and this is exactly the same result as in Table 2.3. Table 2.4 serves to allocate to these parties any number of seats up to nine, and could be extended as required to allocate larger numbers.

A system attributed to Eduard Hagenbach-Bischoff is designed to achieve the same results as D'Hondt's set of tables, but by a shorter and quicker route. In order to avoid the lengthy sets of tables and successive allocation of seats, one by one, when large numbers of seats are involved, the Droop quota is used to allocate as many seats as possible in a first distribution, in exactly the same way as in the highest average system shown in Table 2.3. For any previously determined number of seats, the use of the Droop quota allocates at once to each party the number of seats it is in any case bound to gain. It is for the allocation of the remaining seats that the D'Hondt tables are then applied. For each party it is ascertained from the tables what the average votes per seat would be for each additional seat, beyond those allocated by the Droop quota, and each successive seat is given to the party with the highest average. This D'Hondt/Hagenbach-Bischoff system is used in Switzerland, Belgium and some other countries, and is frequently the one used when a system is referred to simply as 'D'Hondt'.

Hagenbach-Bischoff used the Droop quota. The Hare quota gives exactly the same results, and is in fact used in Belgium and elsewhere, but fewer seats are usually allocated at the first distribution than if the Droop quota were used, and the allocation of seats from the D'Hondt tables is therefore slightly longer.

The versatility of the method which D'Hondt advocated can be demonstrated by another feature it possesses. While the Hare and the Droop quotas commonly allocate too few seats at a first distribution, and the Imperiali and other quotas may allocate too many, it is possible from the D'Hondt tables to identify a quota which will allocate exactly the required number of seats. In Table 2.4 a quota of 250 votes will allocate exactly five seats; a quota of 215 will allocate six seats; a quota of 210 will allocate seven; and so on. (To be more precise, a quota of more than 215 but not more than 250 will allocate five seats; a quota of more than 210 but not more than 215 will allocate six seats; and so on.) This is a function which some electoral reformers have desired that an electoral system should be capable of performing, and some electoral systems have made use of a quota determined in this way, but in practice it is not necessary to use this quota, because for any given pattern of voting the tables themselves can allocate the required number of seats.

The D'Hondt system is criticised because it favours the largest parties and does not ensure that the seats which are allocated to parties are proportional to the votes they have gained. Professor Christopher Hughes once drew attention to the fact that for many years an official Swiss publication explained the working of the D'Hondt system by means of an illustration which sought to show that if in an election with a total of 60,000 votes and ten members to be elected electors had voted for five parties on the pattern:

Party A	36,000 votes
Party B	12,000 votes
Party C	6,000 votes
Party D	5,000 votes
Party E	1,000 votes

then the allocation of seats would be:

Party A	6 seats
Party B	2 seats
Party C	1 seat
Party D	1 seat
Party E	no seat

This would be an understandable and acceptable result, and one which would evidently provide proportional representation, but the illustration

Table 2.5 *Disproportionality of the D'Hondt system?*

Party	Average votes per seat for						
	1 seat	2 seats	3 seats	4 seats	5 seats	6 seats	7 seats
A	36,000*	18,000*	12,000*	9,000*	7,200*	6,000*	5,143*
B	12,000*	6,000*	4,000				
C	6,000*	3,000					
D	5,000						
E	1,000						

was in fact wrong. The application of the D'Hondt system would result in an allocation of seats as indicated by Table 2.5. The result, as indicated by the asterisks, would be:

> Party A 7 seats
> Party B 2 seats
> Party C 1 seat
> Party D no seat
> Party E no seat.

This might, on the face of it at least, be regarded as an unfair and unproportional result, with a bias in favour of the larger parties and against the smaller.

This real or apparent bias in the D'Hondt system led to the introduction of other divisor systems to redress the balance in favour of the smaller parties. The principle of these systems is that if for a larger party which already has one seat or more it is made more difficult to gain each additional seat, then it will be made correspondingly easier for the smaller parties to gain seats. If, for example, in Table 2.4 the second divisor were 3 instead of 2, then for party A's second seat the quotient would be 333·3 instead of 500, and party B would gain a first seat before party A gained a second.

In the various divisor systems, a party's total vote is divided in succession by a particular set of divisors, and the quotients are used as 'priority values' for the allocation of each successive seat. The different divisor systems have different effects on the distribution of seats between parties.

The divisor system which is most widely used instead of the D'Hondt system to achieve results which are more favourable to the smaller parties is the system devised by the Frenchman A. Sainte-Laguë. Instead of divisors in the series 1, 2, 3, etc., divisors in the series 1, 3, 5, etc., are used, that is to say, the odd numbers from 1 onwards. This means that as each party gains an additional seat its 'priority value' for each additional seat thereafter is *reduced more* than it would have been under the

D'Hondt set of divisors. In other words, to gain as many seats as before, a larger party now has to have a larger number of votes in the first place. How the Sainte-Laguë system works by comparison with the D'Hondt system is illustrated in Table 2.6, which uses the same voting figures as in Tables 2.3 and 2.4. When six seats are to be allocated, the results

Table 2.6   *Sainte-Laguë divisor system*

Party	Quotients, or Priority Values				
	1st seat divisor	2nd seat divisor	3rd seat divisor	4th seat divisor	5th seat divisor
	1	3	5	7	9
A	1,000*	333·3*	200·0*	142·9	111·1
B	430*	143·3*	86·0	61·4	47·8
C	210*	70·0	42·0	30·0	23·3
D	125	41·7	25·0	17·9	13·9

under this system, as indicated by the asterisks, are as follows:

> Party A   3 seats
> Party B   2 seats
> Party C   1 seat
> Party D   no seat.

By comparison with the result under the D'Hondt system, as illustrated in Table 2.4, the Sainte-Laguë system gives one seat fewer to the largest party, A, and allocates it to the third-largest, C.

A point which is important for the understanding of the effects of the different divisor systems (and one which will be considered further in the chapter on proportionality) is that it is not the absolute size of each divisor which affects the allocation of seats, but the *ratios between* the successive divisors, or in other words the *relative increment* between one divisor and the next. Under the D'Hondt system, the second divisor is twice the size of the first; in the pure Sainte-Laguë system it is three times the size of the first. For the allocation of the *second* seat, the 'priority value' is more drastically reduced under the pure Sainte-Laguë system than it is under the D'Hondt system, and that second seat is correspondingly more difficult for a larger party to secure. Conversely, a *first* seat is easier for smaller parties to obtain under the Sainte-Laguë system than under the D'Hondt system.

Modified forms of the Sainte-Laguë system have been used since 1952 in Norway, Sweden and Denmark. In this modified form all the divisors except the first are the same as in the pure Sainte-Laguë system, but the first divisor is changed from 1 to 1·4, so that the relative increment between the first and second divisors is greater than under the D'Hondt system, but less than under the pure Sainte-Laguë system. This makes it slightly easier for a smaller party to secure a first seat than under the D'Hondt system, but makes it more difficult than under the pure Sainte-Laguë system.

Another divisor system which has been applied as part of the electoral system for parliamentary elections in Denmark, and is called the Danish system, makes use of divisors in the series 1, 4, 7, 10, etc. This is even more favourable to the smaller parties than any of the other divisor systems which have been mentioned.

Since some electoral systems are much more favourable to the larger rather than the smaller parties, any parties which are able to form alliances, and by this means increase their combined size for the purpose of an election, may gain more seats than they otherwise would. The term *apparentement* is given to party alliances which, for this reason, the electoral law recognises for the purpose of allocating seats to parties. The question of whether or not *apparentement* is permitted can be of great importance to the smaller parties. However, it is a drawback of *apparentement* that it can lead to purely electoral alliances which do not reflect any real co-operation of the parties in the pursuit of common political ends. It is another drawback that *apparentement* may consistently be used by some parties as a weapon against another to which they are hostile – commonly 'bourgeois' parties against socialist or social democratic parties. For these reasons electoral systems have sometimes been changed in order to benefit smaller parties in other ways, so that they will not have to resort to the device of *apparentement*, which then becomes unnecessary and can be abolished.

Finally, there is an electoral system used for parliamentary elections in the Weimar Republic which differs from all of those which have so far been mentioned. Under this system, sometimes called the 'automatic' system, the number of seats in parliament was not fixed in advance. Prior to an election a quota of votes was fixed for the allocation of each seat (in Weimar it was 60,000) and each party was entitled to one additional seat if its remaining votes exceeded half the quota. In an attempt to minimise the 'wastage' of votes which were ineffectual, remaining votes were allocated to parties at the level of 'constituency unions', and again at the level of the nation as a whole. The number of members of parliament was determined by the size of the electorate, by the turn-out at elections and by the number of remaining votes. In Weimar, because of the large number of small parties which failed to gain any quota and any allocation of seats, there was a considerable number of votes which remained ineffectual.

3
Proportionality

It is easy to show that some electoral systems display a greater or lesser bias towards larger or smaller parties. It is more difficult to show which of the systems is the most accurately proportional.

One may first consider the systems based on quotas, which distribute remaining seats to parties which have the highest remainders of votes. On reflection it is evident that such systems cannot be relied upon to be accurately proportional. The size of each party's remainders, which determine the allocation of remaining seats, bears no relationship to the number of votes each party has, yet it is precisely the relationship between the votes and the seats which one is seeking to make as accurately proportional as possible.

Such a quota system cannot even ensure that a party which gains more votes, both absolutely and in relation to other parties, will gain proportionally more seats, nor even prevent such a party from losing instead of gaining seats. Since this is not at first sight obvious it may be illustrated by an example set out in Table 3.1. Suppose that in a country or constituency in which 1 million votes are cast there are held two successive elections, the first to elect 100 members of parliament, and the second to elect 101 members. The elections are contested by three parties, A, B and C, and in each election the method of the Hare quota and largest remainder is used.

In the second election, party C has lost a seat, although its votes increased both absolutely and in relation to each of the other two parties. Parties A and B each gained a seat, although in each case the number of their votes declined. Clearly, an electoral system which can produce such perverse results cannot be relied upon to achieve an accurate proportion between votes and seats. In this example the Hare quota is used, but similar results can in similar circumstances follow from the use of other quotas which depend for their results on the allocation of seats to remainders.

In the USA, for the purposes of allocating seats in the House of Representatives to individual states in *proportion to population*, the

Table 3.1 *Quota and largest remainder system: perverse results*

1st Election
100 members are to be elected.
1,000,000 votes are cast.
The Hare quota is 1,000,000 divided by 100, or 10,000 votes.

Party	Votes	Exact number of quotas	Seats allocated to quotas	Seats after allocation of largest remainder
A	453,320	45·332	45	45
B	443,310	44·331	44	44
C	103,370	10·337*	10	11*
Total	1,000,000		99	100

2nd Election
101 members are to be elected.
1,000,000 votes are cast.
The Hare quota is 1,000,000 divided by 101, or 9901.

Party	Votes	Exact number of quotas	Seats allocated to quotas	Seats after allocation of largest remainder
A	452,170	45·669*	45	46*
B	442,260	44·668*	44	45*
C	105,570	10·663	10	10
Total	1,000,000		99	101

(Asterisks indicate the allocation of the largest remainders.)

largest remainder system was employed after each census between 1850 and 1890. After the census of 1880 it was discovered that if the size of the House were *increased* from 299 to 300, the representation from Alabama would be *reduced* by one seat. This kind of result came therefore to be known in the USA as the 'Alabama paradox'. After the census of 1890 it was found that numerous similar anomalies or paradoxes could arise from various possible increases in the size of the House. For this reason, in 1910, the use of the largest remainder system was discontinued and a divisor system adopted which, for each seat *after the first*, was identical in its results with the Sainte-Laguë system. (Each state was in any case entitled to its first seat under the terms of the constitution.)

The Weimar or 'automatic' system does not provide an escape from such perverse results. It can be shown that if one seat is allocated to each party for every previously fixed quota of votes it has gained, and if the number of members of parliament is not previously determined, then an *increase* in the size of the electorate, or in the turn-out at an election, may result in a *reduction* in the number of members of parliament. Again, such a result will be due to the number and distribution of the remaining votes, and will not be related to the size of the total votes for each party.

Such results justify the abandonment of quota systems and the adoption instead of one or other of the divisor systems, such as D'Hondt, Sainte-Laguë or the Danish system. It is evident from the tables of quotients or 'priority values' in these systems that the allocation of seats is directly related only to the size of the total vote for each party. The results achieved by these systems are consistent and not perverse.

Nevertheless, the various divisor systems yield different results, and they cannot all be equally accurate. The question may then be asked, which is the most accurate of the divisor systems?

First, it may be noted in what significant respects the divisor systems differ one from another. It has already been observed that in the various divisor systems it is not the absolute size of the divisors which determines the result of the system, but the relationship between the numbers in the series. If a set of numbers consisting of, say, 6, 12, 36 and 60 is multiplied or divided by a number, say, divided by 2, the resulting numbers 3, 6, 18 and 30 will bear exactly the same proportion to each other as the original set of numbers. Equally, if the series of numbers in an electoral divisor system is divided or multiplied by a number, the effect on proportionality of the second series will be exactly the same as the effect of the first.

In the USA, for the purpose of congressional apportionment of seats, there was employed after the 1910 and 1930 censuses a divisor system which allocated every seat *after the first* by application of the divisor series 1½, 2½, 3½, etc. For the reasons mentioned, this had exactly the same effect as the series 3, 5, 7, 9, etc. which, for the allocation of every seat after the first, is the Sainte-Laguë series. The values of the numbers in the Sainte-Laguë series are simply twice the values of the numbers in the American series.

The references to systems used for congressional apportionment in the USA are particularly relevant to the question of accurate proportionality, because the constitution of the USA requires that seats should be allocated to states in *proportion* to population. Thus the search for a truly proportional system is an obligation upon Congress, and the search resulted finally in the adoption in 1941 of the present system, devised by Professor E. V. Huntington, and called the method of 'equal proportions'. This system and other alternatives were exhaustively examined by various learned bodies and mathematicians including, finally, at the request of the speaker of the House of Representatives, the US National Academy of Sciences. The expert authorities supported the claim of Professor Huntington that his system was not only the most accurately proportional, but also the only one which had no bias in favour of either larger or smaller states. The system required the allocation to states of every seat *after the first* by application of the divisor series $\sqrt{1 \times 2}$, $\sqrt{2 \times 3}$, $\sqrt{3 \times 4}$, etc., which is in other terms the series 1·414, 2·449, 3·464, etc.

The decision in favour of this series was influenced by the assessment of different *measures* of proportionality which it was possible to adopt. Huntington maintained that in measuring a divergence from proportionality a distinction should be drawn between differences which were *absolute* and those which were *relative*. Thus, the difference between 4 and 5 is smaller in absolute terms than the difference between 100 and 105, but in the first case the larger figure is 25 per cent greater than the smaller, while in the second case it is only 5 per cent greater. Huntington's view was that for a measure of proportionality it was the *relative* divergences which were the most important. The authorities agreed, and they also agreed that of all the systems considered the method of 'equal proportions' was the one which reduced divergences from proportionality to a minimum when measured in relative terms.

In view of these conclusions, it is reasonable that for the assessment of accuracy of divisor systems comparisons should be made with the method of 'equal proportions'. There is an inevitable deficiency in such a comparison, because Huntington's method is not capable of being applied for the allocation of a *first* seat. (The equivalent divisor for a first seat would be $\sqrt{0 \times 1}$, or 0, which could not allocate any first seat, and therefore the series could not allocate any seats at all.) In the case of congressional apportionment this is irrelevant, because under the constitution every state is entitled to one seat, but in the case of elections it would clearly be impracticable to allocate one seat to every *party*, however small, and that method cannot therefore be applied. It can be used, however, as a test of the degree of proportionality of divisor systems in allocating seats *after* the first.

A comparison between various divisor systems and the method of 'equal proportions' is made in Table 3.2 set out in Appendix A to this chapter. The table indicates that, of the divisor systems which are commonly used for elections, those which approximate most closely to the method of 'equal proportions' are the Sainte-Laguë system and the Danish system, and these may be regarded as the most accurately proportional. The D'Hondt system is the least accurate of the systems commonly used.

Since the method of 'equal proportions' is also claimed to be the system which has no bias in favour of larger or smaller states, it may be regarded as the one which, if used in elections for the allocation to parties of all seats after the first, would have no bias in favour of either larger or smaller parties. Those systems which, when compared with the method of 'equal proportions', have *smaller* increments between divisors will favour larger parties, and those which have *larger* increments will favour smaller parties. From this comparison it appears that the Danish system slightly favours smaller parties, and the Sainte-Laguë system slightly favours larger parties, while a bias of the D'Hondt system in favour of the larger parties is more pronounced.

It may be observed from Table 3.2 in Appendix A that the greater the number of seats which each party has been allocated the less difference it makes which divisor system is used. This applies equally, of course, to the systems used for congressional apportionment. In the USA, the method of 'equal proportions' and the equivalent of the Sainte-Laguë system produced identical results after the census of 1930, and it was only after the census of 1940, when the two systems differed in the allocation of one seat, that a decision was finally made in favour of 'equal proportions'.

Moreover, the larger the constituencies in terms of the number of seats which are to be allocated, the more accurate a proportional system is likely to be. If a quota system is used, the greater the number of seats, the smaller will be the quota of votes necessary to secure a seat, the more easily will that quota be attained by smaller parties, and the smaller will be the number of unsuccessful votes which do not contribute to the allocation of a seat. Under a divisor system, the larger the number of seats, the larger will be each successive divisor, the smaller will be the quotients or 'priority values', and the smaller, again, will be the number of unsuccessful votes.

The largest constituency of all is, of course, the entire nation, so that those electoral systems whose allocation of seats takes place, or is completed, on a national basis, can achieve a high degree of proportionality. An electoral system may for this reason provide two or more tiers for the successive allocation of seats, say, at constituency, provincial and national levels.

The establishment of constituencies of different sizes can be of great importance not only for the degree of proportionality achieved but also for the particular interests of large or small parties. Under PR there is still scope for 'gerrymandering' in the fixing of constituency sizes, since a party, wherever it is weak, will benefit from large constituencies yielding a high degree of proportionality, and wherever it is strong will benefit from small constituencies giving a low degree of proportionality. In Appendix B to this chapter examples are given of the extent to which constituencies of different sizes may be an advantage or a disadvantage to parties, according to their share of the total votes.

The adoption of 'additional member' systems is explained by what has been said about the effect of the size of constituencies on the degree of proportionality which is achieved. Disproportionalities are likely to exist in all electoral systems in which electors are divided into many small constituencies. If, however, additional seats are added to those for which elections have taken place in such constituencies, by whatever electoral system, these can be allocated in such a way that, on a national or other basis, greater proportionality can be achieved. This is the purpose of the additional member systems which have been adopted in some countries, including Denmark, Sweden and for a time the Weimar Republic. The additional seats may be regarded as national, and not allocated to any area or constituency; or a predetermined number may be allocated to particular areas; or allocation may be made to constituencies in accordance with the number of votes each party has gained; or it may be made in any other way which is politically acceptable.

APPENDIX A: DIVISOR SYSTEMS

Comparisons with the Huntington method of 'equal proportions'
In the USA the Huntington method of 'equal proportions' has been officially adopted for congressional apportionment on the grounds that this method is the most accurately proportional by the most appropriate tests, and that it displays no bias in favour of either larger or smaller states.

This system cannot be applied for the allocation of a first seat (for which the divisor would be 0), but for the allocation of all seats after the first it may be used for purposes of comparison with other divisor systems.

Since the effects of a divisor system depend on the *ratio between* successive divisors, or in other words the *relative increment* between each divisor and the next, an appropriate method of comparison is to set out for each divisor system the *percentage increment* in the divisor used for allocating each successive seat. That is the purpose of Table 3.2.

Table 3.2 *Percentage increment of divisors in the different divisor systems*

Divisor system	1st seat to 2nd	2nd seat to 3rd	3rd seat to 4th	4th seat to 5th	5th seat to 6th	6th seat to 7th
D'Hondt	100·0	50·0	33·3	25·0	20·0	16·7
Sainte-Laguë: modified						
(1·4, 3, 5, 7, etc.)	114·3	66·7	40·0	28·6	22·2	18·2
pure						
(1, 3, 5, 7, etc.)	200·0	66·7	40·0	28·6	22·2	18·2
Equal proportions	—	73·2	41·4	29·1	22·5	18·3
Danish method	300·0	75·0	42·9	30·0	23·1	18·8

The Sainte-Laguë and Danish systems approximate more closely to 'equal proportions' than the D'Hondt system. The Danish system slightly favours smaller parties, the Sainte-Laguë system slightly favours larger parties, and the D'Hondt system has a more pronounced bias in favour of the larger parties.

APPENDIX B: PROPORTIONAL REPRESENTATION

The possible 'gerrymandering' of constituency sizes
The purpose of this appendix is to show how the relationship between votes and seats may be affected by the size of constituencies, meaning by size the number of seats to be allocated; and how particular parties may gain an advantage or suffer a disadvantage in a constituency of a particular size, depending on their share of the votes.

To measure the degree of proportionality, and how it affects each party, an 'index of proportionality' is calculated by expressing a party's share of all seats as a percentage of their share of all votes. Then an index of more than 100 indicates a *bonus* of seats in relation to votes, and an index of under 100 indicates a *deficiency* of seats in relation to votes. (This index was devised by Cornelius O'Leary, and used by him, in other contexts, in *The Irish Republic and its Experiment with Proportional Representation*, pp. 50–9.)

The operation of the Droop quota is such that in a constituency of three seats the quota is just over 25 per cent, so that any party which secures just over 25 per cent of the votes can be sure of gaining one seat, or 33⅓ per cent of the seats. Similarly, in a constituency of four seats the quota is just over 20 per cent, so that a party with two quotas, or just over 40 per cent of the votes, can be sure of gaining two seats, or 50 per cent of the seats.

Conversely, a party with 40 per cent of the votes in a three-member constituency can be sure of gaining one seat only, or 33⅓ per cent of the seats; while a party with 55 per cent of the votes in a four-member constituency can be sure only of gaining two seats, or 50 per cent of the seats.

Table 3.3 indicates the bonus a party may obtain, or the penalty it may incur, if it has a particular share of the votes in a constituency of a particular size.

The possibilities and hazards of manipulating the size-distribution of constituencies are illustrated by these theoretical examples. If a governing party seek to manipulate the constituency sizes to their own advantage, and expect that in a certain area they will gain 50 per cent of the votes, they may seek to ensure that three-member constituencies are established in that area. If their expectations are fulfilled, they will receive a bonus of seats over votes of 33·3 per cent. If, however, they are mistaken, and secure only 40 per cent of the votes, the three-member constituency will

Table 3.3 *Party advantage or disadvantage in size of
constituency: 'index of proportionality'*

Party's share of total vote	Three-member constituency		Four-member constituency		Five-member constituency	
	Number of seats winnable	Index	Number of seats winnable	Index	Number of seats winnable	Index
16·7%+	0	—	0	—	1	120
20·0%+	0	—	1	125	1	100
25·0%+	1	133·3	1	100	1	80
33·3%+	1	100·0	1	75	2	120
40·0%+	1	83·3	2	125	2	100
50·0%+	2	133·3	2	100	3	120
60·0%+	2	111·1	3	125	3	100

(The plus signs after the percentages showing a party's share of the total votes indicate that the party need 'just over' that percentage to be sure of winning the number of seats shown.)

from their own point of view be the *worst* of the three constituency sizes indicated, incurring for the party a penalty of 16·7 per cent. The four-member constituency would have been the best. However, although a four-member constituency would be the most advantageous for a party which expected to receive 40 per cent of the votes, it would be the *least* advantageous if they secured only 33⅓ per cent of the votes.

Between these 'key' shares of the votes innumerable possibilities present themselves. A 'gambling' element is therefore introduced if attempts are made to manipulate the size of constituencies, so that losses can be incurred as well as bonuses gained.

The larger the number of seats in a constituency, the more accurately proportional will be the allocation of seats, and the smaller will be the penalties incurred by parties with a number of votes which just fails to win a seat, or win an additional seat. So long as constituencies are large, there is no inducement for governing parties to seek to vary the size of constituencies. This tends to confirm the view, which has long been held, that to achieve a reasonable degree of proportionality the smallest size of constituency which is appropriate is one of five members.

4

Voting for Individuals

The Federal German Republic is the only one of the Western European nations having party-list systems of proportional representation which does not offer electors some choice between candidates on the party lists. Even in Germany an elector may vote for an individual candidate in a single-member constituency, and this candidate need not be a supporter of the party for whose list the elector simultaneously gives a second vote; but that part of the election which is conducted by means of party lists offers only 'rigid lists', with candidates named in an order determined by the party, and with no opportunity given to electors to indicate a preference between them. All the other nations, however, offer some element of choice between candidates on party lists.

The methods of electing individuals in list systems of election may be divided into four categories: those in which an elector is allowed only one vote for a single candidate on the list (in Belgium, the Netherlands, Denmark, Finland since 1955 and Austria since 1971); a limited vote system, in which the elector can use more than one vote but fewer votes than there are seats to be filled (Italy since 1946); systems in which electors may have as many votes as there are seats, and in which votes for each candidate are aggregated (Luxemburg and Switzerland); and systems in which electors indicate their choice between candidates in order of preference (Norway, Sweden, Finland between 1906 and 1955, and Austria between 1949 and 1971).

The system of allowing an elector to vote only for a single candidate when more than one candidate is to be elected is, in its simplest form, an example of the single *non*-transferable vote, or the limited vote in a multi-member constituency, when the limit is restricted to one vote. For party elections this has the defects already indicated, and for the election of individuals it has the drawback that if voting is heavily concentrated on one or two popular individuals a choice between the remainder may be left to comparatively few electors who may not be representative of the electors as a whole.

However, this type of election is not used in its simplest form in any of the countries concerned, and in all of them except Finland it is the order of the candidates on the party's list which is the principal determining factor. In Belgium and the Netherlands seats are awarded in turn to each candidate on the party list who achieves a quota of votes determined by the number of seats and votes the *party* have gained. (In Belgium the Droop quota is used, but in the Netherlands the Hare quota.) First, all purely *party* votes are given to the candidate first on the list, his personal votes are added, and his surplus of votes beyond the quota is transferred to the candidate next on the *list*. The personal votes of the second candidate are then added to the votes transferred to him, any surplus beyond the quota is transferred to the next candidate on the list, and so on down the list. Since most electors either vote only for the party list, or for candidates at the head of the list, personal votes seldom result in the election of candidates lower in the list at the expense of those listed higher.

Similarly, in Denmark, the election of individuals is determined mainly by their ranking in the party list. There are three different methods of counting personal votes for each candidate, only one of these gives the electors rather than the parties the determining influence, and it is the parties themselves which can decide which method is to be used. The result is that only a small proportion of candidates are effectively chosen by the electors rather than the parties.

In Finland since 1955 electors have had only one vote for one candidate, and for each party the number of votes each candidate obtains determines the order in which he appears on the party's list. The total votes of all of a party's candidates are credited to the candidate first on the party's list; half that number of votes are credited to the candidate second on the list; one-third are credited to the candidate third on the list; and so on. The final result is exactly the same as if the D'Hondt system had been applied to the total number of votes obtained by the candidates of each party, and each party's seats had then been allocated in turn to the candidates in the order in which they appeared on the party's list. The distinction between this system and the system used in Belgium is that in Finland it is the electors who decide which of the candidates are allocated the seats which a party gains. In Belgium it is effectively the party which decides.

In Italy, the limited vote is used to allocate to candidates the seats won by a party. Electors are entitled to give one vote each to three candidates in constituencies having up to fifteen seats, and to four candidates in constituencies having more than fifteen seats.

In Luxemburg and Switzerland an elector can cast as many votes for individual candidates as there are seats to be filled, and he can cumulate two votes each on particular candidates. Electors can vote simply for a party list, in which case each candidate on the list obtains one vote (or two votes if cumulated in the party list); but electors can also delete names from the party list and substitute others. The number of votes which each candidate obtains will determine not only the allocation of seats to the party, but also the allocation to the individual candidates of the seats which the party gain. These systems therefore give considerable freedom of choice to the electors.

Where the electors can indicate a choice between candidates in order of preference, there is a variety of methods of counting which are used to translate these votes into seats. The simplest method is that which was used in Austria between 1949 and 1970. This was a points system, in which each party could nominate as many candidates as there were seats, and electors could vote for these candidates in order of preference. An elector's first choice was given as many points as there were seats to be allocated in the constituency, his next choice one point less, and so on. The order in which candidates were allocated seats was determined by the number of points each had gained.

In Norway and Sweden the method of allocation is different. In Norway the first party seat is allocated to the candidate with most first preferences; the second to the remaining candidate with most first and second preferences; the third to the remaining candidate with most first, second and third preferences; and so on. In Sweden there is an additional requirement that to gain a first seat the candidate with most first preferences must have gained these from at least half the party's voters; a candidate with first and second preferences must have gained these from at least two-thirds of the party's voters; and so on. Otherwise seats are allocated to candidates with most votes in each category, any ballot papers already used for a successful candidate being reduced in value by half.

A unique system of counting preferential votes was used in Finland between 1906 and 1954. Whatever the number of seats in a constituency, each elector was entitled to vote for a 'list' of up to three candidates only, the candidates being listed by the party in order of preference. All the 'lists' submitted by a single party in a constituency constituted an 'alliance'. The votes for each 'list' were aggregated, that number of votes was credited to the first candidate on the 'list', half as many votes to the second candidate, and one-third as many to the third. The total votes for each 'list' were aggregated for the 'alliance', which was in effect the party. The total votes for each candidate determined the order in which the seats gained by the 'alliance' or party were allocated to candidates. Since the same candidate could appear on many different lists, and in a different order in each list, and since the elector could alter the order and also substitute different names, electors had great potential influence in determining the choice between candidates. However, parties in the course of time ceased submitting 'lists' of more than one candidate, electors seldom exercised their right to formulate their own lists, the system fell out of use, and it was in 1955 finally abandoned in favour of a system which gave electors the freedom to choose only one candidate.

Some systems of proportional representation permit electors to vote for candidates of more than one party, which is called *panachage*. This has been permitted in Luxemburg, Norway, Sweden and Switzerland, but could not apply in those countries in which electors may cast only one vote for an individual candidate, as in Belgium, the Netherlands and Denmark. Since *panachage* is difficult to reconcile with a proportional allocation of seats to parties it should not, it would seem, be permitted in a system which seeks to achieve such an allocation. Those who are opposed to or indifferent to all parties are entitled to vote for independent candidates, but political opinion is not rationally represented in parliament if many electors vote simultaneously for supporters of rival parties which, on the major issues which divide the parties, will vote against each other in parliament. However, from the habits of voting in all countries it is evident that the overwhelming majority of electors vote primarily for parties and only secondarily for individuals, and so long as inconsistency in party voting is confined to small numbers of voters the proportionality of party representation will be distorted to a correspondingly small degree.

5

The Single Transferable Vote

The single transferable vote (abbreviated to STV) is a system which seeks to secure proportional representation by using a method of voting for individuals, and not for party lists. The basic principle is that each elector may exercise one vote only, but each vote takes the form of a schedule of preferences, so that if the candidate to whom the elector gives his first preference does not need the vote, either because he already has enough votes to secure election without it, or because he has no chance of being elected and has been eliminated, then the vote can be transferred to the next continuing candidate for whom the elector has expressed a preference.

The procedure is that after the total votes in the election have been counted, the Droop quota is calculated by dividing the total number of valid votes by the number of seats to be allocated *plus one*, and rounding upwards or adding one. Any candidate who reaches the quota, either on the strength of his own first preferences or with the help of votes transferred to him from other candidates, is deemed to be elected.

A chief merit of STV is that unlike the majority systems it enables surplus votes to be transferred and not wasted in piling up unnecessarily large majorities for popular candidates. Contrasted with the points system it also has the merit that a later preference for an individual candidate cannot operate to the disadvantage of an earlier preference.

An early problem, when the system was invented, was which votes to transfer when a candidate had a surplus. At first the method suggested was to transfer all votes for a candidate which were counted after a quota had been achieved by that candidate, or to examine the votes in the order in which electors appeared in the electoral register, starting at some randomly chosen point. But such methods were later thought to leave too much to chance, and not necessarily represent the views of all the electors who gave the elected candidate their first choice. A method was then worked out to transfer surplus votes to continuing candidates *in proportion* to the next preferences expressed by *all* electors who had voted for the successful candidate.

The method of transferring surpluses in this way may, by means of a simplified explanation, be described as follows. Suppose the quota of votes necessary to secure election is 12. Candidate A is given 18 votes, and therefore has a surplus of 6 votes. The next preferences of *all* the eighteen electors are examined, and it is found that the next preferences of nine of them are for candidate B, of six for candidate C, and of three for candidate D. Thus half the next preferences are for B, one-third for C and one-sixth for D. The 6 surplus votes are therefore transferred in these proportions: 3 (one-half) to B, 2 (one third) to C and 1 (one-sixth) to D.

In practice, for the convenience of the count, the same result is achieved in a different way. Since the 6 surplus votes amount to one-third of all the votes for candidate A in which later preferences for continuing candidates are expressed, the value of *all* the candidate's votes is changed to one-third, and each vote is transferred to the continuing candidate shown as the next preference on the ballot slip. There may be differences in the exact method of counting, but these involve only a choice between simple methods which are easily used and give acceptably proportional results, or else, if required, more exhaustive, complicated and precise methods designed to achieve more meticulously accurate results.

Greater problems arise if, after the transfer of surplus votes, some seats remain unallocated after as many candidates as possible have achieved quotas. The method adopted at this point is to eliminate the candidate who has the fewest preferences, or in other words is 'last past the post', and to transfer each of his votes to the continuing candidate who is found to be the elector's next choice.

There are anomalies inherent in this procedure. To take an example of STV when there is only one candidate to be elected (and in which STV is identical with the method known as the 'alternative vote'), the *only* way in which votes can be transferred is by the elimination of the candidate with the fewest first-preference votes. But the elimination of the last candidate may not accurately reflect the desires of the electors.

In such a case the Droop quota will be just over 50 per cent of the votes, or in other words an absolute majority. If no candidate achieves an absolute majority, then the last candidate is eliminated and his votes are transferred; and this process is continued if necessary until one candidate has an absolute majority. The result may, however, be unsatisfactory. Suppose there are three candidates, A, B and C, for one seat, and there are twenty electors. Of the electors, eight give their first preferences to A, seven to B and five to C, and C is therefore eliminated. But if the supporters of A and B are entirely antagonistic to each other, and if C is more generally acceptable, it could happen that in 'single combat' contests C could defeat A by 12 votes to 8, and could defeat B by 13 votes to 7. The elimination of the last candidate may prevent the true wishes of the electorate from being expressed.

STV is intended to be applied in multi-member and not single-member constituencies, but in such constituencies the difficulty still remains. As one might expect from a quota system whose results depend on the allocation of remaining seats from remaining votes, the results can, as in the case of party-list quota systems, be anomalous and perverse. A candidate may lose a seat between one STV election and the next because the first-preference votes accorded to him have *increased* at the expense of another candidate.

Suppose there is an STV election in which the Droop quota is 12, and after the transfers of votes from successful candidates only one seat remains to be filled. There are three candidates, X, Y and Z, still in contention. Suppose also, for simplicity, that the voters who give their first preferences to a candidate who is eliminated all agree on their choice of candidate for their second preference. The voting in two successive elections could then be as indicated in Table 5.1.

Table 5.1 *Single transferable vote election:*
elimination of candidate with fewest first preference votes

	Votes for Candidates		
	X	Y	Z
1st Election			
1st preferences	8	8	7
2nd preferences		(all for Z)	(all for X)
2nd Election			
1st preferences	10	6	7
2nd preferences		(all for Z)	(all for X)

In the first election Z, with fewest first preferences, is eliminated, all his second preferences go to X, who now has (and exceeds) the quota of 12 votes and is elected. In the second election X *gains* 2 first-preference votes at the expense of Y, who now has fewest first-preference votes. Y is eliminated, all his second preferences go to Z, who now has (and exceeds) the quota of 12 votes and is elected. Thus X has *lost* a seat in spite of (or because of) the fact that he has won more first-preference votes than before. Clearly such a result does not achieve an accurately proportional relationship between votes and seats. (It is not normally possible to ascertain, without access to the individual ballot papers, whether the result of an election could have been affected in this way, since the later preferences of candidates who are 'runners-up' are not counted and published.)

To provide an escape from such anomalies Professor E. J. Nanson in Australia and G. H. Hallett in the USA evolved systems which sought to ensure that a candidate would not be eliminated unless all other continuing candidates were preferred by the electors. The methods to ensure this are complex and sophisticated, but the difficulties are not insuperable in an age of calculators and computers. A more serious objection is that even such methods may not achieve an unambiguous result. It is possible that *no* candidate will be defeated in 'single combat' by all others. How this can be so is demonstrated in the appendix to this chapter.

STV is a 'personal' system of election, in the sense that votes are given to individual persons and counted for individuals only, as distinct from party-list systems, in which votes are counted for parties. In parliamentary elections, however, candidates almost always stand as supporters of a particular party, and the contest for seats is not only between individuals but also between parties.

It is claimed that STV, although it does not set out to achieve proportional representation of parties, does in fact do so. Evidence in support of this claim was presented to the Royal Commission on Electoral Systems in 1909, and to the Speakers' Conference on Electoral Reform in 1965. For this result to be achieved it is necessary, as Lord Courtney, chairman of the Proportional Representation Society, pointed out to the Royal Commission, that electors supporting a party should give not only their first-preference votes but also so far as possible all their next preferences to candidates of the party of their choice; and it was assumed by Lord Courtney that this is what they would do.

If electors supporting a party were to give their votes solely or mainly to one favoured candidate, and failed to allocate subsequent preferences to any other candidates of the party, then they would not elect as many candidates of the party as would correspond to its strength but would only accumulate on their favourite candidate a surplus of votes he did not need. They would be still less likely to secure representation of their party in proportion to their strength if they gave their later preferences to members of other parties.

Party voting adds a complication to STV elections. In the election of *individuals* STV is a system in which a later preference has effect only after an earlier preference has either been elected or eliminated, so that the later preference cannot operate against the earlier. In *party* elections, however, this is *not* the case, since a later preference vote which helps to elect a candidate from an opposing party, instead of from the first preferred party, must be to the disadvantage of the party first preferred.

If voters extensively avail themselves of the facility of voting for members of different parties, then each elector may contribute to the election of members who, on party issues, that is to say on major issues of sufficient importance to justify the formation of rival parties, will extensively vote against each other in parliament. In such circumstances parliament could not, on those major issues, be regarded as representative of the electors in a rational or coherent manner.

This problem for the STV system is no different in principle from that which exists in the party-list systems which allow *panachage*, or voting for individual candidates who support different parties. The confusion which this causes to the representative character of parliament will not, however, be significant if very few voters avail themselves of this facility, but vote consistently for all candidates of one party before voting for the candidates of any other. This is what normally happens in parliamentary elections when more than one choice can be expressed. If electors do behave in this way, as Lord Courtney thought they would, then the result, so far as party representation is concerned, would resemble the result of a party-list election using a quota method, but with the allocation of remaining seats determined by the *smallest* remainders of votes.

However, this system, like others which depend on quotas and remainders, can lead to perverse results, and cannot be relied upon to be proportional. It has already been noted that anomalous results may emerge when STV is used for the election of individuals, and this applies equally to the representation of any parties which the individuals support. Table 5.1 serves to illustrate this point. If candidate X supports party A, and candidate Z supports party B, then between the first election and the second party A will have lost a seat only because it has gained more votes.

On the question of how proportionality in an STV election should be measured, the test most commonly applied is to compare the number of *first-preference* votes for the supporters of each party with the number of seats the party have obtained. It is also argued, however, that since under this system electors can indicate second and later preferences this is not the most appropriate test. Instead, the test should be what the preferences of voters are after all surplus votes and all votes of eliminated candidates have been transferred, and how their preferences at the *final count* correspond to the number of supporters elected from each party. In Table 5.2 both methods are used to measure the proportional relationship between party votes and party seats: first, a measure of the relationship between *first-preference* votes for parties and the seats they have gained; and secondly, the relationship between *final count* votes for parties, as a percentage of all votes cast, and the seats gained by the parties, as a percentage of all seats in parliament. By way of example, these two measures are applied to the STV election held in the Republic of Ireland in 1969.

Table 5.2 is compiled from *Election Results and Transfer of Votes in General Election (June, 1969) for Nineteenth Dáil*, published by the

Table 5.2 *Proportionality of the single transferable vote:*
Republic of Ireland general election of 1969

Party	Percentage of seats	Percentage of total first-preference votes	Final count votes as percentage of total valid votes
Fianna Fáil	51·8	45·7	39·7
Fine Gael	35·0	34·1	27·0
Labour	12·6	17·0	9·6
Other parties	0·7	3·2	0·6
Unsuccessful votes			23·2
Total	100·1	100·0	100·1

(Rounding accounts for additions not yielding 100·0.)

Stationery Office, Dublin. It indicates that in this election representation of parties was not proportional by the criterion of first-preference votes, since Fianna Fáil had more than half the seats, while the opposition parties had more than half the first-preference votes. A circumstance which affected proportionality in this election was the unequal effect on the parties of the size-distribution of constituencies (how this could happen was explained in Appendix B of Chapter 3), but there were several earlier examples of Fianna Fáil achieving more than half of the seats with less than half of the votes; and in 1977, when the size distribution of constituencies was expected to favour Fine Gael, Fianna Fáil obtained a substantial majority of seats, and a substantial 'bonus' of seats in relation to their share of the votes.

Representation of parties in 1969 was even less proportional when measured by the criterion of final count votes. This is explained by the large number of votes which were unsuccessful at the final count in each constituency. These were votes for unelected candidates who were 'runners-up', and also votes indicating first preferences for candidates who were eliminated, but no later preferences for any continuing candidates (i.e. 'non-transferable votes'). The fewer the seats in any constituency, the larger is likely to be the proportion of such unsuccessful votes.

It is also alternatively maintained in support of the STV system that it does not in any case seek to achieve the 'proportional representation of parties', but achieves instead the 'proportional representation of political opinion'. Various political opinions may be held on issues which cut across party lines, such as, in the United Kingdom, membership of the European Community, or devolution for Scotland or Wales. Groups holding a particular opinion on an issue may be referred to as 'parties' with inverted commas. However, it is not satisfactorily established why it is less important to achieve proportional representation of parties (without inverted commas) which will form governments or coalitions or oppositions, and more important to achieve it for 'parties' which will perform no such definable function. Nor is it established that STV will in fact achieve 'PR of political opinion' more accurately than 'PR of parties'. Since the terms of an 'equation' for 'PR of political opinion' cannot be stated, the test of measurement cannot be applied.

Just as it is possible in some party-list systems for parties to gain an advantage through forming alliances for the purpose of the allocation of seats (the device which is known as *apparentement*), so is it possible in STV elections for parties to gain an advantage by forming alliances. (This enabled Fine Gael and the Labour Party in 1973 to gain a majority of seats with a minority of first preference votes.) Under STV, however, there is no need for these alliances to be officially recognised under the electoral law. Parties may agree to recommend to their supporters that they should give their later-preference votes, after votes for their own party, to candidates nominated by their allies, and this is likely to result in the election of a greater number of supporters of each of the allied parties. A merit of this arrangement is the fact that it is the voters themselves who decide whether an alliance contrived between parties shall be effective or not.

In spite of the criticisms to which it is exposed, STV is probably still, for the election of *individuals*, the system which expresses most fairly the desires of the electorate. A later preference cannot, at least, operate to the disadvantage of an earlier preference, as it can under a points system.

If the object is primarily to achieve proportional representation of *parties*, then neither STV nor any other quota system depending on the allocation of remaining seats on the basis of remaining votes is consistent in achieving this aim, as divisor systems are. If the object is to achieve proportional representation of parties as accurately as possible, then a divisor system is to be preferred which resembles as nearly as possible the method of 'equal proportions', such as the Sainte-Laguë or the Danish system.

To achieve both objects as far as is practicable, the divisor system could be used to achieve PR of parties, while STV could be used to enable electors to choose individual candidates within a party list. Alternatively, an STV election could be supplemented by an additional member system, to achieve more accurately the proportional representation of parties.

APPENDIX:
STRAIGHT FIGHTS AND CIRCULAR VOTING

One of the objections which can be made against systems of electing individuals is the unfairness of eliminating candidates who might still have a chance of election. In an attempt to meet this objection it was proposed by Condorcet that the results should be determined by a succession of straight fights between each pair of candidates, and the candidate who defeated all the others should be declared the winner. This system has not been considered for parliamentary elections because of the great complexity when large numbers are involved, although today it could be reconsidered, now that computers can deal easily with much more difficult calculations. Another and less obvious objection is, however, that such a method may not achieve any result at all, because each candidate may be beaten by at least one of the others. It is true that if a single elector is asked to express preferences between three candidates, and if he indicates that he prefers A to B, B to C and C to A, that cannot be regarded as a rational choice. But if a number of electors are expressing their preferences in a variety of permutations and combinations, such a result is possible and not irrational. Suppose that nine electors are asked to express their preferences between three candidates, and suppose also, for the sake of simplicity, that out of all the various possibilities they confine themselves to voting for four combinations of preferences between the three candidates. The election could then be as shown in Table 5.3. Such a method cannot, therefore, be relied upon to solve this problem.

Table 5.3 *Straight fights and circular voting*

Verdicts of 3 voters	Verdicts of 2 voters	Verdicts of 2 voters	Verdicts of 2 voters
A beats B	C beats A	B beats C	C beats B
B beats C	A beats B	C beats A	B beats A

Results:

A versus B:	5 prefer A to B	
	4 prefer B to A:	therefore A beats B.
B versus C:	5 prefer B to C	
	4 prefer C to B:	therefore B beats C.
C versus A:	3 prefer A to C	
	6 prefer C to A:	therefore C beats A.

REFERENCES: PART ONE

A lucid introduction to the conditions necessary for holding fair elections is contained in *Free Elections* by W. J. M. Mackenzie, while Enid Lakeman, in *How Democracies Vote*, is concerned in particular with a description of electoral systems. (Miss Lakeman is director of the Electoral Reform Society, formerly entitled the Proportional Representation Society, whose constitution requires the society to support the single transferable vote method.) In French a useful book is Jean-Marie Cotteret and Claude Emeri's *Les Systèmes électoraux*.

For a description of contemporary or recent electoral systems reference may be made to Wolfgang Birke, *European Elections by Direct Suffrage*, the relevant sections of the Inter-Parliamentary Union's *Parliaments of the World: A Reference Compendium*, and the report on *Electoral Laws of Parliaments of the Member States of the European Communities* issued in 1977 by the European Parliament. Brief reports on any changes which may have been introduced before recent general elections are published annually by the Inter-Parliamentary Union in their *Chronicle of Parliamentary Elections*. (With effect from Volume XII, 1978, the title has been changed to *Chronicle of Parliamentary Elections and Developments*.)

The movement in favour of proportional representation was effectively launched by Thomas Hare in his work on *The Election of Representatives, Parliamentary and Municipal*. He was a pioneer not only in devising the single transferable vote method but also in using a quota system for the allocation of seats. The quota was subsequently modified through the adoption of a system advocated by Henry R. Droop in his *Methods of Electing Representatives*. Later advocacy of the single transferable vote, and descriptions of the refinements which have been made in this method of election, are contained in *Proportional Representation* by J. H. Humphreys, and also in Enid Lakeman's work to which reference has already been made. The rules for STV elections formulated by the Electoral Reform Society are contained in a booklet by Robert A. Newland and Frank S. Britton, *How to Conduct an Election by the Single Transferable Vote*.

Further refinements in STV methods were proposed by Professor A. J. Nanson in a paper on 'Methods of election', which was reproduced in the Parliamentary Paper *Reports from HM Representatives in Foreign Countries and in British Colonies Respecting the Application of the Principle of Proportional Representation in Public Elections* (1907); by G. H. Hallett, in G. C. Hoag and G. H. Hallett's *Proportional Representation*; and by Professor G. Van den Bergh, in *Unity in Diversity: A Systematic Critical Analysis of All Electoral Systems*.

J. W. Gordon gave evidence to the Royal Commission on Electoral Systems criticising anomalies which could arise in STV elections through the elimination of a candidate with fewest first-preference votes, and this was printed in the Royal Commission's *Minutes of Evidence* (1910). The same point has been elaborated in an article by G. Doron and R. Kronick entitled 'Single transferable vote: an example of a perverse social function', published in the *American Journal of Political Science* in May 1977.

The proportional representation movement may be said to have divided into two main streams as a result of the publication by Victor D'Hondt, a Belgian, of his *Système pratique et raisonné de représentation proportionnelle* in 1882. He departed from the system advocated by Hare both in substituting party lists for the election of candidates individually, and in replacing (or supplementing) the quota system by a system of divisors.

Eduard Hagenbach-Bischoff's name has been attached to various electoral devices, and although he was not their original inventor he had a powerful influence on their adoption in his native Switzerland and elsewhere. These were the use of a quota as the preliminary stage in the application of the D'Hondt method; the adoption of the Droop type of quota for this purpose; and the freedom extended to electors to vote for candidates on more than one party list (or *panachage*). His principle work was *Berechtigung und Ausführbarkeit der proportionalen Vertretung bei unseren politischen Wahlen*, published in 1884.

The divisor system advocated by the Frenchman A. Sainte-Laguë as more accurate than that which had been devised by D'Hondt, was outlined by him in a note of less than two pages in the *Comptes rendus hebdomadaires* of the Académie des Sciences, Paris, in 1910. His method was later adopted in a modified form by all the Scandinavian countries.

The first person to devise a systematic 'additional members system' was apparently the Austrian, Siegfried Geyerhahn, in a paper published in 1902 as part of a series entitled *Wiener Staatswissenschaftliche Studien*, but the merits of some such system had already been under discussion, as Count Goblet d'Alviella indicated in his history of proportional representation in Belgium.

The American experience of congressional apportionment has been used as an aid to assess the merits or demerits of quota systems and the various divisor systems. This experience is fully described in Lawrence F. Schmeckebier's *Congressional Apportionment*, and in a report by the US House of Representatives Sub-Committee on Census and Statistics, *The Decennial Population Census and Congressional Apportionment*, 1970. Professor E. V. Huntington had explained his method of 'equal proportions' in an article entitled 'A new method of apportionment of representatives', published in the American Statistical Association's *Quarterly Publication* in September 1921; and in the December 1921 issue of the same journal the method was favourably reported upon by a joint committee of the American Statistical Association and the American Economic Association.

A subject of central interest is whether parliamentary elections should above all provide representation of the electorate as accurately as possible, or whether they should above all provide the basis for strong and stable government. This requires, and has received elsewhere, the more extended study which is beyond the scope of this book. Historical evidence is in any case unlikely to be conclusive when there is no agreement on how stability and strength of government are to be defined, how much or how little government is acceptable, how long a period is appropriate for the measurement of stability, and what degree of mis-representation is tolerable. A suitable starting-point for those who wish to pursue this controversy is John Stuart Mill's *Considerations on Representative Government* on the side of accurate representation, and Walter Bagehot, *The English Constitution*, on the side of strong government. In more recent times, arguments against proportional representation have been developed most forcibly by F. A. Hermens in *Democracy or Anarchy? A Study of Proportional Representation*, while

an opposite case is presented in *Adversary Politics and Electoral Reform*, edited by
Professor S. E. Finer. Judgements offered by Maurice Duverger in *L'Influence des
systèmes électoraux sur la vie politique* have been widely quoted but have tended to
become out of date, since they were based on the experience of proportional
representation in the first thirty years after it was extensively adopted, whereas in
the last thirty years the experience has in many ways been different. A later comparative study was by Douglas W. Rae, *The Political Consequences of Electoral
Laws*. In *People and Parliament*, edited by the late John P. Mackintosh, there is a
chapter by Michael Steed on 'The electoral system and functioning of parliament'.

PART TWO
Belgium and the Netherlands

6

Belgium

When Belgium achieved its independence in 1830, the constitution which was established was based on a limited monarchy, a representative parliament, division of powers between the executive, legislature and judiciary, and the responsibility of ministers to parliament. Until the late 1960s, when attempts were made to resolve cultural and language issues by means of constitutional changes, the constitution of 1831 was revised on only two occasions, in 1892–3 and 1919–21; and on both these occasions the reasons for reform arose out of the need to change the electoral system. This was clearly an issue of central importance, and helps to explain why Belgium was a pioneer in the development of electoral systems.

Also, the electoral system has always been entrenched, or partly entrenched, in the Belgian constitution, and the history of this system therefore serves to demonstrate the advantages and disadvantages of entrenchment. Two electoral provisions in the 1831 constitution which were an obstacle to reform were that the franchise for elections to the lower house had to be restricted to citizens who paid direct taxes varying from 20 to 100 florins in different areas, and that elections had to be held in constituencies which formed divisions within each province. Thus, without a constitutional amendment, which it was difficult to secure, the means-tested suffrage could not be reduced below the level prescribed, and the small-sized constituencies could not be replaced by the province as the electoral unit. Long frustration over the difficulties of achieving wider suffrage and fairer representation helps to explain why, on several occasions, electoral reforms were debated in an atmosphere of acrimony in parliament, violence in the streets, the calling of general strikes, and disturbances which seemed at times to be developing into a revolutionary situation.

At the time of the adoption of the constitution in 1831 there was no demand for universal suffrage, and a means-tested suffrage was taken for granted. The means test discriminated in favour of the rural areas, which were mainly peasant and Catholic, and the one achievement of the revolutionary demands made in 1848 was the abolition of the discrimination by reducing the financial requirements everywhere to their minimum level. From this time onwards there could be no further extension of the franchise without constitutional revision.

Economic developments in the nineteenth century were concentrated heavily in the southern, French-speaking provinces. In spite of the development of parliamentary institutions, this did not for a long time affect the character of popular representation. The means-tested suffrage was so restrictive that everywhere it was the fairly affluent bourgeois class who had the vote, they tended to be the better-educated and French-speaking in Flanders as well as Wallonia, and they elected deputies who represented social and economic interests rather than those of language or race. However, the growing affluence and literacy which accompanied the industrial revolution, and the growing social and economic problems created by industrial and urban development, led to demands for the extension of the suffrage, and the growth of a labour movement which was strongest in the industrial areas of the south.

The elections held under the constitution of 1831, until the reform of the electoral law in 1899, were based on the majority system with a second ballot if necessary, an absolute majority being required at the first ballot, but a relative majority to suffice at the second. Some constituencies were single-member, but most were multi-member, and in the multi-member constituencies the block vote system was used. Through block voting, one party commonly swept the board in each constituency. The Liberals were in office almost continuously from 1848 to 1870, and then alternated with the Catholics until 1882, after which the Catholics became the party permanently in power until the First World War.

It was from about the 1860s that campaigns began to develop both for universal male suffrage and for proportional representation, some advocates supporting both of these causes, and others only one or the other. The earliest important influence in favour of PR was that of Thomas Hare and John Stuart Mill. In 1865 Philippe Bourson published a pamphlet on Hare's system of the single transferable vote, and in the same year a right-wing deputy, Jules de Smedt, also advocated electoral reform. In 1881 Victor D'Hondt was one of the founders of the Association Réformiste Belge pour l'Adoption de la Représentation Proportionnelle, of which Jules de Smedt became president. The committee of the association at this time, and ever afterwards, contained a number of members from both the Liberal and the Catholic parties. In 1882 there began the publication of the association's journal, *La Représentation proportionnelle*, which was prolific in publishing articles on the electoral reform movement in many countries during the following decades. In the same year D'Hondt published his *Système pratique et raisonné de la représentation proportionnelle*, advocating the system which was later the one most widely adopted in Europe.

After 1882, through the bias of the electoral system, the Catholics consolidated their position as the party with a constant majority of seats in parliament. Opposition parties now sought remedies for the inequitable results of the existing system, but at this time it was the campaign for universal manhood suffrage that was gaining ground to a greater extent. The case for 'one man, one vote' was easier to understand than the case for a more sophisticated electoral system, it had a wider popular appeal, and it was supported by many left-wing Liberals, not only on principle, but also because they despaired of gaining greater Liberal representation except through the extension of the franchise.

The means-tested suffrage had led to many corrupt practices and much 'electoral engineering'. There arose an absurd situation in which citizens strove to become liable to pay direct taxes in order that they might become eligible to vote – in the knowledge, however, that they would be recompensed from the funds of the party they supported. Each party, when in government, adopted measures to exempt their opponents from direct taxes. A Liberal government, for example, removed tax liability from farm horses which were used by Catholic peasants as (taxable) 'coach' horses on Sundays; while a Catholic government transformed into indirect taxes those direct taxes which had previously been levied on Liberal-voting wineshop proprietors.

With industrialisation and urbanisation, a socialist party, the Parti Ouvrier Belge, was finally formed in 1885, and from the outset universal manhood suffrage was a principal item of their policy. For the Liberals, proportional representation was the means by which they could achieve fair representation for their voters. For the labour movement, the extension of the franchise beyond the limit now reached within the terms of the constitution was the only way in which they could achieve representation at all. Nevertheless, there were also Socialists who, on principle, favoured proportional representation, just as there were Liberals who favoured universal manhood suffrage. The most powerful of the Socialist supporters of proportional representation was their leader, Emile Vandervelde. His influence, at critical stages of later events, in spite of opposition from many members of his own party, especially the radical left wing, contributed to the eventual adoption of proportional representation. On the Catholic side, supporters of proportional representation were not entirely lacking. The Catholic prime minister, Beernaert, had himself joined the Association Réformiste in 1885.

As regards the franchise, the right wing had actually less to fear from universal manhood suffrage than the Liberals. The Liberal vote was mainly bourgeois, but the right wing could count on the mass of peasant voters who were Catholics. In face of the mounting campaign for universal suffrage, Beernaert was willing to concede it provided the *limited* vote were introduced as some safeguard of minority representation. He had already expressed himself in favour of PR, but did not think he could carry this over the obstacles which were entrenched in the constitution, and against the opposition of the Catholics in the north who were secure in their constituency majorities. Eventually a full general election was held in 1892, which returned a solid Catholic majority, and a commission was appointed to submit proposals for constitutional reform.

A compromise was achieved on this occasion, but only after the Socialists had launched a general strike, and after the threat of serious disturbances. Constitutional amendments of 1893 introduced universal manhood suffrage at the age of 25, but with plural voting allowed for certain categories of the electorate. This was called the *vote capacitaire et censitaire*, or the 'qualifications and property-assessment franchise'. An extra vote was granted to married or widowed taxpayers and landowners, and two extra votes to those holding higher qualifications in education, or occupied in certain professions, or employed in certain offices. No one might exercise more than three votes. The compromise was meant as a safeguard against the domination of parliament by the 'masses', and against the sweeping aside of the better-educated and property-owning classes, who were presumed to have more mature judgement and a higher sense of responsibility.

The effect of this reform was to increase the electorate tenfold. In the general election which followed in 1894 the results showed a victory for the Catholics, which was achieved overwhelmingly at the expense of the Liberals, though the Catholics themselves had a reduced majority. The Liberals lost votes to those electors who feared above all the prospect of a Socialist majority in parliament. The Socialists, whose supporters had the vote for the first time, gained substantial representation in the industrial areas of Wallonia, and this also was at the expense of the Liberals. In parliament, the Catholics still had more than two-thirds of the seats with only half the votes, but the Socialists now had more seats than the Liberals.

The majority system with block votes had produced results which were already highly distorted when there were only two parties in existence. The introduction of universal manhood suffrage created a three-party system which, under the same method of majority voting, produced results which were even more distorted than before. It was not PR which created the three-party system – that was created in 1894 while the majority system still existed. Nor did PR result later in the creation of additional parties which had any significant impact, during the first half of the twentieth century at least, on the structure of the party system. It was only from about the middle of the 1960s that this three-party system was seriously challenged by regional parties based on linguistic and cultural differences.

After 1894 the anomalous election results, and the invidious privileges embodied in the system of plural voting, led to renewed campaigns both for further reform of the franchise and for proportional representation. Some Catholics were becoming alarmed at the prospect that the Socialists, now the second-largest party, could become their main rivals for office, and that in due course, under the majority system of election, they could become the governing party on the strength of a minority vote.

In 1894 Beernaert, already himself a supporter of PR, presented a Bill to adopt the D'Hondt system, subject to the retention of such single-member constituencies as still existed at that time, and to the stipulation of a 'quorum' of votes which a party must secure in a constituency in order to gain representation. These reservations were designed to satisfy at that time both those Catholics who opposed the representation of such splinter parties as the left-wing Catholic Democrats, and those Socialists who opposed the emergence of a rival anti-clerical left-wing party. Beernaert's Bill encountered opposition as well as support from all sides of the house, the Bill foundered and he resigned as prime minister.

However, the disrepute into which the electoral system had now fallen was such that the moment was ripe for a new campaign in favour of reform. Count Goblet D'Alviella's own account of events discloses very little about the part which he himself played, but it may well have been decisive. At his suggestion, the Association Réformiste adopted as a subtitle La Ligue Nationale pour la Représentation Proportionnelle, and embarked on an active campaign of publicity and political pressure. An important development was that Beernaert and other members of the Catholic Party in favour of reform were willing to consult with the Socialists about policy, and this was the first time that the Catholics had collaborated politically with the Socialist left. Emile Vandervelde, the Socialist leader, himself sympathetic towards PR, played an important part, and some other Socialists also participated.

The right-wing Vandenpeereboom, who was now prime minister, thought that in the face of a possible Liberal and Socialist alliance some change in the electoral system should be proposed, but his ministry and the Catholic Party as a whole were divided on what should be done. He submitted proposals which purported to be a compromise, but which were heavily biased in favour of the Catholic Party. In effect, PR was to be introduced in all constituencies which had six deputies or more, which happened to be industrial constituencies where the Catholic vote was weak, and where all or most of the seats were likely, under the majority system, to be held by the opposition; but the majority system was to continue in thirty-five constituencies where the opposition would have gained from PR. The Catholics would have been strengthened where they were weak, and reinforced where they were strong. The proposals were so one-sided that even many Catholics refused to support them.

The Socialists issued a manifesto denouncing the proposals as unconstitutional, because they would set up two electoral regimes, and this would violate the principle of equality which was embedded in the constitution. The Socialist demand, now as ever, was primarily for universal suffrage 'pure and simple', which now meant the abolition of plural voting; but Vandervelde held together the alliance of the Socialists and the Liberals by persuading a Socialist conference at Louvain that PR should continue in the party programme.

Vandenpeereboom thought that the storm which had been created would pass, and he offered no concessions. Towards the end of June 1899 there were on several occasions scenes of uproar and physical violence in parliament which were without precedent in Belgian history. A general strike was called, and there were meetings, marches and disturbances in the streets. At last Vandenpeereboom agreed to an adjournment of parliament so that a commission could re-examine proposals for reform, and the disturbances subsided. However, the all-party commission failed to reach any agreement on any single proposal, and Vandenpeereboom resigned.

De Smet de Naeyer now became prime minister, and without delay he announced proposals for proportional representation using the D'Hondt system. The general council of the Ligue Nationale pour la Représentation Proportionnelle declared that the proposals had its full support. Some Socialists complained that they had been betrayed by the Liberals, and wanted to resume agitation in the streets in favour of universal suffrage 'pure and simple', but their leader, Vandervelde, opposed any obstructive tactics. In local government elections, which were held while the debate continued, the Socialists had little success, and it was evident that they could not raise a popular campaign against the proposals. Most Catholics were now resigned to electoral reform, and in the end it was overwhelmingly the Catholic vote which succeeded in carrying the proposals by 70 votes for and 63 against. The proposals were enacted and became law on 29 December 1899.

There was little jubilation as yet in the ranks of the electoral reformers. Since the constituencies were numerous and small, and since there was widespread resentment against a suffrage still based on discriminatory plural voting, the circumstances were not entirely favourable. The new system was, however, the salvation of the Liberals, who soon recovered, and maintained until the First World War their position as the second-largest party in parliament after the Catholics.

Nevertheless, owing to the small size of the constituencies, the results in elections still fell short of proportionality. The Catholics received considerably more seats than they would have done if the provinces, instead of the constituencies, had been the areas within which proportionality was to be achieved, and the Liberals and Socialists received considerably fewer seats in relation to their votes.

Over the previous five years public support for proportional representation had been greatly strengthened. The last bastion of opposition was in the house of representatives itself, where many members owed their seats to the working of the majority system. The coming of PR was a triumph of public opinion over the repugnance of many members of parliament.

The history of Liberal and Socialist rivalry in seeking further reforms now repeated itself, with the Liberals attempting to improve the proportionality of the electoral system, and the Socialists demanding 'one man, one vote' instead of the existing system of plural voting. There was naturally no urgency for further reform in the Catholic Party as a whole, but many Catholics were more favourably inclined than the Socialists were to the introduction of *women's* suffrage. It was commonly believed that under the influence of the priesthood women would be more inclined than men to support conservative and Catholic policies.

At first it was the Socialists who pressed most strongly for reform. In 1902 there were once again violent disturbances, and six people were killed in the so-called *fusillade de Louvain*, but these were quelled by the security forces and the agitation was for the time being a failure. During the next ten years, however, the movement in favour of universal suffrage 'pure and simple' once again gained momentum, and it had support from the Liberals and some left-wing Catholics. War broke out before any proposals were implemented. During the war, Liberals, including Count Goblet d'Alviella, and Socialists, including Vandervelde, accepted office in the government. The way was prepared for reform when the war was over.

Meanwhile the Liberals, recently rescued through the adoption of PR, had reason to press for the further improvement of the electoral system. The small size of the constituencies continued to favour the Catholics who, in 1904, 1908 and 1914, had a majority of seats in the chamber after having secured only a minority of votes in elections. It would have been possible, after an amendment of the constitution in 1893, to make the province the electoral unit instead of the constituencies, but this would have been strongly opposed by the Catholics. As a compromise Van de Walle, a writer on electoral systems, proposed the device of *apparentement*. This permitted parties to form alliances, so that jointly they might secure the advantage, in terms of increased allocation of seats, which larger parties enjoyed at the expense of the smaller. This advantage would be gained at the provincial level, and additional seats would be allocated to the alliances and the parties in the constituencies by the successive application of the D'Hondt system.

As soon as the war was over a government of 'national unity' was formed under the Catholic leader Delacroix, who announced a programme including universal suffrage 'pure and simple', and the reduction of the voting age to 21. This is what the Socialists wanted, and, as a concession to the Liberals, *apparentement* at the provincial level was introduced in a law of October 1919. There was more prolonged debate over women's suffrage, but in a constitutional amendment of 1921 the compromise arrived at was that the suffrage might in the future be extended to women if it was carried by a two-thirds majority in parliament. Constitutional changes made in 1920 and 1921 confirmed the adoption of universal suffrage 'pure and simple', the inscription of proportional representation into the constitution, and the holding of elections for the chamber every four years, instead of, as hitherto, renewing the composition of only half the chamber every two years.

Proportional representation did not lead, as it was feared, to a proliferation of parties. The three major parties which had emerged at the end of the nineteenth century, before proportional representation, continued to dominate the party political system. There were periods when other parties appeared to be gaining in strength, but on each occasion their success was short-lived. Flemish nationalist parties under various titles achieved substantial representation in the 1930s, and several parties, including the Communists and others which tended to be violent and fascist, constituted a block of 'anti-system' votes in parliament, which amounted to 25 per cent of the total in 1936, but their support fell away again thereafter. In Belgium, parliamentary institutions, in spite, some would say, of proportional representation, survived the world economic depression and the 'anti-system' movements of the 1930s. The constitution of 1831, changed only in the provisions for suffrage and elections, survived intact until the late 1960s.

Although *apparentement* changed the electoral system to the advantage of the Liberals, the reform of the suffrage changed it even more to the advantage of the Socialists. After the First World War there was no occasion on which the Socialists did not gain more seats in parliament than the Liberals, and in 1936 for the first time they gained more seats than the Catholics. The Catholics and the Socialists had become the main rivals for power.

Another consequence of universal suffrage and electoral reform was that the role of political parties became of greater importance, particularly because the need to form coalition governments required consultation between the parties. There was inevitably a fear that parties might come under the control of caucuses or closely knit minorities who did not accurately reflect the views of the electors. In the early days of PR, Count Goblet d'Alviella was optimistic on this account, and assured the British Royal Commission on Electoral Systems that in Belgium party organisation was democratic. The most important point at which democracy should be expressed within each party was in the nomination of candidates for election to parliament, and the count declared that it was quite common for party members to choose candidates using the system of the single transferable vote. However, the control of party members over party affairs does appear, in the course of time, to have diminished rather than increased. After party managers had prepared a list of candidates, the final settling of the order of the candidates on the list by all the party members in the constituency was increasingly abandoned.

Suffrage for women, debated for generations and half-conceded in 1921 as a possible reform in the future, was at last implemented in 1948. This doubled the electorate, but contrary to the expectation of parties of both left and right it made no significant difference to the distribution of votes between the parties.

Of great importance was the emergence of new parties on the political scene from 1965 onwards. These were the rival Flemish and Walloon nationalist parties for whom the questions of language and culture are of the greatest concern. These parties together outnumbered the Liberals in 1971 and 1974. The Catholic and Liberal parties themselves also tended to be divided into Flemish and Walloon factions, although the Socialists for a time retained greater cohesion. The issues between the communities have been of growing importance since the Second World War. Commissions were appointed to seek constitutional solutions of the problems in 1946, 1962 and 1964, and finally a joint parliamentary commission succeeded in introducing constitutional reforms between 1967 and 1971. The solution resolved upon was to divide the nation into four linguistic areas for Dutch-speaking Flanders, French-speaking Wallonia, bilingual Brabant and a small German-speaking area in east Belgium. Cultural councils were established for the main language communities, with powers of legislation in certain fields, including education, cultural activities and industrial relations.

The constitutional changes have been concerned with devolution of power and federalism, which are intended to combine the unity of the state with autonomy for the cultural and linguistic communities. Discussions of reforms in the electoral system have been very much secondary to these major issues, and have had little or no contribution to make to the problems which exist. There is so solid a Catholic vote in Flanders, and so solid a Socialist vote in Wallonia, that majority voting, if it were introduced, would divide the state so deeply that its continued existence would be in doubt.

The Belgian electoral system has remained essentially the same as it was after the reforms of 1919–21, except that a constitutional amendment of 1971 fixed the number of seats in the house of representatives at

212. The number of seats allocated to each constituency is determined after each census of population. The number of the total population is divided by 212, and the quotient (which is the Hare quota) is used to determine the number of seats to be allocated to each constituency, remaining seats being allocated by the method of the 'largest remainder'.

In an election, each elector votes either by casting one vote for a party list in the order in which the party has presented the candidates, or else one vote for one candidate on the list. In allocating seats to parties, the votes for the party list and for individual candidates on the list are aggregated to ascertain the total vote for the party. There are then several stages involved in allocating seats to parties, constituencies and individuals.

First, in each constituency the Hare quota is used for a first distribution of seats in each constituency.

Secondly, for the distribution of the remaining seats at the level of the province, the votes of each party in each constituency are added together; but only a party which has obtained at least two-thirds of the Hare quota in at least one constituency may participate in this second distribution. The total votes for each participating party in the province are then ascertained, the D'Hondt system is applied to these totals, and this determines how many of the remaining seats in the province are to be allocated to each party.

Thirdly, within the province, the additional party seats are allocated to individual constituencies by application of the D'Hondt system to the quotas of votes obtained by the party in each constituency, starting with the party which has obtained the highest number of additional seats. If the highest quota of a party is in a constituency which has already received all the seats to which it is entitled under the constitution, then the party's seat is allocated to a constituency which still has a seat vacant.

Fourthly, for the allocation of seats to individual candidates on a party's list, a Droop quota is obtained by dividing the total number of votes for the party in a constituency by the number of seats which the party has finally been allocated *plus one*, and rounding upwards or adding one. From the party's total vote in the constituency, the first candidate on the party's list is allocated a number of votes which, together with any personal votes he has gained, will reach the Droop quota, and at this point he is deemed to be elected. Remaining party votes are transferred to the next candidate on the party's list in the same way, until he reaches the Droop quota and is elected. This process is repeated until as many candidates have been elected as there are seats allocated to the party in the constituency. Electors can seek to influence the order in which candidates of the party are elected by helping their favoured candidate to achieve a Droop quota with the aid of personal votes, but the odds are heavily weighted in favour of candidates at or near the head of the party's list.

REFERENCES: CHAPTER 6

Belgium has been well served with literature on electoral reform since 1881, when there was founded the Association Réformiste Belge pour l'Adoption de la Représentation Proportionnelle. This continued to issue copious reports and articles up to the end of the century, when its objective was achieved. The electoral system also has two main historians, Count Goblet d'Alviella, in *La représentation proportionnelle en Belgique: l'histoire d'une réforme*, and John Gilissen, *Le régime représéntatif en Belgique depuis 1790*. A briefer account is contained in an article entitled 'L'évolution des idées concernant la représentation proportionnelle en Belgique' by Léon Moureau and Charles Goossens, in the *Revue de droit international et de droit comparé*, 1958. The constitutional background is described in Robert Senelle's *The Belgian Constitution: Commentary*, and the modern electoral system in *Parliamentary Elections in Belgium* by F. Coppieters. An article which examines a particular aspect of the Belgian electoral system is 'Le rôle et la place de l'apparentement dans les élections législatives belges à la lumière du calcul de la dévolution des sièges selon différents modes', by H. Brény and J. Beaufays, in *Res Publica*, 1974.

7

The Netherlands

During the Napoleonic wars the Republic of the Netherlands was converted into a monarchy, with Napoleon's brother, Louis, installed as king. Upon the withdrawal of French troops in December 1813, the Prince of Orange was invested with sovereign powers, and a union with Belgium was established in August 1814. A constitution adopted in August 1815 included, at the insistence of the Belgian notables, the establishment of an upper chamber of parliament, called the 'first' chamber, as well as a lower chamber. In this lower chamber Belgium and the Netherlands were to be equally represented, having fifty-five members each. The original intention was that the legislature should meet alternately in Brussels and The Hague, but this was discontinued after 1819, when Dutch was made the only official language in the new kingdom. The language question was one element in the independence movement in Belgium, which resulted in rebellion and the declaration of Belgian independence in November 1830.

The independence of Belgium required a revision of the constitution of the Netherlands, but this was not completed until 1840. Under both the 1815 and 1840 constitutions the second or lower chamber was indirectly elected by the eighteen provincial councils. These in turn consisted of members representing different 'Estates', or classes of society – the nobles, burgesses and the rural classes. The entire first or upper chamber was nominated by the Crown, reinforcing the considerable powers which the Crown then exercised.

From 1840 onwards liberal reformers sought to achieve constitutional changes which would limit the powers of the monarch and extend those of parliament, and in the course of the revolutionary movements of 1848 this purpose was fulfilled by means of the constitutional revision in October of that year. While the Crown retained the power to dissolve parliament, the first or upper chamber was no longer nominated but was elected by the provincial councils. The principle of government responsibility to parliament became a source of lengthy conflict between the Crown and parliament, but from 1868 onwards the responsibility of ministers to parliament was firmly established.

The authority of parliament was eventually reinforced by a gradual extension of the franchise. In 1850 elections for the second chamber were for the first time direct instead of indirect, and the franchise was extended to males over 23 whether resident in town or country, subject to a means test which varied from province to province. This limited the electorate to about 2·5 per cent of the population. In the 1880s there were growing demands for the extension of the franchise, but only a limited reform took place in 1887, which had the effect of increasing the electorate to 6·5 per cent of the population. Another reform in 1896 increased the electorate further to 12 per cent of the population. In the years before the First World War there was a mounting campaign for universal suffrage, which was achieved for men in 1917 and for women in 1919.

The electoral system established at the same time as the first direct elections in 1850 was based on two-member constituencies, with one member elected alternately every two years, and each serving for four years. At elections, therefore, a candidate stood in what was in effect, for electoral purposes, a single-member constituency. An absolute majority was required at a first ballot, but if a second ballot was necessary a simple majority sufficed. One member was to be elected for every 45,000 of population, so that with a growing population the number of members increased from sixty-eight in 1850 to eighty-six in 1878, but the number of constituencies with two members each was steadily reduced in favour of single-member constituencies. In 1887 the number of deputies in the second or lower chamber was for the first time made constant and fixed at 100. Elections were now, except in municipalities, in single-member constituencies, with an absolute majority required in a first ballot and a relative majority sufficing in any second ballot. From 1896, all constituencies returned a single member only, and second ballots were confined to the two candidates who had most votes in the first. This electoral system remained essentially unchanged until 1917. The boundaries of the constituencies also remained unaltered, and unequal increase in population gave rise to considerable discrepancies in the size of different constituencies. This added force to arguments in favour of electoral reform, which culminated in the adoption of proportional representation in 1917.

Until the powers of parliament had been asserted, first partially in 1848 and then decisively in 1868, there was little scope or need for party organisation, and political efforts were largely confined to the campaign by liberals for constitutional reform. After 1848 a structure of rival political parties began to take shape, reflecting the social and cultural differences within the Dutch nation. At first, in 1850, the Liberals, who were the champions of the constitutional rights of parliament, were the strongest single party, but the Conservatives, on whom the Crown relied for support, became their chief rivals until 1866. After the final assertion of the powers of parliament in 1868 the Conservatives eventually ceased to be a power to be reckoned with, and their representation progressively dwindled in successive elections. The Liberals, on the other hand, became from 1868 the dominant party, and always, until 1901, had an absolute majority of seats in the lower chamber, or else not far short of half the seats. It was only after the turn of the century that the power of the Liberals began to decline, but when it did the decline was rapid and already considerable before the outbreak of the First World War, and before the adoption of proportional representation in 1917.

The other parties reflected the religious and social divisions within the nation. The Catholics were in 1853 permitted to re-establish the episcopal hierarchy which had been proscribed since the Reformation. An overwhelming majority of the population in the southern provinces of Northern Brabant and Limburg were Catholic, and elsewhere in the nation, except in the farthest north-eastern provinces, they comprised a substantial minority. The principal political issue with which they were concerned was whether and to what extent state aid should be given to denominational schools.

The fourth group were the Calvinists, who supported the Catholic Church against the Liberals on the issue of state aid for denominational schools. The most politically active of the Calvinists, and the most dogmatic in matters of doctrine, formed the Anti-Revolutionary Party in 1879. As distinct from political factions within parliament, this was the first effectively organised political party having its base in the electorate and not confined largely to deputies. Socially, the party had adherents among the lower as well as the upper classes. When, however, the party gave its support to the extension of the franchise, one faction split off from the party in 1894, and after successive unions with other groups and consequent changes of name, this group became the Christian Historical Party in 1908.

In the 1880s there emerged a fifth party, a Labour Party, which reflected the growth of industrialism in the Netherlands from about 1870 onwards. In 1881 there was formed a Social Democratic Alliance which had extreme left-wing policies and sought to overthrow the parliamentary system, but more moderate leaders detached themselves from this alliance and the dissident group developed into the mainstream of the labour movement. The Social Democratic Workers' Party, representing this movement, contested the election of 1894 without success, but as support for the Liberals declined they grew in strength and won three seats in 1897, which they increased thereafter to fifteen seats by 1913. After the Second World War the party changed their name to the Party of Labour.

These five parties all survived to contest every election from 1894 to 1972 inclusive. Until 1963 their joint share of the total votes and seats was remarkably stable. In 1913, while the electoral system was still based on majorities in single-member constituencies, the share of the five main parties was 82 per cent of the votes and 83 per cent of the seats. Since the average share of these parties in votes and seats in the six elections between 1918 and 1937, after the adoption of PR in 1917, was respectively 81 per cent and 84 per cent, this suggests there was no weakening in the strength of the main parties as a result of PR. This applied equally to the role of the three main confessional parties (Catholic and Calvinist). Their joint share of the total votes and seats averaged just under 50 per cent before the First World War, and a little over 50 per cent both throughout the interwar period and in the postwar period from 1946 to 1963.

On the issue of electoral reform, the Labour Party were naturally the strongest advocates of the extension of the franchise. The Liberals, mainly a middle-class party, were divided on this issue, and although on the whole in favour of an extension of the franchise they wished to impose a literacy test and to extend the electorate in the urban rather than the rural areas. The Anti-Revolutionary Party, on the other hand, desired an extension of the franchise especially in the rural areas, while the Christian Historicals, socially a more upper-class party, were opposed to any substantial extension of the franchise.

On the issue of the electoral system, the experience on which the calculation of party self-interest might be based was not unambiguous. On the whole, of the three major parties at the end of the nineteenth century, the Liberals normally had a much larger share of the seats than of votes, and so, to a lesser extent, did the Catholics. The Anti-Revolutionary Party, on the other hand, were almost always at a serious disadvantage. These differences were not based consistently on the differences in the size of the parties, the greatest advantage going to the largest. The Anti-Revolutionary Party between 1897 and 1913 always secured far more votes than the Catholics, yet almost always secured far fewer seats. Also, contrary to what might have been expected, the small parties were not particularly disfavoured. The newly emerging or splinter parties did not consistently receive an appreciably smaller share of seats than of votes, and not infrequently received a larger share. This applied to the Christian Historicals, the Labour Party and some other parties. Discrepancies were due more to the geographical distribution of votes than to any critical levels of size of each party; and a further characteristic of the system was that discrepancies varied considerably from one election to another.

If the results of successive elections influenced the eventual decision to adopt PR, the unpredictability of the relationship between votes and seats was probably as cogent a reason for reform as the bias there was in favour of some parties and against others. Also, towards the end of the First

World War, the climate of opinion in many countries was in favour of PR, of which, moreover, Belgium, the immediate neighbour of the Netherlands, had earlier been the pioneer. Although the Catholic Party in the Netherlands had enjoyed a bias in their favour under the majority system, the example of Belgium suggested that PR might well in the future be a safeguard for Catholics in the Netherlands, as well as in Belgium, against the inroads of a growing and popularly based socialist movement.

Proportional representation was adopted in 1917 in a form which, with some modifications, has lasted ever since. The nation was divided into eighteen electoral districts or 'rings', with Amsterdam, The Hague, Rotterdam and seven out of the eleven provinces each forming one district, and the remaining four provinces each being divided into two districts. Nominations of candidates in party lists took place in each district, and it was for these lists that voting in each district took place. However, it was at the national and not at the district level that the allocation of seats to parties took place and proportionality was achieved. District parties were permitted to ally themselves into so-called 'groups' of parties at the national level, but these alliances really consisted of unions of district branches of the same national party. In form, therefore, *apparentement* was permitted, but alliances between different parties in the same district were excluded. Until 1970 it was not possible for separate small parties to improve their electoral chances by entering into an electoral alliance within a district.

The allocation of seats at the national level was based on the simple or Hare quota, that is, the number of votes divided by the number of seats. In 1918 remaining seats were allocated by the method of the largest remainder. All parties which had participated in the election were eligible to share in the allocation of remaining seats, even those which had failed to gain a single electoral quota. It was possible for a party to gain a seat with a share of the national vote which was little more than $0 \cdot 5$ per cent (that is, one-half of the national quota), as one party did in 1918. In that year, of nineteen parties which contested the election, seventeen succeeded in gaining at least one seat. The Catholics had most seats, with thirty, followed by the Labour Party with twenty-two and the Anti-Revolutionary Party with thirteen. The number of parties which succeeded in gaining seats contrasted with the experience before the First World War when, under the majority system, in eight elections between 1888 and 1913, there was no occasion on which the number of parties which succeeded in gaining seats was larger than seven, and the average was between five and six.

The proliferation of parties, and the consequent difficulty of forming viable coalition governments, soon led to changes in the electoral system. An amendment of 1921 provided that in order to share in the allocation of remaining seats a party must have secured at the national level at least 75 per cent of the quota for one seat. (This would have excluded six of the parties which had gained seats in 1918.) In the 1922 election four parties with less than 75 per cent of the quota were excluded, and the number of parties which gained seats was reduced from seventeen to nine.

An amendment of 1923 provided that if, in the first allocation of seats by the Hare quota, fifteen seats or more remained unallocated, then the remaining seats would not be allocated on the basis of the largest remainder, but instead by the application of the D'Hondt method to the *remaining* votes. This meant that a party with a particularly large *remainder* of votes might receive two additional seats before some other party received any. In this respect the small and large parties were on an equal footing, and it might be the smallest party which gained most from the allocation of remaining seats. Thus the application of the D'Hondt system to *remaining* votes could give an advantage to the smaller parties which was even greater than the advantage conferred by the system of the largest remainder. In the elections of 1925 and 1929 the number of parties which gained seats was eleven on each occasion.

A further amendment in 1933 provided that if the number of seats unallocated by the Hare quota exceeded nineteen, then the D'Hondt method should be applied to the *total* votes for each party, and not merely the remaining votes. This meant simply the adoption of the normal D'Hondt method in such cases instead of the largest remainder system, and the change of system tended to favour the largest parties instead of the smallest. At the same time, in order to qualify for the allocation of seats, parties were required to have achieved at least one *whole* quota, and not merely 75 per cent of a quota. In spite of this measure, the number of parties which gained seats was fourteen in 1933 and ten in 1937.

As regards the allocation of seats to individual candidates on party lists, the parties decide the order of preference of their candidates, and place their names on the party lists in that order. Electors have only one vote which they can cast for one candidate on the list, and this vote counts for the party as well as for the candidate. When the number of seats gained by each list has been determined, the number of votes which the party gained is divided by the number of seats it has won, and the figure so obtained is treated as the quota of votes which will secure a seat for a particular candidate. If a candidate secures more personal votes than the quota, his surplus is transferred to other candidates in the order in which they appear in the *party list*; and as many votes are transferred as may be necessary to ensure that all party seats are allocated to individual candidates. Should some seats remain unallocated after the transfer of votes has been completed, the remaining seats are allocated in order to those remaining candidates who received most personal votes, provided they have received at least half a quota of party votes. Any seats which still remain are allocated to candidates in the order in which they appear on the party list. In practice, the candidates elected have almost always been those who appeared at the head of the party lists, and the only value of the personal voting has been to give the parties some indication of the personal popularity of individual candidates on the party list.

The extension of the suffrage in 1917 to all men aged 25 or over led to an increase in the electorate from 15 to 23 per cent of the population, which was increased further to 49 per cent when the suffrage was extended to women aged 25 or over in 1919. With the increase in the number of agricultural and industrial workers who were enfranchised the chief political beneficiaries were the Catholic and the Labour parties. Since the Calvinist confessional parties held on to their share of the seats the chief losses were incurred by the Liberals, who had already suffered a severe decline before the First World War. The once-dominant party of the nineteenth century were at this time no longer able to exert much influence in parliament.

The representation of the four other main parties, on the other hand, remained remarkably stable throughout the interwar period. There was a slight tendency for the Calvinist share of the seats to increase, but this was at the further expense of the Liberals, and the representation of the Catholics and of the Labour Party was virtually the same in 1937 as it had been in 1918. Apart from these parties, the only other to achieve a consistently significant number of seats was the Radical Party, which always obtained between five and seven. The Communists succeeded in winning four seats in 1933, but with this exception no other party succeeded in gaining more than three seats at any time between 1922 and 1937. Although there was a rather large number of parties which succeeded in gaining one or two seats, the major parties, including the Radicals, always had around 90 per cent of the total number of seats, declining somewhat from 94 per cent in the 1920s to rather less than 90 per cent in the 1930s.

All governments were inevitably coalitions, and after general elections, or after the not infrequent breakdown of previous coalitions, these often took a considerable time to form. The Labour Party (Social Democratic Workers) never participated in government during the interwar period, although they were the second-largest party. Cabinets were composed of the confessional parties (Catholic and Calvinist) which had before the war established habits of co-operation through a common interest in safeguarding the right of denominational education. An element of continuity was to be found in the fact that although there were frequent changes of Cabinet it was commonly a limited number of politicians who assumed the leadership or took office in successive governments. Cabinet formation was, moreover, quite different from the practice in countries such as the United Kingdom, since, by convention, ministers did not serve simultaneously as members of parliament. This convention, to which there had been very few exceptions since 1848, was made mandatory and embodied in the constitution in 1938. Although governments depended on parliamentary majorities to pass legislation, this arrangement made it easier to form coalitions, since a prominent party member might enter a government without feeling obliged to adhere in a rigid manner to his party's policy.

After the Second World War the suffrage was extended by lowering the voting age successively from 25 to 23 in 1945, 21 in 1956 and 18 in 1972. From 1956 the number of deputies was increased from 100 to 150, but there was no change in the requirement (introduced in 1933) that to be eligible for the allocation of seats a party must gain one whole quota. With the increase in the number of seats in the lower chamber, the quota was now equivalent to 0·67 per cent of the total vote, instead of 1 per cent, which made it easier for a very small party to gain a seat.

Nevertheless, the party system functioned until about 1963 very much as it had done before. There remained the same five principal parties which between them had dominated the lower chamber since before the First World War. Some parties (as a result of mergers in some cases) had changed their names – the Catholics to the Catholic People's Party, the Social Democratic Workers' Party to the Party of Labour, and the Liberal States Party to the People's Party of Freedom and Democracy. If the continuing Anti-Revolutionary Party and the Christian Historical Party are added, these five parties obtained a higher average proportion of both votes and seats than they had done in the interwar period. The Communists had emerged from the Second World War in formidable strength, as a result of the prestige they had gained in their underground struggle with the German forces of occupation; but the party's popularity did not survive the Cold War, and the share of the seats they gained declined from 10 per cent in 1946 to 2 per cent in 1959.

From 1963 onwards the party system underwent considerable changes, and the political situation became increasingly confused. Among the main changes up to and including 1972 was a substantial decline in the representation of the two largest parties – the Catholic People's Party, which was the largest party in the lower chamber until 1967, and the Labour Party, which was the largest from 1967 onwards. These two parties had between them nearly two-thirds of the seats in 1956 and 1959, but less than half in 1971 and 1972. The decline was particularly marked in the Catholic Party, whose share of seats fell from one-third in 1962 to less than one-fifth in 1972. The share of the Christian Historicals also declined, but support for the Liberals at this time remained fairly steady.

The decline of the two main parties could be accounted for by the new 'splinter' parties which burst upon the scene in the early 1960s. These were of a very varied character. One of them was the Farmers' Party, which was a 'Poujadist' party of protest against the failure of governments to safeguard their particular interests, and which contested elections for the first time in 1963. More significant were the party calling themselves 'Democrats '66', a name derived from the year in which they were formed. This was a 'populist' party, impatient with the 'old guard' and 'the establishment', and anxious to achieve democracy of a direct character. They sought to bring about changes which would ensure greater responsiveness of the legislature to the desires of their constituents. They demanded that prime ministers should be appointed by direct popular election, and that referenda should be held on issues of major importance.

Another new party was a group of Radicals, who were dissidents on the left wing of the Catholic Party, and who formed a separate party of their own in 1968. On the other hand, Democrats '70 were disaffected members of the Labour Party, who objected to the growing influence of the extreme left wing upon that party; and the Roman Catholic Party, formed in 1971, were a right-wing and doctrinaire group who were opposed to liberal tendencies within the Catholic Church.

During this period the overall support for the five main parties greatly declined, from 90 per cent of the seats in 1963 to 82 per cent in 1967, and to little more than 75 per cent in 1971 and 1972. It appeared that the old system in which five principal parties had consistently predominated in the lower chamber of parliament had now disintegrated, and that the effects of PR, so often predicted but so long unfulfilled, were becoming manifest at last. The form of PR in the Netherlands, being based on the nation as a single constituency, offered the possibility of representation to very small parties, provided only they succeeded in gaining a single quota of votes. It now seemed that this had given excessive power to dissident groups within parties, and there developed a body of opinion which favoured changes in the electoral system to make the representation of the smallest parties or factions more difficult. This, it was thought, would have a stabilising effect on the party system, and would reduce the difficulty of forming coalitions. There was little desire to abandon PR altogether, since this had come to be regarded in the Netherlands as part of the essence of representative democracy, and was practised not only in parliamentary elections but also in other sectors of public life. There was, however, in some quarters, a desire to render more difficult the representation of the smallest political groups, commonly regarded as the least politically responsible.

There were two possible reforms of the electoral system which were chiefly under consideration. One proposal was that instead of the whole nation being designated as a single constituency for the purpose of allocating seats to parties, the allocation should instead be made within the eighteen districts in which the nomination of candidates took place and party lists were submitted. In the 1963 and 1967 elections, if the allocation of seats had been made within the eighteen districts, the number of seats gained by the smaller parties other than the main four would have been three and eight instead of fifteen and twenty-seven. (This assumes that the pattern of voting would have remained the same.) A committee on the constitution established in 1967 recommended that allocation of seats should be made within twelve districts with ten to fifteen seats each, but this was strongly opposed by the Liberals and the smaller parties. It also had little support from the politicians of the left wing, who attached greater importance to a proposal that a Cabinet *formateur*, responsible for the formation of a ministry, should be elected by a popular vote, thereby introducing something in the nature of a presidential form of government.

The other possible change was to adopt some form of the German exclusion clause, which limited the allocation of additional seats to parties which had achieved a stipulated proportion of total votes, say, 3 or 5 per cent. If, as in Germany, parties which had failed to secure at least 5 per cent of the votes were excluded, then in the 1963 and 1967 elections the smaller parties other than the main five would have failed to gain any seats at all. This would clearly have been a more drastic solution than the first.

The only material change which was made was the recognition of the *apparentement* of separate parties within an electoral district for the purpose of the allocation of seats. This encouraged the formation of combinations or alliances of parties, but it also favoured the continued existence of separate parties which could now, through *apparentement*, gain more representation than if they had remained wholly independent as before.

No other substantial reform had been made in the electoral system before the situation was transformed once again as a result of a change in the behaviour of the electors and in the tactics of some parties. In May 1973 a coalition government was formed by the Labour Party leader, Joop Den Uyl, supported by the Labour Party, the Catholics, the Anti-Revolutionary Party, the Radicals and Democrats '66. For the next four years the principal opposition party were the Liberals, who had strengthened their representation in the 1972 election. In December 1976 the three confessional parties of Catholics and Calvinists formed a new interdenominational party entitled the Christian Democratic Appeal, to counteract the tendency, which had existed since the Second World War, for their joint share of the votes to decline. This new consolidation of parties contrasted with the recent disintegration of parties and the formation of new ones.

The general election of 1977 also reversed the recent tendency for parties to split up and proliferate. On this occasion the main parties, reduced from five in number to three, secured 83·7 per cent of the votes and 86·7 per cent of the seats, against 73·1 per cent and 75·4 per cent respectively in 1972. Ironically, it was not the newly combined confessional parties which gained the votes and seats − their share of both remained almost exactly the same. The gain was achieved mostly by the Labour Party and the Liberals. With the exception of the Democrats '66, whose representation increased from six seats to eight, the losses were incurred by the new 'splinter' parties which had appeared since 1963, and also by the Communists, whose votes and seats fell to less than one-third of their level in 1972.

The role of the political parties before 1963 had been of such a kind and so consistent as to suggest that the politics of the Netherlands were distinguished by special characteristics of their own described as the 'politics of accommodation'. Beginning in the nineteenth century, and long before the introduction of PR in parliamentary elections, problems arising from the existence of separate social and cultural sectors within the community, particularly divisions between Catholics and Calvinists, were resolved not by the victory of one party or faction over another, but by agreement on a compromise acceptable to each side. For example, state finance for denominational schools was provided on the basis of the number of pupils in each school, that is to say, on a proportional basis. The principle of proportionality was also applied in other fields, such as the composition of the civil service. However, an accompanying feature of the 'politics of accommodation', or compromise, was the dominant part played by the leaders of the parties or interests concerned. Agreements were commonly reached through private negotiation, rather than public debate, which reduced the scope for democratic control.

The adoption of PR made it easier for small parties to exist, but did not lead to a transformation of the party system, which on the contrary, in its main features, remained remarkably constant for several decades. This stable party system was reinforced in the course of time by the development of social and cultural organisations having an allegiance to one or other of the major parties, or to the community which a party particularly represented. Corresponding to each of the Catholic, Calvinist and Labour parties there were trade unions, newspapers, radio and television programmes, social and recreational clubs and charitable institutions, composed of members of the different communities, or serving their interests. It is not simply PR which has accounted for the long-continued existence of the four or five major parties. They have been based on separate community organisations, and they would probably have continued in existence without much change if the electoral system had been different.

For generations, the system of parliamentary government seemed to be under no special threat from 'anti-system' parties or movements. It was only in the mid-1960s that such a threat appeared to have come into existence, reflected in the rise of extremist parties and the decline of the 'establishment' parties in the elections between 1963 and 1972. It seemed then that there was a breakdown in the 'politics of accommodation'. The results of the election of 1977 may have allayed the fears which had only recently been aroused, but it is too early to judge whether the more volatile habits which electors developed in the 1960s are likely to be followed by the resumption of a stable pattern of voting and of party structure in the future.

REFERENCES: CHAPTER 7

The historical development of the electoral system is described by Arend Lijphart in an article entitled 'The Dutch electoral system in comparative perspective: extreme proportional representation, multipartism, and the failure of electoral reform', in the *Netherlands Journal of Sociology*, 1978. The working of the electoral system is also considered by Lijphart in *The Politics of Accommodation: Pluralism and Democracy in the Netherlands*. Hans Daalder has a chapter on 'Extreme proportional representation: the Dutch experience', in *Adversary Politics and Electoral Reform*. The current electoral system is described in *The Electoral System in the Netherlands*, a memorandum issued by the Royal Netherlands Embassy in London.

PART THREE
The Nordic Countries

8

Denmark

Four institutions in Denmark's history have at different times exerted great influence in shaping the constitutional and political framework of the nation. The three most ancient were the monarchy, the popular legislative assembly and provincial autonomy, or at least separate provincial identity. The fourth was the council or chamber of the nobility, which emerged towards the end of the thirteenth century, and was the ancestor of the upper chamber which existed for over a century up to 1953.

In Denmark the monarchy experienced through the ages all degrees of power from absolutism to virtual impotence. After a period of three centuries in which control had lain principally with a great council of the nobility, the constitution was redefined in the Act of Royalty of 1665, which conferred on the Crown an extreme degree of absolute power, with almost no limit except the requirement to maintain the Christian faith in the Protestant form of the Augsburg Confession. This was the regime which lasted until the revolutions of 1848, tempered in the eighteenth century by social and economic reforms, and by the recruitment of office-bearers and government officials from the middle classes.

In the earliest times, provincial assemblies had the power of electing the king, and were responsible for legislation, while the king acted mainly as a military commander and relied for his power on the extent of his own estates. There has persisted a separate identity of the different provinces, Jutland, the Islands, at one time Schleswig and Holstein, and Copenhagen when it achieved a degree or urbanisation which distinguished it from the rest of the country. These separate identities were reflected in the constitutions which were successively formulated, and are still reflected in the electoral system.

In the nineteenth century there were economic and social changes which had an effect on constitutional and political developments. Like the other Scandinavian countries, Denmark in the middle of the century was a poor country compared with others in Western Europe, but a hundred years later it had become one of the richest. Unlike the other

Scandinavian countries, and unlike most other countries in Western Europe, Denmark's economic development was based overwhelmingly on agriculture. In the generations before 1870 there had already taken place an agricultural revolution in Denmark which included a transformation of the industry away from arable crops and in the direction of livestock and dairy farming. Agricultural exports, mainly in these products, accounted for 80 per cent of total exports in the 1870s and about 90 per cent at the end of the century. Britain alone accounted for some 40 per cent of the export market in 1880 and some 60 per cent in 1900. Denmark depended much less than Sweden on industrial development, and the industries which expanded were mainly those directed to the domestic market, based on crafts and small-scale enterprises, while industrial exports remained insignificant. The continued dominance of agriculture in overseas trade accounts for the great emphasis given to agricultural interests in government policies, and the continued importance of agriculture in party politics.

There were, however, divisions of interest between large landowners, working farmers and rural labourers, which were reflected in the structure of the party system and the composition of party membership. The farmers in Denmark, unlike those in most other European countries, were progressive, not only in the practice of their occupation but in political and economic outlook as well. Since they had developed an efficient farming industry which relied on exports and depended on the free flow of international trade, they were as much in favour of free trade as the industrialists were in Britain. There was a division of interest between the working farmers and the wealthy landowners, who continued to enjoy political privileges and the receipt of ancient rentals. Opposition to these privileges and payments made liberals out of the farmers, and it was they who pressed for constitutional reforms which would reduce the influence of the privileged classes on the Crown and on the government of the country.

For a long time the demands for parliamentary forms of government were resisted by the Crown. After 1830, provincial assemblies were established with functions which were purely consultative. After the revolutions of 1848, however, a constituent assembly was elected by direct, equal and universal suffrage of all self-supporting males over 30 years of age, and its proposals for reform were adopted in the 'June Constitution' of 5 June 1849. This established a two-chamber parliament (Rigsdag), with a lower chamber (Folketing) and an upper chamber (Landsting). King Frederick VII renounced the absolute powers of monarchy, and accepted that ministers should be responsible to parliament. For the Folketing, direct elections were to be held in single-member constituencies, and voting was by relative majority, but not by secret ballot until 1901. For the Landsting, the elections were indirect, but both the suffrage and the system of voting were the same as for the Folketing until elaborate changes were introduced in 1866.

Since the Napoleonic wars the incorporation of Schleswig and Holstein in Denmark had been a source of domestic trouble with the German minorities and of dispute with Prussia. An attempt to solve this problem was made in 1855 by setting up a federal council of the realm (Rigsråd) in which all the provinces were to have elected representatives, from Jutland, Zeeland, Lolland-Fallster and Funen, and also from Schleswig and Holstein-Lauenburg. To this council twenty members were to be appointed by the Crown, but thirty were to be directly elected, and another thirty were to be indirectly elected by the provincial assemblies. It was for these elections that the minister, Carl Andrae, devised the first parliamentary election system in Europe which was based on the single transferable vote. However, the system was introduced in most unfavourable circumstances. Schleswig insisted on the retention of single-member constituencies for its elections, to gain the greatest advantage for its German majority; Holstein refused to participate in the federal regime; and finally the incorporation of Schleswig and Holstein in the Danish state led to war with Prussia and Austria and the loss of these two provinces in 1864.

In 1866 there followed a constitutional revision in which the large landowners and the wealthier middle classes succeeded in introducing changes which conferred electoral privileges upon themselves, and ensured that there would be a Conservative majority in the Landsting. This was one of the few occasions in any country in which the suffrage was deliberately made more restrictive. For the Landsting, the suffrage was now limited largely to electors who satisfied high property qualifications. Twelve of the sixty-six members of the Landsting were appointed by the Crown, one by the Faroese assembly and the remaining fifty-three by indirect election. Only half of the college of electors was now to be elected (by the relative majority system) by those electors who were enfranchised for the Folketing elections. For the other half of the college of electors, only those from Copenhagen were to be elected, and for these elections the franchise was restricted to persons eligible under a high property qualification. The rural members of the college of electors were to consist of persons with high property qualifications, who had the right of membership of the college without election. The system of election was to be Andrae's version of the single transferable vote, which had been used for the now defunct Rigsråd, but the element of fairness or 'proportional representation' which that system contained was in marked contrast with the highly restricted nature of the franchise – it was virtually only the wealthy and the conservative who were 'proportionally' represented.

In the Folketing, on the other hand, the system of voting by relative majority soon reduced the Conservatives to a permanent minority. The liberal farmers in 1870 formed the party called the Venstre, meaning 'the left', though Liberal is the term usually applied to the party. The Venstre were anxious above all to secure the reality of parliamentary democracy by requiring that governments should be responsible to the popularly elected Folketing. In 1872 the Venstre gained a majority of seats in the Folketing, and retained that majority for the rest of the century.

Meanwhile, with the growth of the industrial population, the foundations of the Social Democratic Party were laid in 1871, and in 1884 that party gained two seats in the Folketing. Nevertheless, the king always appointed ministries which had Conservative support in the Landsting. From 1875 to 1894 the prime minister was J. B. Estrup, who had to endure the permanent opposition of the Folketing, and after 1885 governed by means of 'provisional' legislation without the authority of parliament. With Estrup's departure in 1894 the government made concessions to the Venstre by introducing some progressive social legislation, but this led to a division of the party between the 'Negotiating Venstre', or collaborators, and the uncompromising 'Venstre Reform Party'. The Venstre reformers gained seventy-six seats and an absolute majority in the Folketing in 1901, compared with fourteen for the Social Democrats and only eight for the Conservatives.

The Social Democrats united with the Reform Venstre in demanding a parliamentary system in which the government would be responsible to the Folketing. The Crown capitulated, a Venstre government was formed in 1901, and the aim of responsible parliamentary government was at last achieved, more than half a century after the attainment of universal male suffrage for the Folketing.

Changes in the political party system were not slow to follow. Having achieved their main constitutional aim, the Venstre reformers failed to satisfy the electorate in other respects. Taxes fell heavily on the small farmers, the government compromised with the Conservatives in the Landsting by maintaining what many regarded as too high an expenditure upon defence, and nothing was done about reforming the invidious franchise for the Landsting. Another party split took place, the Radical Venstre Party was formed in 1905, and after financial scandals had shaken the government in 1908 the Radical Venstre formed a government with the support of the Social Democrats, and then, after an unsettled period, another government which lasted from 1913 until 1920.

One policy which the Radical Venstre and the Social Democrats had in common was the reform of the electoral system, not only for the Landsting but also for the Folketing. Under the existing system neither party could hope to gain representation corresponding to their electoral strength unless they entered into an electoral agreement with the other. The existing system was favourable to the numerically largest party, the

Venstre, which in 1901 had received 67 per cent of the seats with 43 per cent of the votes, and even in 1913 gained forty-four seats when on a proportional basis it should have gained only thirty-two. The Conservative right wing were now the chief sufferers under this system in the Folketing – for example, in 1913 they gained more than 22 per cent of the votes but only 6 per cent of the seats. The Conservatives had therefore been anxious for a long time to introduce PR for the Folketing elections, but on the other hand they were opposed to the reform of elections for the Landsting, for which, in 1906, the electors with high property qualifications formed 7 per cent of the electorate, but returned more than 38 per cent of the electoral college. From 1910 onwards there were interparty negotiations about electoral reform, but it proved possible to achieve this only within the context of wider reforms of the constitution.

The constitutional amendment of 5 June 1915 abolished the property qualifications previously required for the Landsting elections, and admitted all male and female citizens over the age of 35 to the suffrage to elect a college of electors. The king's power to nominate members was transferred to members of each *old* Landsting, who were to nominate eighteen members for each *new* Landsting. The election of the members of the electoral college now took place by means of the D'Hondt system, while the election of the members of the Landsting by the electoral college continued to be by the Andrae system of the single transferable vote. In spite of these reforms, the Landsting continued to be more conservative than the Folketing, because its election was still indirect, each Landsting continued to be elected for eight years compared with four for the Folketing, and there was a higher voting age than for the Folketing (for the Landsting, 35 years; for the Folketing, 30 years in 1915, 29 years in 1918 and 25 years in 1920).

For the Folketing elections of 1918, when women were admitted to the franchise for the first time, a hybrid system of election was used. For the elections in Copenhagen, the D'Hondt system was applied, and for the provinces elections in single-member constituencies by relative majority, with additional seats allocated to the parties to secure more proportional representation through the application of a quota system. By means of this measure of PR the Conservatives were able to gain considerably increased representation in the Folketing after they had surrendered their bastion of power in the Landsting. The hybrid system continued, however, to favour the Venstre Party, since the additional seats were too few to ensure accurate PR, and the Radical Venstre and the Social Democrats were still compelled reluctantly to form alliances for electoral purposes.

In 1920 there was introduced a single electoral system for the whole country, the framework of which has existed ever since. There was then established the system of geographical electoral divisions distinguishing between the smallest unit, the nomination constituency, from which an individual candidate was nominated for each party; the district, within which constituency members were elected by application of the D'Hondt system; and finally the principal electoral areas, within each of which PR was achieved more exactly by allocating additional seats to parties through the application of the Sainte-Laguë system proper. The main innovation in the system introduced partially in 1918 and then comprehensively in 1920 was the achievement of PR by allocating additional seats, while retaining an element of the old single-member constituency system in the form of the nomination constituencies.

The year 1920 marked the end of a period of constitutional changes which had been in progress since 1901, and in the light of future developments two points are here particularly worth noting. One is that already, before the first elements of PR had been introduced for elections to the Folketing in 1918, there had been established, under the relative majority system, the four-party structure which continued to exist with little modification until the 1960s. Proportional representation neither created a multi-party system nor resulted in a proliferation of additional parties. There were a few smaller parties which sometimes gained representation, but even when such parties reached a peak in 1939, five small parties apart from the main four parties succeeded between them in gaining only fourteen seats in the Folketing. The second point is that the constitution of 1915 provided that the revision of the constitution itself could take place only after a lengthy procedure. Any proposal for a constitutional amendment, after it had been approved by parliament, was to be submitted to a new parliament after a general election. If it was then adopted by a two-thirds majority of at least two-thirds of the members of parliament present and voting, it had to be approved by a majority in a popular referendum, the majority being equivalent to at least 45 per cent of the registered electorate. This rendered it difficult to achieve any further amendment of the electoral system, or of any other provisions of the constitution.

Social and economic changes led to the rise of the Social Democratic Party, with the result that in 1926 they achieved the largest number of seats in the Folketing, and from 1929 to 1940 they formed the government with the support of the Radical Venstre. In 1929 they announced a programme of further reforms including the abolition of the Landsting. This was still a Conservative stronghold, with power to delay legislation though not to prevent it. In 1936 the government achieved a majority in the Landsting as well as the Folketing, and reform now seemed to be possible, but by this time the Venstre, which had been the reforming party of the left in the nineteenth century, had become the ally of the Conservatives against socialism. When the constitutional proposals were submitted to the electorate in a referendum in 1939 they were accepted by an overwhelming majority of some 966,000 votes to 86,000, but the majority constituted only 44·46 per cent of the electorate and thus did not reach the constitutional requirement of 45 per cent. By so narrow a margin was reform of the constitution frustrated in 1939.

Immediately after the Second World War there was a swing to the left, and then, as a result of the Cold War, a swing to the right, until, after alternations of government, the Venstre and the Conservatives formed a government in 1951. Wartime collaboration between parties had led to consultation over changes in the constitution, and a commission set up in 1946 by a Venstre government had submitted proposals for reform. The Venstre, having held out for bicameralism until 1951, yielded to the demands of the Radical Venstre and the Social Democrats for the abolition of the Landsting. The Constitution Act of 5 June 1953 was carried by an overwhelming majority of votes in the referendum, but by only a tiny margin over the requisite 45 per cent of the registered electorate.

By way of compensation for the abolition of the Landsting the Act introduced the device of the legislative referendum. This meant that any contentious legislation could, on the vote of one-third of the Folketing, be made the subject of a referendum, and could be rejected by a majority vote, provided at least 30 per cent of the registered electorate voted against it. Ten years later this constitutional device was used when four Land Acts of the Social Democrat government were decisively rejected in a referendum. Another constitutional revision made it possible to carry out future amendments of the constitution if, in a referendum, at least 40 per cent instead of 45 per cent of the registered electorate were in favour. The constitutional revisions of 1953 also provided that elections must be by proportional representation, but left it to electoral laws to determine whether elections should be based on single-member or multi-member constituencies. In successive constitutional amendments and referenda the voting age was reduced to 23 in 1953, 21 in 1961 and 20 in 1971.

As regards the electoral law, a principal change which was introduced in 1953 was the substitution of the modified Sainte-Laguë system in place of the D'Hondt system for the allocation of district seats to parties. The manner in which the electoral system has operated since 1953 is considered below, but here it may be noted that although the change from D'Hondt to Sainte-Laguë made it slightly easier for a party to gain a first district seat, another important provision of the electoral law restricted the right of participation by parties in the allocation of additional seats to those parties which had fulfilled certain conditions. Small parties were, as a result of this, generally unsuccessful in qualifying for the allocation of additional seats. Under an electoral law of 1960 it was provided that to share in the allocation a party had to win one constituency seat, or have received 60,000 votes in the whole country, or have received in each of the electoral areas (Jutland, the Islands and Copenhagen) as many votes as the average required to win a constituency seat. In 1961 an amendment provided that it would suffice for a party to have gained 2 per cent of the votes in the whole country, instead of 60,000 votes, and this was a slight concession, because in the 1960 election 60,000 votes had been equivalent to 2·46 per cent of the valid votes which had been cast. However, with an increase in the electorate and in the number of votes, 60,000 votes was in 1966 equivalent to only 2·15 per cent of the votes, so this concession was already proving to be of doubtful value. Another concession made in 1961 was that allocation might be made to parties which attained the average number of votes required to gain a seat in only two of the three principal areas instead of in all of them.

From 1953 until 1968 the Social Democrats always formed the government, but ministries were short-lived and existed sometimes with only minority support in the Folketing. One of the reasons for instability in the party system was difference of opinion over neutrality and defence. The Radicals had always, since the party was first formed in 1905, been in favour of neutrality in international conflicts and against defence expenditure and commitments, and in this they were in agreement with the Social Democrats. After the Second World War the Social Democrats changed their policy, and favoured Denmark's membership not only of the United Nations, the International Monetary Fund and the International Bank, but also the North Atlantic Treaty Organisation and later the European Economic Community. Because of Denmark's membership of NATO, the Radicals refused to join the Social Democrat government formed in 1953.

In 1960 the Social Democrats gained strength in the Folketing, but the Socialist People's Party, formed by Aksel Larsen in 1959 after his expulsion from the Communist Party, also gained steadily in strength in the 1950s. In 1961 Denmark applied for membership of the EEC, which alienated both the Radicals and the Socialist People's Party, but on the other hand the Social Democrats were defeated in 1963 in a series of referenda over their land legislation, which was regarded by most of the electorate as too socialist in character. In this confused situation the Social Democrats and the Socialist People's Party were returned in sufficient strength to the Folketing in 1966 to form the first socialist majority in Denmark's history. However, the Socialist People's Party held out for a programme of uncompromising socialist legislation, the government fell, and a coalition of Venstre, Conservatives and Radicals was formed in 1968. In 1971 the Social Democrats were back in power with the support of the Socialist People's Party.

The early 1960s appear to have been a turning-point in Danish party history, with parties other than the main four beginning to play a more important role in the Folketing. The Socialist People's Party, emerging as a fifth party, had more votes than the Radicals and as many seats in 1960 and 1964, and in 1966 had more seats as well. After the Radicals once again achieved more seats than the Socialist People's Party in 1968 and 1971 the latter were still well represented in the Folketing. Another left-wing splinter party had less success. A group of dissidents broke away from the Socialist People's Party in 1967 in protest against anti-inflation measures and the level of expenditure on defence, and in opposition to the application made for membership of the EEC. This group formed the Left Socialist Party which, in 1968, succeeded in qualifying for four supplementary seats in the Folketing, but failed to do so in 1971.

Only five parties were represented in the Folketing after the elections in 1971, four others, including the Communists and the Left Socialists, having failed to secure 2 per cent of the votes. After 1971 there was a marked decline in the support for the Socialist People's Party and the Radical Venstre, and in 1973 all the five major parties lost heavily, especially the Social Democrats. Apart from these, five other parties succeeded in gaining seats in 1973 and 1975, and six in 1977. The most remarkable increase in representation was gained by a new Progress Party founded in 1973, a 'Poujadist' party resolved to abolish income tax, the defence forces and the diplomatic service, and to reduce manpower in the civil services by 90 per cent. This party gained twenty-eight seats in 1973, then twenty-four in 1975 and twenty-six in 1977. Both in 1973 and in 1977 this was the second-largest party in the Folketing after the Social Democrats. Another new party established in 1973 were the Centre Democrats, who considered that the Social Democrats were moving too far to the left under the influence of the extremists. Their success, however, was more limited than that of the Progress Party.

Other small parties which, in one or more of the elections from 1973 onwards, succeeded in gaining representation were the Communists, the Left Socialists, the Single Tax Party (disciples of Henry George) and the Christian People's Party (opposed to abortion and pornography). One element of stability during this period was that in spite of a large loss of seats in 1973 the Social Democrats always gained substantially more seats than any other party. But those four parties which had been formed before the First World War were no longer the only rivals for power and office, as they had been until the middle of the 1960s.

The electoral system of 1953, under which this situation arose, was constructed in such a way that representation was determined at three different geographical levels, which were the nomination constituencies, the districts and the principal areas or provinces. The manner in which the electoral procedure is carried out is best understood by following the stages of an election from the smallest unit, up through the districts to the principal areas, and then back again down through the districts to the nomination constituencies.

The nomination of individual candidates or of party lists of candidates takes place in the nomination constituency. Excluding the Faroes and Greenland, which have two members each, 135 constituency members are elected from the mainland and adjacent islands in (after 1970) seventeen districts. To these constituency or district members forty additional members are added to give more accurately proportional representation between the parties within the principal areas. How the lists of nominations are prepared determines, at the end of the whole electoral process, how the choice between individual candidates is decided.

The number of members to be elected from each principal area and each district is fixed on the basis of population every ten years after a census, subject to adjustments in favour of sparsely populated parts of the country. Electors vote by placing a cross against the name of either one individual candidate or one party, on the separate nomination lists presented in each nomination constituency; and if the candidate is on a party list a vote cast for him counts also for his party. Within each of the seventeen *districts* the total votes for each party are aggregated, and district seats are then allocated to each party by application of the modified Sainte-Laguë system.

Supplementary seats are then allocated to each party which fulfils the conditions which have already been described above. The district votes of the eligible parties are aggregated at the principal area level (that is, in Jutland, the Islands and Copenhagen respectively). There is a predetermined number of supplementary seats which may be allocated in each principal area, which was in 1975 nineteen for Jutland, fourteen for the Islands and seven for Copenhagen. Within each principal area the Sainte-Laguë system proper is applied to the total votes of each eligible party within the area, having regard to the constituency or district seats each party has already won. Thus, if a party has already gained three seats, the fourth Sainte-Laguë divisor is applied, which is 7; if it has already gained four seats, the fifth divisor is applied, which is 9; and so on. The supplementary seats are now awarded in turn to the parties in any area which have the highest quotients after the divisors have been applied to their total votes within each area; provided that any area which has reached its maximum number of seats ceases, of course, to participate any further in the allocation of supplementary seats.

All supplementary seats having been allocated to parties within each of the principal *areas*, they are now allocated to *districts* within the areas. This is done by applying to each party's votes in all districts of the area the Danish system which has divisors of 1, 4, 7, 10, etc., having regard, as before, to the number of district seats which the party has already won.

What has next to be decided is which *candidate* on each party list is entitled to each seat which the party has won in each district. The electoral law provides for three ways in which this may be done, depending on the way in which the party lists have been presented by the parties. The commonest type of list gives a candidate not only all his own personal votes in the district but also all party votes in his own *nomination constituency*; another type of list operates in such a way as to allow the choice between candidates to be determined chiefly by the *personal* votes which have been cast in the whole district; while the third, used by the Social Democrats and the Communists, is weighted heavily in favour of the *party*'s order of preference among the individual candidates. These rules were prescribed in an electoral law of 1920. The purpose was to establish PR while retaining as far as possible the advantages of the old single-member constituencies, and at the same time giving electors as much choice as possible between several candidates. It was the intention that the voter should, without forsaking his party, have a choice between candidates, but he was not offered the opportunity of cross-party voting.

It may be noted that the parties themselves decide which type of list they will present to electors, and therefore how much influence the choice of electors will have in deciding between individual candidates. It seems, also, that the tendency has been for the number of personal votes to diminish and the number of party votes to increase. Moreover, a high proportion of personal votes has been for candidates who would in any case have been allocated the party votes in their nomination constituencies, and if these are excluded the number of 'effective' personal votes has been a small proportion of the total.

The electoral system produces a relatively high degree of proportionality between votes and seats, but the regulations restricting access to the supplementary seats can result in serious discrepancies in the distribution of seats to small parties which are just above or just below the permitted level of participation. In 1968, for example, the Left Socialist Party gained 57,184 votes, which was 2·003 per cent of the total number of valid votes, and the party was thus only just eligible by the slenderest margin to receive supplementary seats, of which it was entitled to, and received, an allocation of *four*. If it had received 93 fewer votes it would have received no seats at all.

The relatively high degree of proportionality in the Danish electoral system removed the need for those electoral alliances which were found necessary by the Social Democrats and the Radicals before the First World War, and since the electoral reforms of 1920 no such alliances have been formed. However, it is evident that if *apparentement* were permitted it could make a great deal of difference to the small parties, because this would make it much easier for them to gain the right to participate in the allocation of the supplementary seats.

Restrictions on the allocation of supplementary seats have been criticised by the Independent Party on the extreme right wing and the Left Socialists on the farthest left, which have both suffered on occasion from a failure to receive any. On the other hand, once a party have reached the threshold and achieved the right to participate in the allocation of supplementary seats, they gain a considerable advantage over those which have failed to do so.

The comment has been made about the Danish electoral system that although every change in the electoral law establishing PR has been an improvement when considered in isolation, the system as a whole has become so complicated that only a few specialists understand it. Even these may find it difficult to know who, in the end, gets the benefit of their vote, after supplementary seats have been allocated to parties, and party votes have been allocated to individual candidates. Nevertheless, having had the experience of PR for more than fifty years the electors and almost all of the political parties seem to regard the complexity as a matter of minor importance compared with the advantages of a proportional system.

REFERENCES: CHAPTER 8

The early experience with the single transferable vote in Denmark is described by Poul Andrae in a work on his father, Carl Andrae, *Andrae and His Invention: The Proportional Representation Method*. Works by Kenneth E. Miller on the representative system include *Government and Politics in Denmark*, and an article on 'The Danish electoral system', in *Parliamentary Affairs*, 1964–5. A particular aspect of the Danish electoral system is examined by Mogens N. Pedersen in his article 'Preferential voting in Denmark: the voters' influence on the election of Folketing candidates', in *Scandinavian Political Studies*, 1966. The representation of parties in parliament is examined by Alastair H. Thomas in *Parliamentary Parties in Denmark, 1945–1972*.

9

Norway

The establishment in Norway of parliamentary institutions based on popular elections was part of a process of constitutional developments which led to the assertion of Norway's identity as an independent nation. The issue of independence was complicated by the accession to the throne of Norway, through the centuries, of different dynasties, which linked it in some periods to Denmark and in others to Sweden. In the nineteenth century, aspirations for constitutional reform were inspired by a demand for independent nationhood as well as by a desire for radical changes in the direction of representative democracy.

At the time of the Napoleonic wars there was a union of the Norwegian and the Danish crowns. In the last stages of the war, from 1812 onwards, Denmark was in alliance with France, but Sweden with Britain and Russia. By the terms of the Treaty of Kiel in January 1814, after Napoleon's defeat at Leipzig in the previous year, Norway was to be ceded by Denmark to Sweden. After King Frederik of Denmark had renounced the Norwegian throne the claimant was Prince Christian Frederik, who advocated independence for the Norwegian nation, not union with Sweden; and in support of his claim to the throne he agreed to the convening of a constitutional assembly to settle the form of the Norwegian government. This assembly was held at Eidsvold from March to May 1814, and it agreed upon the basic terms of a constitution which, with amendments, has been in force ever since.

The assembly also elected Christian Frederik to be King of Norway. This provoked diplomatic intervention by the allied powers to insist upon the implementation of the Treaty of Kiel, and resulted in an armed incursion by Marshal Bernadotte (Carl Johan), who in 1810 had been elected by the Swedish estates to be the heir apparent to the Swedish throne. By an armistice signed in August 1814, both sides agreed to a union of Norway and Sweden, the terms of which included the provision that the two nations should be regarded as equals, and that the constitution established at Eidsvold should be recognised and adopted for Norway. It was also agreed that Christian Frederik should renounce his claim to the Norwegian throne.

The Eidsvold constitution provided that there should be a separation of the legislative, executive and judicial powers; that the power to legislate and impose taxes should be exercised by the people through representatives in their parliament, or Storting; and that no hereditary privileges should be recognised or granted to anyone.

Hostility to Sweden's hegemony in Norway was later expressed in the form of opposition to the office of Viceroy of Norway, as a symbol of inferior status; and it was expressed also by the assertion of the Storting's exclusive power to pass legislation, and by demands for the appointment of separate diplomatic and consular representatives to protect Norwegian interests abroad. The office of viceroy was abolished in 1872, when Norwegian affairs were entrusted to a minister of state; and as regards legislation the king in 1884 accepted that while he himself would retain the power of veto ministers should be responsible to the Storting for the exercise of their functions. On the question of overseas representation, however, an amendment of the Swedish constitution in 1885 provided that the Swedish parliament alone should be directly responsible for foreign policy. The proposal of separate diplomatic and consular organisations for Norway was rejected, and Norwegians were seldom appointed to posts abroad.

The demand for independent representation abroad was ultimately the occasion for the separation of Norway from Sweden. With the expansion of Norwegian trade and navigation this became a matter of major importance towards the end of the nineteenth century. On the eve of the First World War the tonnage of the Norwegian mercantile fleet was nearly two and a half times as great as the Swedish, substantially greater than the French, and about half as great as the German. This issue remained a constant grievance, and provided a focus for nationalist sentiment.

In 1905 a Bill introduced by the Norwegian Cabinet for the establishment of a Norwegian consular service was passed by the Storting but vetoed by the king. The government resigned, no other Cabinet could be formed, and in June 1905 the Storting passed a resolution declaring that the union with Sweden was dissolved. At this point the Swedish parliament conceded that the continuance of the union should be made the subject of a referendum in Norway. The referendum was held, and separation was decided upon by 368,208 votes in favour and only 184 against. Oscar II abdicated as King of Norway, and as a result of a plebiscite Prince Carl of Denmark was offered the crown of Norway with the title of Haakon VII. He accepted, and there was thus re-established, after a lapse of nearly six centuries, an independent royal house in Norway. At the same time, the power of the Crown was limited by removing its veto over legislation and its control of foreign affairs.

The victory for Norwegian independence was simultaneously a victory for the Norwegian parliament which had been established by the constitution of 1814. The Storting was a unique type of legislature which combined the features of both a single-chamber and a dual-chamber parliament. The Storting as a whole was elected by a popular vote, and then the Storting themselves elected one-quarter of their own members to form an upper chamber of parliament, or Lagting. The initiative for legislation lay with the lower chamber, or Odelsting. When the Storting considered the passing of 'laws', which were definable as provisions which regulated the rights and obligations of the people as a whole, the Lagting acted as a revising chamber; but since representation in the Lagting was a reflection of that in the Odelsting conflicts of interest were seldom likely to arise.

The constitution of 1814 provided a very narrow basis for parliamentary suffrage. It was confined to government officials, freehold and leasehold farmers, owners of urban property, and citizens who were licensed to trade as merchants or craftsmen. The size of the electorate was in practice limited even further by a requirement that of those who were eligible to vote only those would be permitted to vote who had taken an oath of allegiance to the constitution and then had their names entered on the electoral register. In 1829 the registered electors constituted only 5·6 per cent of the population, and this was much less than half of the eligible population. In 1882 the registered electorate was still only 7·6 per cent of the population. It was therefore only a limited section of the population which was represented in the struggle for an increase in the power of the Norwegian parliament.

A significant stage in this struggle was reached in 1869 when a Liberal majority passed an Act to ensure that in future parliament should meet at least annually, and not merely at the king's discretion. In 1882 the Liberals gained 63 per cent of the votes and 73 per cent of the seats in the Storting, and the Odelsting successfully brought an action against the king's ministers for having permitted a misuse of the royal veto. The king sought to govern in defiance of parliament with a Cabinet of Conservative ministers, but finally he was obliged to invite Johann Sverdrup, the Liberal leader, to form a government. It was from this time that the principle of ministerial responsibility to parliament was established in practice, though not embodied in the constitution.

It was in the 1880s, also, that a system of political parties began to take shape. The distinctive interests of different sections of the community had already begun to emerge soon after the adoption of the new constitution in 1814. Some 90 per cent of the population were rural and some 80 per cent were engaged in agriculture and forestry, but it was government officials who were most commonly elected to be members of parliament and appointed as ministers of the Crown. An agitation for farmers' representation was successful, and by 1833 they formed the largest single group of members. After 1845 a farmers' party sought representation in the government but did not succeed, and until 1884 the king continued to nominate ministers at his own discretion. Among the middle and professional classes ideals of constitutional and parliamentary government became widely accepted, and led eventually to the organisation of a Liberal Party. This was founded in 1882 with the title of Venstre, or party of the left, which sought to secure responsible parliamentary government.

In opposition to the Liberals there was founded, also in 1882, the Conservative Party, consisting of higher civil servants and wealthy burghers, who supported the authority of the Swedish Crown. The election of 1882 was the first which was essentially a contest between opposing political parties, and on this occasion the Liberals gained 73 per cent of the seats and the Conservatives all the remainder. The Liberals thereafter, until 1903, won an absolute majority of both votes and seats in every election except one. The exception was the election of 1888, when a section of the party representing farmers, who had dissident views on economic policy, split off to form a separate Moderate Left Party, and generally to combine with the Conservatives.

During the revolutions of 1848 on the Continent a labour and trade union movement had come into existence in Norway. In the absence of much factory industry its strength lay chiefly among the small peasants, farm labourers, sawmill workers and miners. One of the demands of this movement was for universal manhood suffrage, to gain for the working population some access to the seats of political power. A constitutional amendment of 1884 extended the suffrage to citizens paying taxes on income above a certain level, and this enfranchised many of the sawmill workers and miners, but still, in the election of 1885, the electorate consisted of only 9·4 per cent of the population. The formation of the Labour Party in 1887 induced the Liberals to compete more strenuously for popular support, and in 1897 they passed legislation which introduced universal manhood suffrage at the age of 25, and also abolished the requirement to take an oath to the constitution as a condition of being entered on the electoral roll. The effect of these measures was to increase the electorate to 19·7 per cent of the population in 1900.

Until 1905 elections for the Storting were indirect, and held in multi-member constituencies. In the cities, the 'primary' electors, or eligible voters, elected one 'secondary' elector for every fifty eligible voters in the constituency, but in rural districts one 'secondary' elector for every hundred eligible voters. Moreover, the number of deputies who might be elected by the 'secondary' electors was substantially greater for the urban than for the rural constituencies. This unequal representation, which survived in some degree long after the adoption of so-called 'proportional' representation in 1919, ensured that although originally the urban population constituted only 10 per cent of the population of the country, they were represented by one-third of the deputies in parliament. It was expressly provided in the constitution that this should be the balance of representation between urban and rural areas. The result was that until this requirement was removed in 1953 the rural areas were always under-represented. It was not until 1960 that the share of the towns in the total population rose to about as much as one-third.

In 1905, when Norway gained her independence from Sweden, the system of indirect elections was abolished. The country was divided into single-member constituencies from which deputies were directly elected. The system of election was one requiring an absolute majority in the first ballot, but only a relative majority in a second ballot, in which all candidates who had stood in the first were entitled to stand again. The change from indirect to direct elections was largely the consequence of the adoption of universal manhood suffrage in 1897, because the large increase in the number of electors made the organisation of indirect elections so difficult that in some constituencies it broke down altogether.

The Labour Party, though formed in 1887, did not succeed in electing a representative to the Storting until 1903. Thereafter, also, the bias of the majority system of election was such that their share of seats was always much less than their share of votes. The growth of the party was nevertheless steadily maintained. In 1915 and 1918, with 32 per cent of the votes on each occasion, they attained 15 per cent and 14 per cent of the seats respectively.

After national independence had been achieved, the Liberals no longer enjoyed the popular support they had received as leaders of the independence movement, and were deserted by factions which differed on particular issues of policy. After the reforms of 1905 the Storting was no longer dominated as it had been by Liberals, Conservatives and (since 1888) the Moderates. A larger number of parties was represented in the Storting, including not only the Labour Party but also National Liberals, Worker Democrats and members of the Agrarian League. This proliferation of parties took place during the period of majority elections in single-member constituencies, and *before* the introduction of proportional representation.

After the First World War, in Norway as in several other countries, public opinion was strongly in favour of strengthening democratic institutions in reaction against the autocracies held responsible for the war. There was also growing support for the adoption of PR in parliamentary elections, so that within the representative institutions the representation should be accurate and fair. Of the particular interests liable to be affected by a change in the electoral system, the Liberals in Norway had almost always enjoyed a considerable bias in their favour under the majority system of election, on almost all occasions gaining a much greater share of seats than of votes; but since 1905 their share of both had declined. In 1906 they had 59 per cent of the seats for 45 per cent of the votes, and in 1918 40 per cent of the seats for 28 per cent of the votes, but it seemed inevitable that they should soon lose altogether the advantage they had once enjoyed as the largest party. Also, the Liberals had a long history of advocating radical reforms in favour of more representative forms of government, and could not consistently oppose further changes in the same direction.

The Labour Party's interest at this time also seemed to favour reform. In 1915, for example, they obtained only 15 per cent of the seats for 32 per cent of the votes. The Conservatives were not so obviously affected, but usually their share of the seats had been less than their share of the votes, and sometimes much less. There was no strong reason for them to resist reform; and the interest of all the small parties also was clearly on the side of PR. It was therefore without much opposition, or even debate, that proportional representation was adopted.

The introduction of PR was effected by means of a constitutional amendment of 1919, which established a party-list system in multi-member constituencies, with seats allocated by the method advocated by D'Hondt. However, the system fell distinctly short of true proportionality. The Norwegian constitution specifically determined the number of deputies to be returned from each constituency, and this allocation did not correspond with the number of the population or of the electors in each. The constitutional requirement that one-third of the seats should be allocated to urban constituencies, although they had less than one-third of the population, was not removed until 1953. Moreover, for the allocation of seats on a proportional basis, the country was divided into twenty constituencies, within each of which the proportional allocation of seats was to take place. The chances of the smaller parties were less than they would have been if there had been fewer and larger constituencies, and much less favourable than if the allocation had been on a national basis.

Under the new electoral system electors were given the opportunity to express preferences between individual candidates by voting for as many candidates as there were seats to be filled, and seats were allocated to parties on the basis of the number of votes a party's candidates obtained. A vote for a party list without any preference between candidates was counted as a vote for all the party's candidates in the order of preference shown on the list. *Panachage*, or voting for candidates of more than one party, was permitted, and two or more parties were entitled to submit joint lists of candidates which would be treated in the same way as single party lists.

This last device was intended to permit combinations of small parties to benefit from the bias of the D'Hondt system in favour of the larger parties. Between 1930 and 1949 a system of *apparentement* was allowed, under which two or more parties could form an electoral alliance, presenting separate lists but exhibiting on each list a subtitle to indicate the existence of the electoral alliance. An elector could vote for the party list, but score out the subtitle if he disapproved of the alliance. The allocation of seats was then determined by a method which calculated the party's votes in two ways, one on the basis of each party's votes counted separately, and the other on the basis of the votes cast for the alliance as if it were a single party. The result which was accepted was that which was more favourable to each party in the alliance. This ensured that the elector could express himself against the alliance without diminishing his support for his own party.

In practice it was generally anti-socialist parties which entered into alliances. The Labour Party themselves had by 1927 become much the largest single party, and from that time onwards almost always enjoyed the advantage which the D'Hondt system confers on large parties. Even without forming alliances the Labour Party were now almost certain to gain a greater share of seats than of votes. When the Labour Party had an absolute majority of seats in 1949 they secured the adoption by the Storting of a measure which disallowed alliances of parties in the form of *apparentement*, though separate parties were still entitled to submit joint lists of candidates.

As regards voting for individual candidates, each elector was entitled to cast votes for as many candidates on a party list as there were seats to be filled in the constituency, indicating his choice in order of preference. For the purpose of allocating seats to each party, it was to the total of these votes on each party list that the D'Hondt system until 1953, and then the modified Sainte-Laguë system, was applied. The first seat gained by a party was allocated to the candidate who had most first-preference votes, the next to the remaining candidate who had most first- and second-preference votes, and so on until the party's seats had all been allocated. The elector was entitled to delete names from the party list and insert others, but little advantage was taken of this facility, since most electors were interested chiefly in supporting a particular party, and were not so much concerned with the relative merits of individual candidates on the party lists.

The only important change in the suffrage which took place in 1919 was the reduction of the voting age from 25 to 23 (subsequently reduced to 21 in 1946 and to 20 in 1972). The introduction of PR in the same year not only made it easier for small parties to gain seats, but also improved the prospects for dissidents who withdrew from a party to form another because of a difference over some point of policy. Nevertheless, the number of parties did not in the interwar period show any marked tendency to increase. Between 1906 and 1918, during the period of majority elections in single-member constituencies, there were generally five or six parties which gained representation, and in 1918 there were seven. In the six elections between 1921 and 1936, the number of parties which succeeded in electing at least one member was eight in 1924 and 1933, seven in 1921 and 1927, and six in 1930 and 1936.

As in the period before the First World War, it continued to be the three main parties, Liberals, Conservatives and Labour, which gained the predominant number of seats. In the first two elections held in 1921 and 1924 after the adoption of PR, the joint share of these parties in seats in the Storting, which had been well over 90 per cent before the war, fell to 72 per cent and 67 per cent respectively. There was at this time considerable representation of other parties, including National Liberals, Farmers, Social Democratic Workers and in 1924 the Communists. However, from 1927 the share of the three main parties once again increased, until in 1936 it was 86 per cent.

Before the war all parties, especially the Liberals, had been liable to divide into factions on particular issues. The Labour Party tended to disintegrate on their right and left wings as a result of conflict between those who favoured more extreme measures of socialism on the one hand, or more limited social reforms on the other. When the Labour Party joined the Comintern in 1919, a moderate Social Democratic wing split off and formed a separate party. When the Labour Party later withdrew from the Comintern, the Marxists in the party then seceded to form the Communist Party in 1924, and the Social Democrats rejoined the Labour Party in 1927. The Communist Party gained 6 per cent of the votes and six seats in 1924, but failed to gain any seats in the elections between 1930 and 1936. Of the other smaller parties, the National Liberals failed to elect any members in 1936, and only the Farmers consistently maintained a significant level of representation, returning twenty-six members at the peak of their performance in 1927, and still retaining eighteen members in 1936. None of the other small parties gained more than one or two seats in any of the interwar elections.

The relative strength of the major parties did, however, change in the interwar period. The Labour Party's share of the seats rose from 19 per cent in 1921 to 47 per cent in 1936. This great increase was partly at the expense of the Liberals, whose share fell almost continuously, but it was more at the expense of the small parties. The Conservative share of the votes fluctuated, but also on the whole moved downwards.

No party succeeded in gaining an absolute majority of seats in the interwar period, but no coalitions were formed, only minority governments of single parties which relied on other parties for support. Twelve Cabinets were formed between 1920 and 1940, but an element of stability was provided by the fact that the constitution made no provision for the premature dissolution of the Storting. Under the terms of the constitution each parliament was elected for a term of three years, until in

1938 the term was extended to four years. There was thus no opportunity for governments or oppositions to improve their electoral chances by contriving to hold a 'snap' election.

Conservative, Liberal and Agrarian governments alternated in office between 1920 and 1935. Although the Labour Party were the strongest party from 1927 onwards, it was only in 1935 that they achieved office for the first time. Labour governments continued in office until the country was invaded by Germany in 1940, and after that continued to form a government in exile.

After the Second World War the Labour Party invariably had many more seats than any other party, and continued in government until the general election of 1965. In the four elections between 1945 and 1957 the party had an absolute majority of seats, although they never had an absolute majority of votes. The party continued to benefit, as they almost always had done since 1927, from the advantage which the D'Hondt system conferred on the largest parties; and in the immediate postwar elections the discrepancy between votes and seats in favour of the Labour Party was particularly marked. This bias of the electoral system became a leading political issue, and there was mounting pressure from other parties for electoral reform. To reduce the anomaly, the D'Hondt system was in 1953 replaced by the modified Sainte-Laguë system, which was also introduced about the same time in Denmark and Sweden. The new system made it slightly easier for the small parties to gain seats.

Although the modified Sainte-Laguë system was more accurately proportional than D'Hondt, a substantial element of disproportionality remained in the Norwegian electoral system. This was due partly to the fact that the allocation of seats still took place separately in twenty electoral districts, and not on a national basis. Under the constitution each county constituted a separate constituency with a specific number of seats allocated to each, but these did not strictly correspond to the distribution of the population. The constitutional requirement that seats in Storting should be divided in the ratio of two to one between rural and urban constituencies was removed in 1953, but the number of seats allocated to each constituency was still laid down in the constitution. There was now a bias against the more densely populated areas of Oslo and the surrounding county of Akershus, which was only partially rectified by the allocation of additional seats in 1973.

The disproportionality of the electoral system affected the distribution of seats between the socialist and non-socialist parties, and also between the rival socialist parties themselves. After the adoption of the modified Sainte-Laguë system the Labour Party still, in 1953 and 1957, had more than half the seats with less than half the votes, though the discrepancy between votes and seats was now reduced. The Socialist People's Party, on the other hand, gained only two seats in 1961 and 1965, against the *nine* to which they would have been entitled on a purely proportional basis in the nation as a whole; and even if the Sainte-Laguë system had been adopted in its pure form instead of the modified version, they would still, as a result of the allocation of seats separately in numerous constituencies, have gained only four seats. In 1961 the Labour Party had 74 seats out of 150, and depended on the support of the two members of the Socialist People's Party who had secured election. In the 1965 election the Labour Party lost six seats, and although they were still much the strongest party, with 43 per cent of the votes and 45 per cent of the seats, they fell from power for the first time in thirty years. Under a purely proportional system, the Labour Party could, in spite of gaining fewer seats of their own, have remained in office. This was because they could have counted on the support of the *nine* members who would have been elected from the Socialist People's Party. Paradoxically, therefore, the strongest single party would have retained power under a more purely proportional system, instead of losing it under a system which was less proportional.

After the Labour Party's failure in the election of 1965 a coalition government of non-socialist parties was formed by the Centre (Agrarian) Party, including members of the Conservative, Liberal and Christian People's parties. In the 1969 election the Labour Party recovered the six seats they had lost in 1965, but this time the Socialist People's Party failed to gain any seats (instead of the four they could have won under a purely proportional system), and so Labour could not form a government. However, the non-socialist parties were divided on the issue of Norway's prospective membership of the European Community, and the fall of the government gave the Labour Party the opportunity to form a government in March 1971.

The Labour Party were on the whole in favour of joining the European Community, and resigned when membership was rejected in the referendum which took place in September 1972. A coalition government was formed by members of other parties hostile to membership of the EEC, including the Centre Party, which had consistently opposed membership on the grounds that the interests of agriculture and fisheries would suffer.

In the general election of 1973 the Labour Party lost twelve seats and the Liberals lost eleven, each evidently penalised for having supported membership of the EEC. The greatest gain in seats was achieved by the Socialist Electoral Alliance, formed by the Socialist People's Party and the Communists, who were opposed to the EEC and to the NATO alliance. The Labour Party and the Socialist Electoral Alliance jointly had 78 out of the 155 seats in the Storting, and in spite of their electoral losses the Labour Party were thus able to form a government with a bare majority. The members of the Socialist Electoral Alliance included

Reidar Larsen, leader of the Communist Party, and the first Communist Party member to be elected since 1961. In 1975 the parties of the Socialist Electoral Alliance proposed to convert the alliance into a new Socialist Left Party, but the Communist Party, in a congress held in November of that year, threw out the proposal so far as their own members were concerned, and removed Larsen from the leadership of the party.

On the question of whether the system of proportional representation has led to the disintegration of the party system, the evidence is open to different interpretations. If one takes the two leading parties, Labour and the Conservatives, one finds that their joint share of seats rose from 67 per cent in 1945 to 76 per cent in 1977, with fluctuations in between. In the postwar period there were three other parties which consistently had a significant representation in the Storting. These were the Liberals, the Centre Party and the Christian People's Party, each of which, apart only from the Centre Party in 1949, always had at least 7 per cent of the seats. Between them, the five major parties shared all the seats in 1949 and 1969. In 1953 the Communists had three seats, but apart from this the only two years in which more than two seats were gained by any party other than the principal five were 1945 and 1973. The elections in each of these years had followed a crisis in the affairs of the nation. In 1945, after the Communist achievements in resistance movements during the war, the party gained eleven seats, but with the advent of the Cold War they lost them all in 1949. In 1973, the election followed the sharp division of public opinion during the referendum on entry into the EEC, and on that occasion twenty-one members were elected who did not belong to any of the five major parties. It seemed then that the old party system might well have disintegrated; yet in 1977 only two of the twenty-one seats were retained, and of the five major parties the only one which was still struck down was the Liberal Party, which retained only the two seats they had gained in 1973.

REFERENCES: CHAPTER 9

The text of the 1814 constitution and a description of the electoral system for the Norwegian parliament are published in English by the Norwegian Ministry of Foreign Affairs. Developments in the Norwegian electoral system are reviewed by T. K. Derry in *A History of Modern Norway, 1814–1973*, and by James A. Storting in *Norwegian Democracy*. A case study of the electoral system is contained in an article by S. Rokkan and H. Torstein, 'Norway: the Storting election of September 1965', in *Scandinavian Political Studies*, 1966.

10

Sweden

The Swedish parliament, or Riksdag, claims to be the second-oldest in Europe after the English parliament, having a continuous history since 1435. It was also at an early date more broadly based than parliaments elsewhere, since its four 'Estates' included one for representation of the farming community, in addition to those which represented the nobility, the clergy and the burghers.

Through the centuries, the balance of power swung periodically between Crown and parliament. A period of moderate absolutism was brought to an end in 1809 by the Russo-Swedish War, which resulted in the surrender of Finland by Sweden to Russia, and the deposition of King Gustav IV of Sweden. This was followed immediately by the preparation of a new constitution, which was based essentially on the separation of the powers of the executive, the legislature and the judiciary, but still left the Crown in a very strong position, since it was provided that 'the king alone shall govern the realm', and that he alone should be responsible for the administration, foreign policy and the armed forces.

Between 1809 and 1866 the Swedish parliament continued to consist of the traditional four Estates. The nobility took their seats in their own Estate by right of heredity, and all the senior Lutheran clergy were represented in theirs *ex officio*, only the subordinate clergy choosing a limited number of representatives by election.

The burghers consisted of citizens engaged in trade, whether retail or wholesale, and in manufacturing or crafts. At first all burghers were members of exclusive gilds, until gild privileges were abolished in 1846, but in 1858, for the election of representatives in the burghal Estate, property qualifications were substituted for the occupational qualifications which had previously existed.

For the election of the Estate of farmers, the country was divided into 300 electoral districts, each entitled to return one representative, but in practice two or more districts commonly combined to send only one representative between them, so as to minimise the expenses of representation which they had to bear.

About the middle of the nineteenth century, the nobility and the clergy each represented less than 0·5 per cent of the population, and the burghers not much more than 2 per cent. The agricultural community accounted for two-thirds of the population, but of these it was only the farmers who were represented in the agricultural Estate, not the cottagers and labourers who formed two-thirds of the agricultural population. Also unrepresented was a growing middle class of junior civil servants, doctors, teachers, technicians and other 'white-collar' occupations.

A reform of parliament was achieved by an Act of 1866. Earlier, in 1862, elected provincial councils had been established, and these were now used as electoral colleges for a first, or upper, chamber of parliament, which was to have *equal legislative power* with a second, or lower, chamber – this provision later had an important bearing on the introduction of electoral reforms. The franchise for the elections to the provincial councils was extended to men and women aged 23 or more who paid taxes, but a system of plural voting, based on wealth, enabled a rich elector to cast thousands of votes, limited in 1900 only to 5,000 in county constituencies, and 100 in the towns.

For the lower chamber there was no plural voting, but the franchise was limited to those who had high property qualifications. The election of members was direct in those towns which returned members of their own, but in large constituencies, formed by groups of communes or small towns, elections could be indirect. The Act of 1866 extended the franchise to about 5 per cent of the population, and this had risen to little more than 8 per cent by 1905.

In effect, the reform of 1866 substituted control of parliament by a plutocracy for control by the nobility, and this was achieved by means of the property qualifications for the electors of both houses. When further reforms of parliament were sought, particularly from 1905 onwards, it was in turn these propertied classes which came under attack. Although the four Estates had been swept aside when the two-chamber parliament was established in 1866, the old and new parliaments were otherwise much the same in their social composition, and there continued to be little change for the next forty years.

From 1866 onwards the farmers in the second chamber formed the chief opposition in parliament, and in 1867 they instituted what was at that time the only organised political party, registering members who subscribed to a common political programme. Their chief practical aim was to secure the removal of ancient land taxes they were required to pay, but from which the nobility, in return for services they had once rendered to the Crown, had remained exempt.

Elections contested on party lines date back to the free trade controversy of 1887, resulting from the influx of cheap grain from the USA and Russia. Farmers themselves were divided on this issue, depending on whether they were primarily consumers or producers of grain; and exporting interests were naturally in favour of free trade. In the first chamber a majority of protectionists was formed, whose interests were now the same as those of protectionist farmers in the second chamber. When a reunited Farmers' Party was formed in 1895 this was more conservative than the party of earlier decades. The farmers were now less interested than they had been before in parliamentary reform, and opposed an extension of the franchise, since this could now result in a loss of their seats to middle- and lower-class candidates.

After a Social Democratic Party had been formed in 1889, a Universal Suffrage Association was founded in 1890, which was supported by radical Liberals as well as the Socialists. Co-operation between Liberals and Socialists having once been established in support of franchise reform, it was easier in later years for coalition governments of these two parties to be formed. By 1905 both the Liberal and the Socialist parties had secured effective representation in parliament, and the farmers no longer provided the opposition.

The movement for reform of the franchise was complicated, however, by other issues of a constitutional nature. A second issue involved the doctrine of the separation of powers which was enshrined in the constitution of 1809, and which meant that control over the executive was exercised by the Crown and not by parliament. A third issue was a demand that within parliament itself power should lie effectively with the lower chamber, which was more representative of the people as a whole, and not with the upper chamber, which was more exclusive and indirectly elected. It is only in the context of these three issues that it is possible to understand why and how a fourth issue was raised and resolved, which was the reform of the electoral system by substituting proportional for majority elections.

Although the Crown's executive powers were technically limited by the requirement that decrees should be countersigned by a minister, the ministers themselves were appointed by the king, and they were responsible to him and not to parliament. However, the powers of ministers increased independently of the Crown. E. G. Bostrom, who was chancellor between 1891 and 1900, sought support for his ministry from members of both chambers, and when he resumed office in 1902 he was the first chancellor who was specifically permitted by the king to choose his own ministers. When Christian Luneberg formed a coalition in 1905 to deal with Norway's demand for independence as a separate state, his ministry was composed, not of servants of the Crown, but of parliamentary leaders, as no previous ministry had been, and it included the Liberal leader, Karl Albert Staaff.

As a result of the success of the Social Democrats and the Liberals in the election of 1905, they jointly constituted a majority in the lower chamber, and Staaff was able to form a government. In the course of debates on measures for parliamentary and electoral reform, Staaff claimed that the essential issue was whether the powers of government should continue to be exercised by the king. When his proposals for reform were passed by the lower chamber but rejected by the upper chamber, he demanded the dissolution of parliament and an appeal to the electorate in a general election. The king refused to grant a dissolution, on the ground that under the constitution the two chambers had equal status, and one could not seek powers to over-rule the other. Staaff thereupon resigned office.

The contest between the Liberals and the king was resumed on the eve of the First World War on the issue of defence. The king responded to a public demonstration in favour of measures to strengthen the nation's defences by a statement of concern at the delay in taking such measures for which the government was responsible. When Staaff asked the king to retract his criticisms of the government the king refused, and Staaff once more resigned. Again this appeared to be a victory for the king, but this was the last occasion on which the king publicly spoke or acted against a ministry.

In 1917, after electoral successes by the Social Democrats and to a lesser extent the Liberals, Nils Eden, now the Liberal leader, formed a coalition government consisting of political leaders drawn from the lower chamber and supported by a majority of members of that chamber. He demanded that the king should dissolve parliament if the upper chamber rejected parliamentary reforms which he intended to introduce. The king agreed, and this marked the final establishment of government responsible to parliament, only twelve years after the first serious contest between king and parliament in 1905.

The establishment of the supremacy of the lower chamber was the central aim and over-riding ambition of Staaff, who was on the radical left of the Liberal Party. As a policy for the Liberals it scarcely survived the death of Staaff in 1915, after which it became evident that although it might be in the Liberal interest to curtail the power of the Conservatives in the upper chamber, it was no longer an attractive alternative to concentrate powers in the lower chamber, in which the Social Democrats had by now become the most powerful party, and continued to be the strongest in every subsequent election.

In the last quarter of the nineteenth century, the process of industrialisation in Sweden had led to the growth of a labouring class in industry which was attracted to the Social Democratic Party, and also a lower middle class on which Staaff and the radical Liberals based their support. Both of these growing sections of the population were excluded from the franchise by high property qualifications, and both supported the campaign for universal manhood suffrage, which was the basis for the parliamentary reform movement before the First World War.

From about 1900 the Conservatives reconciled themselves to an extension of the franchise through the reduction of property qualifications for electors, and concentrated instead on ensuring that, in spite of the growth of the Liberal and Social Democratic votes, Conservative representation should be safeguarded in both chambers of parliament. After Bostrom, a Conservative, became chancellor in 1900, he introduced a Bill providing for the extension of the franchise to men aged 25, with a 'safeguard' in favour of mature and responsible (that is, Conservative) voters by confining the vote to taxpayers who were liable to conscription, and by giving an extra vote to married and older men. This proposal was rejected by both chambers.

It was at this point that proportional representation, which had earlier been proposed by Bishop Axel Billing in 1892, was put forward as an alternative 'safeguard' in both chambers of parliament, in place of the traditional 'safeguards' of property qualifications. Sixten von Friesen, who was at that time the leader of the Liberals and a moderate, gave his support to proportional representation, saying that 'no party and no class ought to have anything against it'. However, the more radical Liberals gained strength in the election of 1902. The National Liberal Federation, under the leadership of Staaff, resolved in November 1903 to support proportional representation only if it was adopted for both chambers of parliament, failing which they would demand a limitation of the powers of the upper chamber. Staaff now replaced von Friesen as the leader of the Liberal Party in parliament. He decided that the Liberals could control the lower chamber under elections held by majority voting in single-member constituencies, and he therefore included this system of voting in his proposals for reform, modified only by a second ballot in the absence of an absolute majority in the first. He preferred to leave the upper chamber unreformed, and therefore indefensible, whereas the Conservatives became willing to accept reform of the upper chamber, and also to accept proportional representation in elections for that chamber, if that was the price which had to be paid to preserve their (Conservative) influence.

After Staaff became chancellor, the upper chamber accepted a resolution that elections for that chamber by the electoral colleges (that is, the provincial councils) should be by proportional representation, and that in the majority elections for those colleges the maximum number of votes which any individual might cast for candidates should be reduced from 5,000 to 1,000. However, the real issue now was whether the lower chamber should have supremacy over the first, and on this issue Branting, the leader of the Social Democrats, gave his support to Staaff.

He also supported Staaff's proposal for a majority system in elections for the lower chamber in single-member constituencies.

In 1907, after the resignation of Staaff, Salomon Lindman assumed office and formed a ministry of supporters of proportional representation, consisting largely of Conservatives, but including also some dissident Liberals and some independents. He pressed the view that in order to overcome Liberal opposition to proportional representation for the lower chamber, the Conservatives would have to accept reform of the composition of the upper chamber, and he proposed that this should be achieved by introducing proportional representation not only for the election of the upper chamber by the electoral colleges, but also for the electoral colleges themselves, that is to say, for the provincial and city councils. He introduced a Bill which included these proposals, and which also reduced the number of votes which any single elector might cast from 5,000 to 40. In his opinion, a more conservative element in the upper chamber could be ensured by the indirect elections still to be held for that chamber, and by longer terms of office for its members.

Staaff, and most Liberals, demanded a predominant role for the lower chamber, and also criticised the Bill on the grounds that membership of the upper chamber would still be restricted to candidates with high property qualifications. The Bill was amended by reducing the qualifications for candidates seeking election to the upper chamber from ownership of property to the value of 80,000 riksdaler or an income of 4,000, to property of 50,000 or an income of 3,000. This was supported even by Branting and the Social Democrats. On the other hand Staaff supported (while Branting opposed) the survival of plural voting, which still gave as many as 40 votes to wealthier electors, since he rightly feared that equal votes would favour the Social Democrats rather than the Liberals. Thus, in the later stages of reform the opposition was disunited. The Conservatives favoured PR, the Social Democrats still favoured single-member constituencies, and the Liberals were now divided. The Bill, with successive amendments which had been adopted, was passed in both chambers in 1907, and became law when, in accordance with the constitution, it had been confirmed by a new parliament in 1909.

As regards the changing role of political parties in parliament, it was not until the late nineteenth century that the modern party system developed. The Social Democratic Party was formed in 1889, Branting was their first member to be elected to parliament, with Liberal support, in 1897, and was their only member until 1903. However, the party had thirty-four seats in the lower chamber by 1908, and became the largest party in that chamber in September 1914. The Liberal Party became effectively organised from 1893, and were the leading party in the lower chamber between 1905 and 1911, after which their strength declined as the Social Democrats made further advances. The Conservatives first resorted to systematic party organisation in 1904, in preparation for the election of 1905, and this organisation was used by Lindman in 1906 to secure support for his reform proposals. The Farmers' Party, which had formed the earliest of the political parties, played a leading role in securing the compromises which resulted in electoral reform. They were virtually extinguished in the election of 1911, but were revived as the Agrarian Party in the election of 1924, and became the Centre Party in 1957. These four parties, emerging from majority elections *before* the electoral reforms of 1907 to 1909, have between them almost invariably dominated the party system ever since. Proportional representation did not lead to any significant change in the party system or multiplication of parties.

As a result of the reforms of 1907 to 1909, all elections to the lower chamber were now direct, the suffrage was extended to all men aged 24 or over, and election was by proportional representation using the D'Hondt method. Fifty-six constituencies were designated, within each of which proportionality was to be achieved. At the national level this still fell substantially short of true proportionality, and any party which had less than 30 per cent of the votes was generally under-represented.

The D'Hondt method was also used for elections to the upper chamber, for which the age of suffrage was 21, but for which plural voting based on property was still retained, permitting a wealthy voter to cast up to 40 votes. There was also still a high property qualification for candidates seeking election to the upper chamber.

After Liberal and Social Democrat successes in the election of 1911, Staaff formed another government which, as already indicated, came into conflict with the Crown over the issue of defence. In 1914 there was a slight rise in Social Democrat representation, but the Liberals lost heavily to the Conservatives.

In the election of 1917 the Conservatives lost seats gained by the revived Farmers' Party, and gains were also made by a new left-wing Socialist Party. However, the Liberals and the Social Democrats slightly strengthened their representation, and they formed a coalition under the Liberal leader, Nils Eden, although, since 1914, it had been the Social Democrats who had formed the strongest party in the second chamber.

In the turbulence and unrest which accompanied the end of the First World War, especially after the revolution in Russia, it was possible to rush through further constitutional reforms, since there was a fear, partly justified, and partly exploited by the reformers, that the alternative to substantial reforms would be revolution in Sweden. The Social Democrat leader, Branting, had become a strong opponent of revolution and supporter of reform, and his influence was important at this time.

By the reforms which took place between 1918 and 1921, universal male and female suffrage was established for both chambers of parliament, at the age of 27 for the upper chamber (reduced to 23 in 1936), and at the age of 23 for the lower; and plural voting was abolished for the upper chamber (equal voting already existed for the lower). Another substantial change was a reduction in the number of constituencies for elections to the second chamber from 56 to 28. In the larger constituencies it was possible for a greater degree of proportionality to be achieved. This reduced the bias of the D'Hondt system in favour of the larger parties, and was to the advantage of the 'bourgeois' parties, which collectively outnumbered the Social Democrats in parliament. But the number of constituencies was still so large that in the parliaments between 1930 and 1950 an average of more than seventeen seats were allocated in each parliament in a manner which departed from true proportionality in the nation as a whole.

To counteract this bias in the electoral system, the electoral law between 1921 and 1952 provided that two or more parties might unite in an alliance for electoral purposes – that is to say, *apparentement* was permitted. In the 1920s alliances were infrequent, those which were formed were normally on a local and not on a national basis, and the party alliances formed in some constituencies were often different from those formed in others, sometimes cancelling each other out. However, it became a standing grievance of the Social Democrats that this system of alliances was of the greatest utility to the smaller 'bourgeois' parties. Between 1931 and 1948 alliances were more frequent, they were commonly directed against the Social Democrats, and their effect on results became more pronounced. This became even less tolerable for the Social Democrats when the Agrarian Party joined 'bourgeois' alliances during elections, but were willing to join a coalition government with the Social Democrats thereafter.

When the Social Democrats invited the Agrarians to join the government in 1936, they successfully stipulated that the Agrarians should not in future join electoral alliances with other groups. This resulted, however, in an electoral setback for the Agrarians in 1938, an outcome which was indirectly to the disadvantage of the Social Democrats themselves, since it weakened the coalition of the two parties.

Dissatisfaction with the system of alliances was revived when another coalition was formed between the Social Democrats and the Agrarians in 1948, and it was now resolved that a change should be made in the electoral system. Instead of *apparentement*, a different method was to be devised to make it easier for smaller parties to gain seats. The solution arrived at was the replacement of the D'Hondt system by a modified form of the Sainte-Laguë system, and this was effected by a reform of the electoral law in 1952. Instead of the pure Sainte-Laguë divisors of 1, 3, 5, etc., which were thought to be too conducive to the proliferation of small parties, the first divisor was changed to $1 \cdot 4$.

In practice it was not much easier, under this modified Sainte-Laguë system, for small parties to gain a first seat. Compared with the effects of the D'Hondt system, it was only from the second seat onwards that they benefited to a significant extent, and this was of diminishing value as the number of seats they gained increased. There was not a great deal of difference in 1948 between the results as they were under the D'Hondt system, with or without electoral alliances, and what they would have been if the *modified* Sainte-Laguë system had been employed; but there would have been a considerable difference, and one much closer to true proportionality, if the *pure* Sainte-Laguë system had been applied.

After the limited and somewhat ambiguous reforms of 1952 there was a movement in favour of more far-reaching changes, not confined to the electoral system, but including curtailment of the powers of the upper chamber, and changing its composition. However, the conservative character of the upper chamber now lay, not in the nature of its social composition (the property qualifications required of candidates were removed in 1933), but in the time-lag which delayed the reflection of changes in political opinion in the country by changes in the political composition of the upper chamber. While members of the lower chamber were elected for four years, members of the upper chamber were elected for eight. In the course of time, the upper chamber reflected the dominance of the Social Democrats. In 1941 the number of seats they had in the lower chamber was 134, and by 1949 this had *fallen* to 112. During the same period the number of their seats in the upper chamber *rose* from 74 to 84. In view of the earlier history of constitutional reform, it is ironical that the Social Democrats no longer had a particular motive for reducing the powers of the upper chamber, since they now had a majority in that chamber.

The Liberals in 1953 advocated the abolition of the upper chamber, but were not at that time supported by other parties. A Royal Commission was, however, appointed in 1954 to review the entire constitution, and as a result of its lengthy deliberations its reports began to appear from 1963 onwards. Debate was concentrated especially upon two issues: whether the upper chamber should be abolished, and whether the electoral system should be reformed in favour of a majority system. In the absence of agreement a new Commission recommended in 1967 a total revision of the constitution involving the abolition of the upper chamber. In 1969 parliament agreed, and decided that a single chamber of 350 members should replace the upper and lower chambers of 151 and 233 members respectively. A recommendation that proportional representation should be replaced by majority voting in single-member constituencies was rejected.

However, one important change in the electoral system did gain approval in parliament at this time. It was a defect of the existing system that through the division of the country into many constituencies it did not provide proportional representation in the nation as a whole, but increased the advantage of the larger parties, and favoured those whose support was concentrated in particular geographical areas. These anomalous results could be illustrated from the 1964 election, in which the Centre Party, whose support was highly localised, returned members having an average of 16,959 votes each, while the Communist Party, whose votes were more widely dispersed, required an average of 27,718 votes to elect each of their members.

To make representation more accurate, the solution adopted was to have a two-tier electoral system. In the first place, 310 members were to be elected by PR in the same constituencies as before, and using the same modified Sainte-Laguë system; but forty additional seats were to be allocated to achieve more accurately proportional representation on a national basis. For this allocation, also, the modified Sainte-Laguë system was to be used, and the additional party seats were to be allocated to those constituencies where the party had the highest share of the constituency vote. However, it was also desired to ensure that there should be no proliferation of small parties which might make the formation of governments more difficult, and the allocation of constituency seats was therefore limited to those parties which had secured at least 12 per cent of the votes in the constituency, and the allocation of national seats was limited to those which had secured at least 4 per cent of the national vote. The effect of the reforms was that one part conferred benefits on the smaller parties, while another part took some of the benefits away.

Apart from the four main parties, the Communist Party was the only one which had ever secured as much as 4 per cent of the national vote since 1944, and they had done so in six of the eight elections between 1944 and 1968. In practice, therefore, this was the only one of the smaller parties which was likely to surmount (and gain from) the exclusion clauses. In 1964 they had 5 per cent of the votes, but gained only 8 of the 233 seats ($3 \cdot 4$ per cent of all seats). Now, any party which had at least 4 per cent of the votes would be allocated at least 14 of the 350 seats (4 per cent of all seats).

In the 1970 election the result hinged on whether the Social Democrats and the Communists would receive enough seats between them for the Social Democrats to be able to form a government with Communist support. In the event, the Communists gained $4 \cdot 8$ per cent of the votes, and seventeen seats. The Social Democrats had 163 seats, which left them in a minority in parliament, but able to form a government with the support of the Communists. It was evident from the first election under the new electoral system that it was not going to be much easier than before for a single party to form a government.

In the election of 1973 the Communists again surmounted the 4 per cent barrier, and obtained nineteen seats with 5·3 per cent of the votes. Since the Social Democrats had 156 seats, this meant that the two parties had between them exactly half of the 350 seats in parliament, and the Social Democrats formed a government which had a precarious existence until 1976. (The Christian Democrats had 1·8 per cent of the votes, but the exclusion clause prevented them from receiving any of the *six* seats to which they would have been entitled on a strictly proportional basis.) This experience led to a constitutional amendment to reduce the number of national seats from 40 to 39, in the hope that by fixing an odd number of seats, and reducing the total number of seats from 350 to 349, there would be avoided for the future the situation in which parliament was exactly divided between government and opposition. No provision was made, however, for the possibility that a single independent member might be elected, creating an equally precarious balance between the parties.

This new arrangement had no decisive effect on government formation after the election of 1976. The Communists received 4·9 per cent of the votes and 17 seats, and the Social Democrats gained 152 seats, so that between them the two parties had only a minority of seats in parliament. In October 1976 Hr Thorbjorn Falldin formed a coalition government of the Centre, Moderates and Liberals.

The exclusion clauses introduced in 1970 had a potentially drastic effect, since a single vote in excess of 4 per cent of the votes in the entire nation could ensure that a party had fourteen seats in parliament, while a single vote short of 4 per cent could deprive it of any representation at all. This has to be set against the advantage which it is sought to achieve by preventing a proliferation of small parties in parliament.

Among other changes in the electoral system, the voting age which, for the former second chamber, had been reduced to 23 in 1921 and to 21 in 1945, was for the single-chamber parliament reduced in 1970 to 19 and in 1975 to 18. Another change was a provision in the constitution of 1975 that in parliamentary elections substitutes for members should be elected, who should replace the members if they died, resigned or obtained leave of absence from parliament. The speaker of the Riksdag and ministers might not serve as members of parliament so long as they held office, their places being taken during such period by their substitutes.

As regards the allocation of seats to individual candidates, the elector is entitled to vote for individual candidates in order of preference, provided their number does not exceed by more than two the number of seats to be filled. The elector may vote for a party, and vote for the party list of candidates in the party's order of preference; but he may also delete the names of candidates who are on the list, or add the names of candidates not on the list. If a candidate votes for a party, he must place at the head of the list of candidates for whom he votes the name of a candidate who is on that party's list, otherwise the vote for the party is invalid. Only a vote for a party is counted towards that party's allocation of seats, and in the absence of a vote for a party the elector's vote counts only towards the election of candidates for whom he had indicated a preference.

There are two methods of counting votes for the allocation of seats to individual candidates on a list. First, if a candidate has been given first preferences by votes numbering at least half of the votes cast for the list, he is entitled to the first of the party's seats. Any two candidates who are together given the first and second preferences on a number of votes equal to at least two-thirds of the votes for the party are entitled to the first two seats, and so on. Secondly, if candidates fail to reach the number of votes required by this method, those with most votes in each category are allocated the seats, provided that in counting the votes for this purpose a ballot paper containing the name of a candidate already elected is counted as half.

There are no regulations which prescribe the methods by which candidates are chosen for nomination on the party election lists. This is regarded as an internal matter to be decided by the parties themselves. In general, the selection of candidates is made at the constituency level, and the central party organisations do not have much control.

REFERENCES: CHAPTER 10

On Sweden, works which include accounts of the electoral system are Douglas V. Verney, *Parliamentary Reform in Sweden, 1866–1921*; Dankwart A. Rustow, *The Politics of Compromise: A Study of Parties and Cabinet Government in Sweden*; and Joseph B. Board, *The Government and Politics of Sweden*. Articles specifically on the electoral system are by Nils Herlitz, 'Proportional representation in Sweden', in the *American Political Science Review*, 1925; Raymond Fusilier, 'La représentation proportionnelle en Suède de 1919 à 1952', in the *Revue internationale d'histoire politique et constitutionnelle*, 1954; Björn Molin, 'Sweden: the first year of the one-chamber Riksdag', in *Scandinavian Political Studies*, 1972; and Neil Elder, 'The Swedish General Election of 1976', in *Parliamentary Affairs*, 1977. There is a pamphlet by Olaf Petersson on *New Trends in the Swedish Electorate: A Focus on the 1976 Election*. Official publications include *Constitutional Documents of Sweden*, *Sveriges Riksdag: The Swedish Parliament* and *The Swedish Political Parties*.

11

Finland

Until 1906 Finland had one of the most archaic forms of parliament still surviving in Europe, based on four separate Estates of nobility, clergy, burgesses and farmers, with an exclusive type of representation for the first two, and a highly restricted electoral franchise for the others. Yet in 1906, after the revolution of 1905 in Russia, this nation adopted a liberal, rational and highly sophisticated constitutional system and method of election which could in some respects be regarded as the most advanced in Europe. The rationality was perhaps the product of a long period during which constitutionalism and legalism had been the weapons with which the Finns, and in collaboration with them the Swedish minority in Finland, had defended their autonomy and historic institutions against encroachments by the tsarist government.

This opposition gathered strength after 1863, when the Finnish Estates were convened for the first time in fifty years. They now met more regularly, and passed social legislation which had for generations been neglected. One of the most important of these measures was the provision of universal education from 1866 onwards, the result of which was that by 1900 the population of Finland over the age of 15, overwhelmingly rural as it was, became highly literate compared with other countries. It was to a literate population that universal suffrage was extended in 1906, not only to men but, for the first time in Europe, for parliamentary elections, to women as well; and it was the views of an educated electorate that the system of proportional representation was designed to express as accurately as possible in parliament.

When Finland was in 1809 separated by force of arms from Sweden and incorporated in the Russian Empire, it remained a largely autonomous Grand Duchy, as it had been since 1581, and it continued to be responsible for its own legislation. The tsars now became the grand dukes, responsible for Finland's external relations and defence. Also inherited from the Swedish period was the parliament of the four Estates, which had originated in the fifteenth century. Tsar Alexander I demonstrated his liberalism and desire to rule as a constitutional monarch by guaranteeing to the Finns the continuance of their existing rights, liberties and institutions, including the four Estates. It was normal for subsequent tsars to give similar undertakings, but until the 1860s little interest was taken by the Russian government in the affairs of the Grand Duchy. After meetings of the Estates were resumed in 1863, a Constitution Act of 1866 provided that they should meet at least every five years, and in practice it became normal for them to meet at intervals of not more than three years. At the same time, relations became somewhat closer with Russia, which established free trade with the Grand Duchy between 1859 and 1885.

The representation in the Estates, and the nature of the elections which were held, were very flexible. Between 1863 and 1905 the number of the members of the Estate of the nobility varied between 122 and 201; the Estate of the clergy numbered 40 or more; the burgesses between 38 and 73, and the farmers between 47 and 64. For elections to the Estate of burgesses the electorate in 1900 was less than 24,000, and for the farmers it was slightly more than 100,000. These figures compare with a population of about 3 million at that time. Elections to the Estate of burgesses were by block votes in multi-member constituencies, with electors exercising anything from 10 to 50 votes each, depending on how much they paid in taxes. There was similar voting by farmers in the first stage of their indirect elections, and in the second stage electoral colleges chose members of the Estate by means of simple plurality voting.

Political parties in a modern sense scarcely existed, but movements which developed into political parties were concerned with the promotion of the Finnish language and culture in place of the dominance of Swedish. Before the end of the century Finnish was adopted alongside Swedish as the official language, and also as the language for secondary and university education.

The Swedes predominated in the Estate of the nobility, and also for most of the nineteenth century in the Estate of the burgesses, since the Swedish population was concentrated in the towns of southern and western Finland; but by the end of the century the Finns predominated in the Estate of burgesses as well as the Estates of clergy and farmers. By controlling three of the four Estates they were able to control parliamentary legislation, for which the agreement of three out of the four Estates was required.

With growing Russian encroachment upon Finnish liberties and acts of tsarist oppression before and after 1906, there developed a division between the Old Finns, who favoured co-operation and compliance so far as possible with the tsarist government and officials, and the Young Finns, who insisted on the maintenance of constitutional rights and liberties. The Swedes generally supported the Young Finns and associated themselves with Finnish aspirations for autonomy, which was an element contributing to national unity in the struggle for independence.

The fact that there was before 1906 little development of political parties other than the Finnish and Swedish cultural movements is more readily understandable when one takes into account not only the limited scope for political expression through the Estates, but also the slow economic and social development of Finland during the nineteenth century. Industrialisation was much slower to spread there than in the other Nordic countries, and only began to accelerate in the last decade of the century. In 1900, agriculture, forestry and fishing still accounted for more than two-thirds of the occupied population, compared with 55 per cent in Sweden, and 45 per cent in Norway and Denmark. The slower development of industry in Finland, and the continuing importance of agriculture and forestry, were later reflected in the structure of the political parties. As in other Nordic countries, the parties could eventually be distinguished as extreme left, social democrat, centre, liberal and conservative, but the social democrats, in spite of being the leading party, did not achieve so dominating a position as in the other Nordic countries. The Social Democrat Party was formed in 1903, before the reforms of 1906, but was powerless to have much influence on events through lack of representation in the Estates. Immediately after universal suffrage was adopted in 1906 they gained the largest representation in parliament, and in 1916 won 103 out of the 200 seats. This was the only occasion in Finnish parliamentary history when a single party gained an absolute majority in parliament. In the civil war of 1918 the Social Democrats were absent from parliament since they were engaged in the losing side of the battle to establish a revolutionary socialist regime. In spite of this the desires of the Social Democrats were largely satisfied in the constitutional reforms of 1919.

The origins of the pressure for reform at the end of the nineteenth century lay in a new and oppressive attitude of the tsarist government towards the Finns. Pan-Slav and expansionist ambitions in Russia sought more rigorous control over Finland, and in 1899 the tsar assumed certain powers of legislation in Finland without reference to the Finnish Diet. In 1901 he imposed conscription into the armed forces, which aroused widespread opposition, culminating in 1904 in the assassination of the governor-general in Finland, Nikolai Bobrikov. In 1905 the revolutionary movement in Russia, and the Russian defeat in the war with Japan, gave the opportunity for constitutional reforms in Finland, and for the replacement of the old Diet of Estates by a new unicameral parliament based on universal suffrage.

However, this was not the end of Russian oppression, and from 1907 onwards the new parliament was repeatedly dissolved when it sought to assert itself in domestic policy and legislation. The surviving Finnish senate was packed with Russian officials, and Finnish dissidents were deported to Siberia. When the Russian revolution of 1917 ended the tsarist regime this removed the last link which bound Finland to Russia, and on 6 December 1917 the Finnish parliament declared Finland to be an independent sovereign republic. After a civil war in 1918 there followed, on 17 February 1919, the adoption of a new Constitution Act which, to the unicameral parliament already established, added an elected president as head of state instead of the tsar, and a council of state responsible to parliament as the executive arm instead of the senate.

As regards the electoral system, there had already before 1905 been public interest in alternative forms of election, including proportional representation. It was in the labour movement that the advocacy of electoral reform was strongest and increasingly urgent in the years immediately before 1905. In 1896 a convention of workers' associations demanded a reduction in the means-tested suffrage for the Estates of burgesses and farmers, and the abolition of the graduated scale of votes; in the next convention in 1899 the demand had hardened to the establishment of a unicameral legislature elected by universal male and female suffrage for all persons over 21; and in 1903, when the Social Democratic Party was founded, proportional representation was added to these demands.

After the revolution of 1905 the tsar assigned to the Finnish senate the task of formulating proposals for constitutional reform. The Russian nominees had been removed from the senate, which was now dominated by constitutionalists, and an all-party committee including Social Democrats was appointed to make proposals for a reform of the representative system. All parties except the Swedes (most strongly represented in the former Estate of the nobility) were in favour of a unicameral system, and when the Swedes realised that this would probably prevail they held out for a system of PR for the unicameral parliament, as the only guarantee of the continued representation of minorities in parliament. This argument was accepted by the reform committee.

There were various other circumstances which favoured the adoption of PR at this time. One was that as yet there were no large parties which sought or expected to achieve that sole dominance over parliament which was feasible under a majority system but rare under a system of proportional representation. There had been no history of bitter rivalry between parties, but on the contrary a history of collaboration through the Diet of Estates against the oppressions of the tsarist regime. There was therefore a ready acceptance of the principle that each party should be fairly represented in parliament. Another point which made it easier to accept PR was that in the elections, such as they were, for the Estates of burgesses and farmers, there had already been experience of the multi-member constituencies which were, at some point in the electoral system, essential for the achievement of PR. There were some pleas on behalf of the majority system, on the grounds that it was easier to understand, and on behalf of small constituencies, to restrain the power of large-scale party organisations, but these were not strongly supported.

Finally, a subcommittee came down in favour of a chamber of 200 members elected from fifteen constituencies, designed to be numerous enough to avoid excessive centralisation, but each large enough to secure a fair degree of proportional representation. These recommendations were accepted by the senate, subject to the fixing of the number of the constituencies at sixteen, and the suffrage was now also extended to all men and women over 24. What was evidently the decisive consideration in favour of PR was that this compensated for having only one chamber of parliament instead of two.

The Constitution Act of July 1906 provided for the abolition of the old Estates and the establishment of the new parliament. A Parliament Act which was passed at the same time, as a basic, fundamental or constitutional law, provided that parliament should be unicameral and have 200 members; that elections should take place every three years (changed in 1955 to every four years); and that members should be elected by direct, equal and proportional elections in constituencies numbering between twelve and eighteen. All men and women aged 24 (amended by stages later to 18) were to be entitled to vote, subject to the exclusion of certain defined categories.

Article 67 defined what Bills were of a constitutional nature, and the special procedure which must be adopted in enacting, amending or abrogating such laws. The procedure required was that a proposal adopted in one parliament must, after a general election, also be accepted without amendment by a two-thirds majority of a new parliament. Alternatively, in case of urgency, such a Bill might be passed in one session by a five-sixth majority of parliament. The electoral provisions of the Parliament Act were entrenched in the constitution in this way, including the requirement that representation should be proportional.

The other electoral provisions were contained in electoral laws which were revised from time to time, but which, from the electoral law of 1906 onwards, remained unchanged as regards the method of counting *party* votes and determining the proportional representation of parties. Essentially, the method adopted was the D'Hondt divisor system, and this was originally linked in an ingenious way with the method of selecting individual candidates within each party.

Parties, or 'associations of electors', were entitled to nominate up to three candidates on a 'list', the names of the candidates being arranged in order of priority. These lists could in turn be associated in 'alliances' between lists, provided these alliances were notified to the returning officers before an election. Each elector could cast only one vote for one list, and all votes for a list counted also as votes for the 'alliance' (if any) of which it formed part. Candidates could be nominated in more than one constituency, and on more than one list in each constituency.

The method of counting votes for each *candidate* may be regarded as a variation of the D'Hondt system operated, as it were, in reverse. The candidates having been arranged in order of priority on a list of three, the candidate first on the list is awarded a number of votes equal to the total number of votes cast for the list; the candidate second on the list is awarded half as many; and the candidate third on the list is awarded one-third. The number of votes which a candidate gains in this way is called his 'comparison number'. If the candidate has been nominated on several lists, whether in first, second or third places (which can be varied in different lists to give the electors a choice of preferences between candidates), then all his 'comparison numbers' are added together to ascertain his total vote within the 'alliance'. When the number of votes for each candidate in the alliance has been ascertained, they are then ranked within the 'alliance' in the order of the number of votes each has obtained.

The total number of votes for each alliance is now ascertained, by adding together the total number of votes cast for the candidates who were first on each 'list'. When this has been done, the candidate first in the order of ranking in each alliance is given a number of votes equal to the number of votes for the alliance; the second candidate one-half as many; the third candidate one-third as many; and so on. Within the constituency, the first seat is awarded to the candidate of any alliance who has most votes; the next seat to the candidate of any alliance with the second highest number of votes; and so on until all the seats in the constituency have been allocated.

At this final stage, the procedure is simply another way of arriving at exactly the same result as if the D'Hondt system had been applied to the total votes of every alliance. It was the first stage of the count, when 'comparison numbers' were awarded to candidates appearing on a list, or on several lists, which was really an innovation, and which was unique to the Finnish electoral system.

The alliances of the Finnish electoral system were the real equivalent of the lists in other list systems of PR; and it was the number of votes given to a party's alliance in a constituency which determined the number of seats which a party obtained. It was the D'Hondt system which determined that allocation, and therefore in essence the Finnish system was the same as other list systems of PR using the D'Hondt method; and in this respect the Finnish electoral system has remained unchanged. The lists of up to three candidates were intended to be a means of providing electors with a choice between candidates of the same party. Another advantage claimed for this system was that it enabled a popular candidate, nominated on several lists, to help others of the same party to gain votes, since each of these would gain a share (larger or smaller, depending on his place on the list) of the votes which the popular candidate was able to attract. For the same reason a popular candidate would be nominated in more than one constituency, though he was entitled, of course, to a seat in only one of them.

Other variations in voting procedure were also permitted. Electors could alter the order of the candidates on a list; or indicate that their vote was only for one candidate and not for the list; or write in the name of a candidate not nominated on the list.

All these devices for choosing between candidates on lists were eventually removed from the electoral system, not because they favoured one party rather than another, or because they aroused any controversy, but simply because they fell out of use. Parties ceased, for the most part, to prepare lists of three candidates, with the result that by 1933 80 per cent of the so-called lists contained one name only, for whom the 'comparison number' was simply the number of votes cast for the list, or candidate. After an Election Act of 1935 had reduced from three to two the number of candidates who might be nominated on a single list, the number of one-person lists in the first election under the new law in 1936 accounted for 95 per cent of all lists, and after this the so-called lists were almost wholly a fiction.

Lists of more than one candidate were abolished for the election of 1954, and finally for all future elections in 1955. From this time onwards electors could vote for only one candidate on the list of names of a party alliance. The Finnish system now became similar to the Belgian, but without the possibility of voting for a list of candidates in the party's order of ranking, and only with the possibility of voting for one individual candidate.

Parties had availed themselves to a greater extent of the possibility of putting up the same candidate in more than one constituency. So long as it was possible to nominate lists of two or three candidates, a popular or hard-working candidate could be linked with others who had little chance of gaining votes on their own account. Usually only well-known party leaders stood as candidates in this way. Parties in search of electoral support continued to nominate some candidates in this manner even after lists were restricted to single candidates from 1954 onwards. The greatest use of this facility appears to have been made by new parties seeking to establish themselves. Parties with strong organisations in the constituencies seldom availed themselves of this facility, because they did not need to. There was therefore little influential support for such candidatures, and in the Electoral Act of 1969 they were finally prohibited.

Of greater consequence for the working of the electoral system was the method of converting party votes into seats, and the effect it had on the degree of proportionality which was achieved. In spite of many proposals for a change or modification of the system it has remained essentially unaltered since 1906, but the attitude of individual parties towards the existing system and the various proposals for reform has varied according to their interests and experience.

One characteristic of the Finnish party system is that, allowing for mergers and changes of name, there have been six parties, owing their origin to the period before 1919, for which the support of the electors has remained fairly steady from one election to the next, and a number of smaller parties for which the support has been more volatile. Of the main parties, the Finnish equivalent of the Conservatives were the Old Finns, who in 1919 became the National Coalition Party. The equivalent of the Liberals were the Young Finns, who in 1919 became the National Progressive Party, and in 1951 the Finnish People's Party, and who in 1966 joined with the Liberal League to form the Liberal People's Party. The Swedish People's Party have had consistent support from the Swedish-speaking community. The Agrarian Union, founded in 1908, became the principal 'bourgeois' party, and eventually, to broaden their appeal beyond the declining farming community, changed their name in 1965 to the Centre Party. The Social Democrats, formed in 1903, have depended heavily on support from rural as well as urban labourers.

To the left of the Social Democrats after 1958 were the Social Democratic Opposition or League. Farther left still were the Communists, when they were not banned, operating in the 1920s through the Socialist Workers' Party, and from 1945 as the Finnish People's Democratic League.

After 1906 the Social Democrats emerged as the strongest single party, having more than 40 per cent of the seats until 1922, and more than 50 per cent in 1916. In the 1920s their share of seats declined to less than 30 per cent, through the rivalry of the Socialist Workers' Party, but recovered once again in the 1930s when that party was banned. Since 1945 their share of seats has once again been limited through rivalry on the left, both from the Finnish People's Democratic League and, later, from the Social Democratic League.

The Agrarian Union/Centre Party became consistently the second party after the Social Democrats in the interwar period, and a close rival to that party after the Second World War, regularly obtaining more than 25 per cent of the seats. Since 1970 this has fallen below 20 per cent.

The Conservatives, or National Coalition, were the second-largest party before 1919, the third in the interwar period, and the fourth since the Second World War, but have recently maintained a respectable share of about 12 to 17 per cent of the seats. The Swedish People's Party, who also tend to be conservative, regularly secured over twenty seats before the Second World War, and regularly more than a dozen since.

It is the Finnish equivalent of the Liberals who have suffered most from a decline in representation, their share of seats having fallen steadily after the First World War. On the other hand the Communist-dominated

People's Democratic League have since the Second World War had a share of seats comparable with those obtained by the Social Democrats and the Agrarian Union.

Under the D'Hondt electoral system, as adapted in its particular way in Finland, it is possible for parties to increase their share of seats by joining together in electoral alliances. In Finland it has been possible to do this only at the level of the constituency, and not at a higher level, for example, a province or the nation as a whole, as in Belgium. Moreover, in Finland, parties which join an alliance do not retain a separate identity within the alliance, which is really a joint list of candidates. The dilemma for the parties in an alliance of this kind is the same as that which arises under the limited vote. If a party puts up too many candidates their support may be too thinly spread, so that their candidates may fail to gain a place high enough in the order of priority to win one of the seats gained by the alliance.

Electoral alliances have, nevertheless, always been frequently formed, but there has been a great difference in the extent to which particular parties have been willing to enter into alliances. The Social Democrats, as the strongest party, have had less need or have felt less inducement than other parties to form alliances, and in fact did so on only one occasion, in 1924, with the Socialist Workers' Party. The (Communist) People's Democratic League, on the other hand, have been consistently in favour of collaboration between left-wing parties, but have seldom been successful in persuading other parties to collaborate, apart from constituency alliances with the Smallholders' party in 1945, and with the Social Democratic (Opposition) League in 1966. All other alliances have been between non-socialist parties.

The Social Democrats have, in any case, been opposed on policy grounds to alliances with socialist rivals, especially the Communists. The electoral alliances which have been formed most frequently have been those entered into by the various parties capable of being designated as 'liberal', which have normally co-operated either with the Centre or with the Conservatives.

The past experience of the parties is reflected in their attitude to proposals for the introduction of *apparentement* between parties. The Social Democrats have been consistently against this, suspecting, in the light of past evidence, that it would be non-socialist parties which would take and gain most advantage out of this facility. Parliamentary committees proposed *apparentement* between 1922 and 1924, and again in 1965–6, but although there was some support for this from the Centre Party, the Conservatives and the Liberals, there was not enough to secure its adoption.

The issue of major importance in proposals which have been made from time to time for reforming the electoral system was what degree of proportionality ought to be secured, and to what extent a bias should be permitted in favour of the larger parties. There was seldom any serious suggestion that the system should be changed in order to secure *greater* advantage for the larger parties, but between 1918 and 1933 many proposals were put forward, chiefly by the Swedes, the Conservatives and the Liberals, in favour of reforms which would have improved proportionality and benefited the smaller parties. Almost annually, such proposals were debated but came to nothing through lack of general agreement.

The Finnish Swedes were the first to introduce, in 1918, a proposal that additional seats should be allocated at the national level to repair deficiencies in proportionality which resulted from the allocation of seats at the level of constituencies. This was the innovation being introduced in Denmark at that time. Their specific proposals were that 180 of the 200 seats in parliament should be allocated to constituencies, and 20 additional seats at the national level. This proposal was linked with others in favour of *apparentement*, but a Bill including these proposals was defeated in 1924, chiefly through the opposition of the Agrarian Union. It was, in fact, the largest parties, the Social Democrats and the Agrarian Union/Centre Party, which consistently opposed reforms designed to achieve more accurate proportionality.

In 1953, and again in 1962, the Finnish Swedes proposed another measure by which proportionality might be improved, which was the adoption, as in Norway, Sweden and Denmark, of the modified Sainte-Laguë system instead of the D'Hondt. A government committee in 1964 expressed the view that nationwide proportionality was not the only consideration, since local circumstances varied; and that Finland did not have the large parties and small constituencies which appeared to have motivated the reforms in the other three countries. The committee considered that the existing Electoral Act adequately satisfied the constitutional requirement of proportional representation.

The subject was not dropped thereafter, since the participation of smaller parties in government, when a larger party needed their support, could, as it did in 1964 to 1966, depend on the willingness of the major party to support reform; but proposals by the government in favour of *apparentement* of parties were defeated in 1966 by the opposition of left-wing parties.

For the various reasons which have been indicated, the electoral reforms which were introduced after 1906 left essentially unaltered the system of allocation of seats to parties, but in other respects a number of changes were introduced. As already noted, lists of up to three candidates which had been permitted up to 1935 were limited to two candidates in that year, and then to only a single candidate from 1954 onwards. The abolition of candidatures in two or more constituencies which had also often been proposed was at last accomplished in an Act of 1969, to have effect after 1970. Also, in 1969, the nominations procedure was amended to provide that only political parties registered with the Ministry of Justice might nominate candidates for election, except in Aalund Province. The Political Parties Act laid down certain requirements for registration, including a programme or statement of policy, and the adhesion of at least 5,000 members. The procedure for the nomination by parties of candidates for election was still, however, left to the discretion of the parties themselves. The Social Democrats were the only party which regularly arranged primary elections among their members to decide upon the nomination of candidates. The (Communist) People's Democratic League were one of the parties whose organisation exercised the closest direct control over nominations.

Since a single party has succeeded in gaining an absolute majority of seats on only one occasion (in 1916), governments have inevitably been coalitions, and they have generally been short-lived. Several elements of stability have nevertheless been set against this to provide a greater continuity of administration than might have been expected. One element of stability has been the role of the president, who, though not the leader of the government, is able to exercise greater power than a purely ceremonial head of state. The president's only positive involvement in government is his responsibility under the constitution for the nation's foreign relations, and also, as commander-in-chief of the armed forces, for its defence, but he has considerable influence in other ways as well. Apart from the advice and mediation he may offer in the formation of Cabinets, he can suspend laws which appear to be unworkable or contrary to the national interest, and he can also promulgate decrees. He cannot, however, exercise these powers without the advice of ministers, except in times of emergency.

REFERENCES: CHAPTER 11

Finland is one of the countries for which there is a book giving a detailed and systematic history of the electoral system. This is *The Electoral System of Finland* by Klaus Törnudd. The constitutional background is outlined in a chapter on 'The Finnish constitution and its development' by Paavo Kastari, in the official *Constitution Act and Parliament Act of Finland*.

PART FOUR
Austria and Switzerland

12

Austria

In Austria, as elsewhere in Europe, constitutional aspirations and movements in the nineteenth century owed their origin or their impetus to the
French revolution, but for a long time the demands for popular representation and for political rights and liberties were successfully repressed.
However, the growth of liberal and democratic movements before and
after the revolutionary disturbances of 1848 led to the promulgation of
the first of many more or less democratic constitutions. After reversals as
well as successes, these culminated in the adoption of universal manhood
suffrage in 1907.

Austria is one of the most conspicuous examples of a country rent and
riven by disaffected national minorities of many races and languages, for
whom aspirations for democratic forms of government were combined
with, or subordinated to, demands for political and cultural autonomy,
and finally for complete independence. Universal manhood suffrage was
not directly relevant to the aspirations of nationalism. When liberal and
democratic reforms which had for generations been resisted were at last
adopted, in the hope that they would appease the disaffection of the
national minorities, it became evident that this could not stem the tide of
nationalism.

The history of reform before 1907 consisted of a period from 1848 to
1867, in which there were a number of abortive and short-lived constitutions, and a period from the year 1867, when there was introduced a
constitution which survived in the imperial parliament until 1907, and in
the Länder or provinces until 1918.

Since 1861, the assemblies of the provinces had been elected in
separate Curiae, or Estates, for different sections of the community. This
system was adopted in 1867 for the imperial parliament itself. Four
separate Curiae were established for the great landowners, the towns, the
chambers of trade and industry, and the rural community. The constitution of 1867 came after the establishment of the dual monarchy of
Austria-Hungary, and the virtual autonomy of Hungary under the
Imperial Crown, subject to imperial control of foreign affairs, defence

and imperial finance. The new constitution was largely an attempt to gain support for the new regime by granting concessions to the peoples and nationalities of the western, or Cisleithanian, half of the empire, as well as to the Hungarians.

The constitution now provided for a bicameral parliament with an upper house and a house of representatives, the latter elected indirectly by the Landtag, or assembly, in each province. It was later provided by a law of 1868 that if a Landtag were obdurate and failed to return members, then they should be elected directly by the people in the province. The Czechs refused to send representatives from their Landtags in Bohemia and Moravia, since they demanded the same degree of autonomy as the Hungarians, and direct elections were therefore held in those provinces under the law of 1868. This constituted a step towards a directly elected parliament, but only at the expense of antagonising the national minorities. From 1873 it was provided that all elections for the imperial parliament's lower house should be direct, but carried out through the four Curiae established for each Landtag in 1861. This curial form of election lasted until 1907.

The constitutional structure in 1867 was highly complex, the Cisleithanian half of the empire being fragmented into nineteen units, consisting of kingdoms, grand duchies, archduchies, duchies, margraves, counties and the city of Trieste, each with some degree of local autonomy. From these areas deputies were sent to the imperial parliament under a highly unequal system of representation. There were direct elections for the first three Curiae (great landowners, towns and chambers of trade and industry), with separate means-tested franchises for the first two, and a restricted membership franchise for the third. In the rural communes, elections were indirect and subject to the same means-tested franchise as for townsmen. This constitution was heartily opposed by the Czechs, Poles and Slovenes. The Czechs refused to attend the imperial parliament, the Poles refused to vote in the parliament, and the German representatives easily secured a two-thirds majority for the adoption of the constitutional changes.

There was a great disparity in the representation of the classes included in the various Curiae. In the election of 1879, for example, there was one representative for every 63 of the great landowners, one for every 27 members of the chambers of trade and industry, one for every 1,600 urban voters, and one for every 7,900 voters in the rural communes. Only a few radicals at this time advocated universal manhood suffrage, but German liberals as well as representatives of the national minorities advocated a more equitable suffrage. In the 1880s there was a campaign for the extension of the franchise, in the 1890s for the abolition of the curial system and the establishment of universal manhood suffrage, and in 1893 there were street demonstrations in support of these demands.

In 1896 Count Badeni produced a compromise in the form of a fifth Curia, for which there would be no means-tested franchise, but a suffrage for all men aged 24 or over. To render this more palatable to the Conservatives, members of the first four Curiae were to vote for representatives of the fifth as well, so that universal manhood suffrage was combined with plural voting. Elections were to be direct for the first three Curiae, but indirect for the fourth and fifth. In the elections for the fourth and fifth Curiae, voting in the colleges was to be by absolute majority. This reform was adopted in 1896.

The elections of 1897 and 1901 demonstrated what a huge disparity still existed in the representation of the different Curiae. In the fifth or 'universal' Curia 69,000 votes were required to elect one representative, compared with 12,000 for the fourth, 4,000 for the third, 26 for the second and 64 for the first. As regards the representation of the different nationalities, there was a bias in favour of the wealthier German community, but the Germans were slightly outnumbered in the house of representatives by the non-German communities. The major discrepancy lay in the gross under-representation of the Ruthenes. This was a poor community, largely migratory in search of work, without an aristocracy, and resentful of exploitation by the Poles in Galicia. The protection of the Poles against the disaffected Ruthenes was one of the problems which later confronted the electoral reformers in 1906 and 1907. But apart from this the electoral injustices incurred by the various nationalities were slight compared with those which discriminated between social and economic classes.

From the time of the Badeni electoral reforms onwards there was agitation for the further extension of the franchise, and in particular for universal manhood suffrage pure and simple. In Hungary the independence movement led by Kossuth gained a majority in the Hungarian parliament in 1905 with universal manhood suffrage as one of its aims. The Social Democrats in Cisleithanian Austria demanded this as well, and held demonstrations in favour of reform. An impetus was given to these demands by the Russian revolution in 1905, and the movement was supported by social democrats and liberals of all nationalities. Those who were most opposed to the demands were the German clericals, the great landowners in Bohemia, and the Polish Club representing the upper-class members of the Polish community.

In response to street demonstrations in November 1905, the emperor came down in favour of universal manhood suffrage, and a committee of parliament was set up to work out the details. The essence of these reforms, contained in an Act of 1907, was that the curial form of representation for the imperial parliament was now ended, and universal manhood suffrage was established. Direct elections were to be held in single-member constituencies by a form of absolute majority voting everywhere except in Galicia, where separate arrangements were made in the interests of the Polish minority. Here there were to be two-member constituencies, one seat to be awarded to a candidate with 50 per cent of the votes or over, and another to a candidate with 25 per cent or over. Where Poles were in a minority they could expect to gain at least 25 per cent of the votes and one seat.

The most important problem was how seats were to be apportioned between constituencies on a geographical basis, and it was this that occupied most of the deliberations of the reform committee. It was calculated in careful detail what representation was likely to be gained for each nationality by any proposed division of constituencies, and this was all the more important since a majority system was to be employed in single-member constituencies.

However, population was not the only criterion which was adopted for the apportionment of seats. The theoretical basis which was adopted was that representation of each province should be based equally on its contribution of direct and indirect taxes to the imperial treasury. Thus, in principle, a province's percentage share of the imperial population and its percentage share of direct and indirect taxes were to be added together and divided by two, and the average was to indicate its share of representation in the imperial parliament. This was to the advantage of the wealthier German community, who were favoured also by the requirement of one year's continuous residence in a locality as a qualification for exercising the franchise there. Much of the Slav and the Ruthene population were migratory in search of labour, so this requirement reduced their electorate and contributed to their under-representation. It was such considerations that reconciled some German interests to reform.

Proposals for the enfranchisement of women were rejected with little debate, and so were proposals for proportional representation. A proportional system would have been to the advantage of the Slav nationalities, and the lack of any campaign in its favour can be accounted for only by ignorance among those communities of the benefits it might have conferred upon them.

The extent to which the various nationalities were represented in the imperial parliament was not substantially changed as a result of the reforms of 1907. The German share, still appreciably higher than it should have been in terms of population, was about 45 per cent, while the share of the Ruthenes was only about half what it should have been on a proportional basis. There were disputes over urban and rural constituency boundaries between Germans and Slavs. There was rivalry between Germans, Romanians, Poles and Ruthenes in Bukovina; between Germans and Slovenes in Styria, Carinthia and Carniola; between Italians, Serbs and Croats in Dalmatia; and between Poles and Ruthenes in Galicia, where the Polish governor was shot by a Ruthene in

1908. There was probably no system of apportionment of representatives and division of boundaries which could have resolved or greatly modified these differences and disputes under a majority system of election. In some respects reform served only to aggravate the problem of the nationalities, since the extended suffrage increased the political power of the peasantry, many of whom had been imbued by their parish priests with a devotion to their own cultural identity and institutions as well as to their church.

One of the inadequacies of reform was that parliament had no control over foreign affairs and foreign policy. The Czechs and Poles objected to the Triple Alliance with Germany and Italy which had been formed in 1882, and the Slav communities vehemently opposed the annexation of Bosnia by Austria in 1908. In the end it was war which ended the constitution of 1907, but even before that it was clear that fair and accurate representation in the imperial parliament would not have satisfied the claims and aspirations of the various nationalities. What they wanted, more particularly after the establishment of the dual Austro-Hungarian monarchy in 1867, was the same degree of autonomy as the Hungarians had been granted. A possible solution without a dissolution of the Habsburg Empire would have been a federal constitution combined with democratic reforms. However, the Christian Socialists and the Social Democrats, both of whom favoured electoral reform and universal suffrage, were both also in favour of a centralised form of constitution, the first in support of imperial institutions, and the second with a view to the ultimate creation of a united socialist state. On the other hand, the Polish and Czech landowners were federalists, but entirely opposed to universal manhood suffrage. In each case it was still within the framework of the empire that autonomy for the various nationalities was sought, and total independence was the aim as well as the achievement only of the postwar period.

Towards the end of the First World War, on 16 October 1918, the emperor issued a manifesto in which he authorised the formation of separate autonomous states within the empire. The 208 elected German deputies in the house of representatives then met as the provisional national assembly of what was now called German Austria. They concluded, on 27 October, a separate peace with the Allies, and later recognised Czechoslovakia and Yugoslavia as separate independent nations. The emperor did not formally abdicate, but on 12 November the assembly declared German Austria to be a democratic republic, and the committee of parliament became the government. In the following year the national assembly announced that a new parliament would be elected by direct, equal and universal suffrage for both men and women aged over 20, by a newly introduced system of proportional representation.

The adoption of proportional representation aroused little debate or opposition or even, it seems, much interest. In Austria the majority system had always been used in elections, usually, before 1907, in single-member constituencies, and from 1907 universally so except in Galicia. But for some time before the war radicals and social democrats had advocated PR, and this was now conceded by the bourgeois parties. One reason for the easy acceptance of this system was that before the war, and in the 1918 assembly, there existed no party or parties which dominated representation in parliament, and which could hope to exploit a majority system in order to gain a majority of seats in parliament. There were dozens of parties split up among the various nationalities before the war, but even among the Germans themselves there was consistently a large number of parties after universal manhood suffrage had been established, first partially in 1896 and then completely in 1907. As a result of the election of 1897 there were fifteen German parties in parliament, and in 1911 there were still eight. So far from a multi-party system being the product of PR in Austria, the number of parties was very much smaller in the interwar period after PR had been established.

The two principal parties elected in the 1911 parliament were seventy-six Christian Socialists, who at that time adhered to the empire and the monarchy, and fifty Social Democrats, who planned a people's republic and union with Germany. The elections of 1919 were based on the D'Hondt system in a single-stage ballot in twenty-five multi-member constituencies, with *apparentement* permitted. The result was the election of seventy-two Social Democrats, sixty-nine Christian Socialists, twenty-six German Nationalists, one Czech and one Zionist. Karl Renner, the Social Democrat leader, formed the government.

The new parliament adopted in 1920 a new constitution which had a federal structure, including a lower house, or Nationalrat, which was elected by direct universal suffrage, and an upper house, or Bundesrat, which represented the Länder, or states. As regards the electoral system, a law of 1920 introduced a two-stage system, with a first stage for which the twenty-five constituencies were preserved, and a second stage in which proportionality was determined at the level of the nation as a whole. There were 170 seats, of which 155 were allocated at the con-stituency level and 15 at the national level, in each case in accordance with the D'Hondt system of allocation. *Apparentement* was no longer permitted, and the party lists were 'rigid', allowing no expression of preferences between candidates.

A further change in the electoral system was made in 1923. The twenty-five constituencies were still retained, and also a two-stage system of allocation of seats, but for the second stage the twenty-five constituencies were divided into four 'constituency unions', within each of which, instead of in the nation as a whole, proportionality was to be achieved. For the first allocation of seats, the Droop quota was calculated from the total number of votes and seats in each constituency, and seats were allocated to parties in accordance with the number of quotas their votes were able to secure. For the second allocation, the D'Hondt system was applied at the level of the constituency unions, to allocate the remaining seats on the basis of each party's remainder of votes.

Constituency seats were allocated to individual candidates in the order in which they appeared on the party lists. For the allocation of the remaining seats to individual candidates, the parties might submit separate lists of nominees for the constituency union seats, or alternatively the remaining seats might be allocated to individual constituencies within the constituency union by the application of the D'Hondt method to the party's votes and seats in each constituency. A seat which had thus been allocated to a constituency would be awarded to the next unelected candidate on the party list in that constituency.

The elections of 1920 and 1923 revealed the nature of the party system established under the constitutional and electoral reforms which had been made since 1918. The Christian Socialists and the Social Democrats emerged as the two most powerful parties and the only real contenders for power, while a third party, or group of parties, frequently held a balance of votes in the Nationalrat. In the interwar period this third group consisted of various German nationalist parties, which varied from the moderate to the extreme, but which collaborated with each other in parliament. After the Second World War, as a result of the experience of German invasion and occupation of Austria, and the subjugation of the country by the National Socialist police state, the German nationalist element virtually disappeared from the party system in Austria. However, there still existed a third party, sometimes holding the balance, which was now the Liberal or Freedom Party, representing a mixture of political conservatism and economic individualism. There were also at particular times incursions by smaller parties into the party system, representing movements on the extreme right or extreme left.

The two main parties upheld respectively the social and economic interests of the wage-earners and the middle classes. In the aftermath of the First World War they collaborated to achieve economic and social reconstruction, and formed what came to be called the Great Coalition. But the conflicts of interest between the parties proved stronger than the demands of national unity in a period of adversity, and the coalition failed to outlast the 1920s. The problems with which the country was faced were so intractable, and involved such drastic measures, that governments which sought to deal with them were virtually bound to be unpopular and arouse opposition in the electorate. Austria was isolated among hostile powers after the war, the economic situation was catastrophic, reparations imposed a crippling burden, inflation was rampant, state finances were chaotic, industry was starved of investment, and most goods were in short supply. Governments could scarcely exercise authority, since their own survival was constantly in doubt.

In 1920 the Christian Socialists replaced the Social Democrats in power, and the Social Democrats remained in a minority in the Nationalrat during the rest of the interwar period, though they once again gained the largest number of seats of any party in 1930. The Christian Socialists, on the other hand, had an absolute majority of seats in 1920 and 1927, and very nearly an absolute majority in 1923 as well. A bipartisan policy was pursued with some success between 1922 and 1928, but in the meantime the social and political tensions became so acute that the entire fabric of the state began to crumble. The intrusion of armed bands into the organisation of political activity was a new and explosive element in the situation, and led to competitive preparations for physical conflict on both the extreme right and extreme left, with the risk of violence greatest in the vicinity of contested frontiers. The army began to assume a more powerful influence in political life.

An attempt was made to strengthen the authority of the government by a constitutional reform in 1929, which provided for the direct election of the president by the enfranchised population instead of by parliament, and to confer on him increased powers of government formation, dissolution of parliament and legislation by emergency decrees. In fact no presidential elections were held until 1951, because the presidential term of office was extended by parliament in 1933, dictatorship and war followed, and at the beginning of the period after the Second World War, when the country was still occupied by foreign troops, the president was once again nominated by parliament.

The Christian Socialists lost heavily in the elections of 1930, but the Social Democrats were still in a minority in parliament and could not form a government. Parliamentary business became chaotic, and in 1933 an impasse was reached when the speaker precipitately resigned, leaving no method under the constitution by which a new speaker could be appointed, and no way in which the Nationalrat could be legally convened.

Meanwhile, the seizure of power in Germany by the National Socialists alienated the support for union with Germany which had long existed within both the Christian Socialist and Social Democratic parties. The chancellor, Dolfuss, came to depend increasingly on the political and financial support of Mussolini, and on the backing of the army at home. At the beginning of 1934 a paramilitary organisation of the left, the Republican Defence Union, rose in revolt, to anticipate disbandment by the government, but were forcibly put down by the army and police, and the Social Democrat Party were declared illegal.

The chancellor, Dolfuss, was assassinated in July 1934 and the National Socialist Party, to which was attributed responsibility for the crime, were banned by the new chancellor, Schuschnigg, who now depended for his authority on the army and the police. However, a change of policy by Mussolini and the formation of the Rome–Berlin 'axis' in 1936 deprived Schuschnigg of his main protector, and early in 1938 he was forced to legalise the National Socialist Party, and take members of the party into his government. His desire to consolidate popular support for himself through a referendum was the pretext for the German invasion of Austria, and the total absorption of the country into the German Reich.

Towards the end of the Second World War, in April 1945, representatives of three Austrian political parties, the Communists, the Socialist Party of Austria (formerly the Social Democrats) and the Austrian People's Party (formerly the Christian Socialists), united to proclaim the re-establishment of the Austrian state and the constitution of 1920. With the consent of the Russian occupation forces Karl Renner, the Socialist leader, formed a government, in which he included representatives of all the three parties. In September 1945 the four-power control of Austria was established, and the Renner government was recognised by the Western Allies. In November 1945 elections were held under the provisions of the electoral law of 1923. The People's Party had a decisive victory, with eighty-five seats, against seventy-six for the Socialists and only four for the Communists.

Although the People's Party and the Socialists emerged once again, under different names, as much the most important contenders for power, as they had been immediately after the First World War, history did not, in other respects, repeat itself. The two parties formed a coalition which lasted for twenty years until 1966. The lessons of the collapse of parliamentary government in the 1920s appeared to have been learned. The Socialists did not wish to retreat once again into permanent opposition and impotence, but were prepared to exercise their influence on legislation and on the processes of government.

The existence of the coalition was reflected in domestic social and economic policy. The Socialists put forward demands which the People's Party were unable to resist for nationalisation and for the representation of the workforce in industry and on administrative bodies. By way of compensation, other institutions were established which gave an effective voice to representatives of management and the professions. Chambers of industry, agriculture and labour were created which had considerable political influence through the examining or drafting of laws and statements of policy affecting their own particular spheres. The coalition was reflected in this way not only at the level of parliament and government, but in other spheres of public life as well. It was interparty committees as well as the government and debates in parliament which decided details of policy and the distribution of offices.

In a regime of such a nature the electoral system of proportional representation had a vital part to play. The effect of each election was to alter the balance between the parties, but the electors could not easily throw one party out of office in favour of the other, and apparently did not want to. Until 1966 electors seemed to be satisfied that the coalition should continue.

There was, however, one important change in the electoral law in 1949, when it was provided that electors might express preferences between the candidates placed on a party's list. This was done by a points preference system, with an elector's first preference given as many points as there were candidates to be elected in the constituency, his second choice given one point less, and so on. The elector might also strike out the name of a candidate altogether. If an elector voted simply for a party list, then the points were awarded to each candidate in the order of the party's ranking of the candidates. The great majority of voters exercised a vote for the party rather than for individual candidates, and it was seldom that the order of the candidates was changed as a result of the electors' votes.

There were certain anomalies in the practical operation of the electoral system. The allocation of 'remaining' seats to 'remaining' votes was of much greater importance for the smaller parties than it was for the larger. In all the elections between 1945 and 1959 a total of 734 seats was gained by all parties at the first distribution at the constituency level, compared with only 91 at the constituency union level in the second distribution; but whereas the minor parties during this period won 27 seats at the first distribution they won 33 at the second. This emphasised the discriminatory nature of the 'exclusion clause', which provided that no party might share in the allocation of seats at the level of the constituency union unless they had gained at least one seat in a constituency. Moreover, this rule worked in a rather arbitrary fashion, since constituencies varied in size. In a small constituency of three seats a party would need more than a quarter of the votes to be sure of gaining a seat, whereas in a constituency of eleven seats they would need only one-twelfth. A party's success could depend upon whether their votes were concentrated in large or small constituencies.

After 1962 the Great Coalition showed signs of breaking down. Its main objects, which were national independence, political stability and economic reconstruction and expansion, had by now been achieved. The restraints of the coalition upon party policies became increasingly irksome, and a new generation of younger politicians was not greatly influenced by the warnings of what had happened in the 1920s. At the same time there was increasing impatience with the working of the electoral system, which had more often than not failed to provide any party with an absolute majority of seats, and the People's Party, with new ambitions for power, declared before the election of 1966 their desire for electoral reform in favour of a majority system. Ironically, under the then-existing PR system, the People's Party secured an absolute majority of seats in 1966, thereby greatly weakening their argument in favour of reform.

There was a reversal of fortunes in the next election of 1970, when the Socialists gained a larger number of seats than any other party and formed a minority government. They then succeeded in implementing an electoral reform, through the electoral law of 1971, which was largely opposite in effect and intention from that which the People's Party had earlier proposed. This involved the first major reconstruction of the electoral system since 1923. The number of constituencies was reduced from twenty-five to nine, which corresponded exactly with the Länder represented in the Bundesrat; and instead of the four constituency unions there were to be two constituency regions, one for Vienna, Lower Austria and Burgenland, and one for the rest of Austria. The allocation of seats at the first stage of the election was now to be based on the Hare quota instead of the Droop quota, and the number of seats in the Nationalrat was increased from 165 to 183.

This electoral reform was carried out as a result of collaboration between the Socialists and the Liberals, on whose support the Socialists depended during a period of minority government; and in a number of respects it was to the advantage of each. The larger constituencies and constituency regions meant not only that proportionality could be achieved more exactly, but also that smaller parties would find it easier to gain a first seat in a constituency, and therefore qualify for the allocation of 'remaining' seats. The Socialists also stood to benefit in certain respects, since the goodwill of the Liberals, who benefited directly from the electoral reform, diminished the likelihood of an alliance between the Liberals and the People's Party.

One other change related to the preferences which an elector had been able to express between candidates on the party lists. Electors were now entitled to cast only one vote for one candidate. If, in a constituency, a candidate received a number of votes equal to or greater than the (Hare) quota, he was elected. All seats not allocated in this way were allocated in accordance with the order of the candidates on the party's list. This system had less of a 'personal' element in it than that which was removed, but in practice neither system had much influence on the election of individual candidates, which was determined mainly by the parties.

Although the electoral changes of 1971 tended to favour the smaller parties, the choice of electors thereafter resulted in the return of the Socialist Party with an absolute majority of seats for the first time in the general election of 1971, and this was repeated in the general elections of 1975 and 1979.

Austrian experience has in some respects been such as to defy the expectations of what the workings of an electoral system are likely to be. Under the PR system established immediately after the First World War the number of parties was much fewer than it had been under the previous majority system, and this remains true even if one refers to the German parties alone, and not to the numerous parties representing national minorities. The number of parties did not increase during the interwar period, and after the Second World War it diminished. In the interwar period, when parliamentary government collapsed, this was the consequence, not of any proliferation of parties, but of external events which were devastating in their effects. The electoral system could not be regarded as responsible for the breakdown of parliamentary government, otherwise, under the same electoral system, government could be expected to have collapsed again before now. As time passes, the longer the period during which government and parliament are based on the PR system, and succeed in achieving political stability and social and economic development, the more attractive do the advantages of that system seem, and the more remote its dangers.

REFERENCES: CHAPTER 12

A history of the electoral system in Austria is contained in an extensive article by Herbert Schambeck in the *Jahrbuch des Öffentlichen Rechts der Gegenwahrt*, 1972. A particular phase of reform is studied by William A. Jenks in *The Austrian Electoral Reform of 1907*. The operation of the electoral system since the Second World War has been the subject of articles in the journal *Parliamentary Affairs* by W. W. Kitzinger, 'The Austrian electoral system' (1958–9), and John Dreijmanis, 'Proportional representation and its effects: the Austrian experience' (1970–1). A publication of the Federal Press Service, Vienna, gives the *Documentary Background of the General Election in Austria on October 5, 1975*.

13

Switzerland

The Swiss Confederation is a legendary cradle of democracy in modern Europe, and a stronghold of resistance against despots and tyrants. Inevitably, the history of the confederation is more complex than the legend, and its development was not always in the direction of greater liberty and progress. The complexity arises for several reasons, one of which is the diversity of the origins of the confederation. It was created out of the union of numerous cantons, which differed in size, race, language and religion, and although the struggle for liberty was a force which bound the confederation together when they were united in resistance against the dominance of great powers, it could work also in the opposite direction, since cantons and their inhabitants demanded freedom from domination by other cantons and by the authorities of the confederation.

The evolution of democratic institutions was not, moreover, a continuous process, since the tendency throughout the cantons in the seventeenth and eighteenth centuries was for power to be concentrated in exclusive gilds or oligarchies, and confined to a few wealthy families.

After the fall of Napoleon, the Peace of Paris of November 1815 guaranteed the independence and neutrality of Switzerland. Its territory was now also augmented by the addition of three cantons which had earlier been incorporated in the French Empire, so that the cantons had now reached the number of twenty-two. Within the confederation the cantons were represented in an assembly in which each canton had one vote, and in which each delegate was bound by the instructions of his cantonal government.

The July Revolution of 1830 in France launched a liberal movement in Europe which in Switzerland had the aim of transforming the union of separate and independent cantons into a united federation, and converting the central council into an assembly elected by direct, universal and equal suffrage. However, a draft revision of the constitution in 1832 was rejected by the Catholic cantons, which demanded that there should be unanimity among all the cantons for the adoption of any constitutional change. There developed an alignment of mutually antagonistic forces, with the conservative and Catholic cantons hostile to the centralisation of power in the confederation, and an increasingly anti-clerical liberal movement anxious to increase the authority of the central legislative body, and to strengthen its popular base. Conflict over religious issues finally precipitated a crisis within the confederation. In 1841 the Protestant canton of Aargau dissolved monasteries within its territory; this provoked the Catholic canton of Lucerne to allow the return of Jesuits, who had earlier been forbidden to establish their organisation in Switzerland. The hostile reaction of the Protestant cantons to this measure led to an attempt by several Catholic cantons to secede from the confederation in 1845, and to form a separate confederation, or Sonderbund. Civil war followed, in which the Protestant cantons were victorious, and the central authority of the confederation was successfully asserted.

A revised constitution was adopted by a referendum in May 1848, and this, with amendments, has been in force ever since. A federal assembly was established, including a popularly elected national council, and a states council in which the cantons were each equally represented regardless of population. A federal council, or national executive, with authority only over customs, defence and foreign affairs, consisted of seven members, each directly elected by the federal assembly to serve for the period between general elections. Thus the executive were directly appointed by the legislature; and in the legislature power was shared between representatives of the people voting as individuals, and representatives of the cantons functioning as independent and largely sovereign states.

The members of the federal council have usually been re-elected by each assembly until they decided to retire. The principle of proportional representation came gradually, in the course of time, to be reflected in the composition of the federal council. Between 1848 and 1892 all seven members of the council were always Liberal Radicals; from 1892 until 1919 there were six Liberals and one Catholic; from 1919 to 1929 five Liberals and two Catholics; from 1929 to 1943 four Liberals, two Catholics and one Farmers' representative; and from 1943 to 1953 three Liberals, two Catholics, one Farmers' representative and one Social Democrat.

The compromise in the federal assembly between federal and cantonal interests was reflected in the electoral arrangements for the national council and the states council. For the national council the constitution provided that its elections should be regulated by federal legislation, while the method of the election of the members of the council of states was within the jurisdiction of the individual cantons. In some cantons the members of the council of states were elected in popular assemblies of all citizens; in others by the members of the cantonal grand councils; but in most they were popularly elected at the same time as the members of the national council. The periods for which members of the council of states held office also varied from one canton to another, but most cantons elected them for the same period as that for which the national council were elected.

A federal law of December 1850 laid down the system of election which was to be used for the national council. The number of seats was at first fixed at 119, and the nation was divided into forty-nine constituencies, the boundaries of each one lying wholly within the territory of a canton or half-canton. The number of members in a constituency depended on the size of the population it contained. Originally there were twelve constituencies returning one member each, thirteen returning two members, fifteen returning three and nine returning four. As population increased, the total number of seats in the national council was increased correspondingly after each federal census, until by 1911 the number had reached 189. The rate of increase of population varied considerably from one constituency to another, and the allocation of seats to constituencies was periodically varied accordingly. The largest constituency had four seats in 1850, but nine in 1902.

The voting system provided for three ballots, each elector having as many votes as there were seats to be filled in the constituency. In the first two ballots a candidate had to gain an absolute majority of votes to secure election, and if any seats remained unallocated a relative majority sufficed at the third ballot. There was no restriction on candidatures for the first two ballots, but the third was restricted to three times as many candidates as there were seats to be filled. The selection of candidates eligible to stand in the third round of the election was determined if necessary by an extra ballot.

In essentials, these regulations remained in force until proportional representation was established in 1919. Meanwhile, some minor changes were made. In 1900, the third ballot was discontinued, a relative majority was accepted as sufficient for election in a second ballot, and no restrictions were placed on candidatures for election in the second ballot. Experience had shown that no candidate who failed to gain an absolute majority in a first ballot was ever likely to gain one in a second ballot, and it was therefore pointless to require an absolute majority in that ballot. The restriction on candidatures was removed, since it was found that electors increasingly voted for party nominees, and seldom nominated non-party candidates. There was little danger, therefore, of a flood of nominations at the later stages of an election.

It was in individual cantons that majority systems of election first came under criticism, and that demands were made for methods of voting which would give more equitable results. In Geneva, in 1842, as a result of popular disturbances which arose out of the distorted results of recent elections, a constituent assembly was convened, and Victor Considérant, who was then in Geneva, proposed a system of proportional representation. This was regarded at the time as an eccentric idea. In 1846 a similar situation arose, Considérant was again in Geneva, and he addressed a letter to the grand council which was printed and published and much quoted thereafter. He argued that elections by majority systems were based on a fundamental error which confused two quite distinct purposes. In the making of decisions it was appropriate to be guided by majority votes, but in choosing representatives the only fair result was one in which the electors were proportionally represented. His arguments were again unavailing, and a majority system of election was still used for elections under Geneva's revised constitution of 1847.

In 1864 serious riots broke out in Geneva in protest against continued misrepresentation, and the canton fell into a state of anarchy from which it was rescued only by the intervention of other members of the Swiss Confederation. The disturbances were an expression of the passionate antagonism of the two main political parties, the radical Protestants and the conservative Catholics, which finally led to the paralysis of government. It was through these events that the Swiss philosopher, Ernest Naville, became convinced that the root of the trouble was the abuse of power by majorities, and the oppression of minorities, which resulted from the majority system of election. Together with others of a like mind he helped to found in 1865 the Association Réformiste de Genève. He later became the editor of regular bulletins issued by the Société Suisse pour la Représentation Proportionnelle, and was himself a prolific contributor to the bulletins.

The Geneva association favoured a system recommended by Antoine Morin, which involved voting for lists of candidates (a method of voting already familiar to the electorate in the form of the 'block vote'), with the allocation of seats determined by a quota of votes required for each seat. This system was called *la concurrence libre des listes*, or, for short, *la liste libre*. At first it was resolved that electors should be able to vote only for a single list, in which the order of priority of the candidates would be fixed by the nominators (in practice this would be the political parties) and could not be changed. In 1870 it was decided to allow electors to exercise a 'double vote', that is to say, to vote both for a list and for individual candidates they preferred on that list, and this modification eventually formed part of the electoral system adopted for the national council. Meanwhile, however, in spite of sustained advocacy by the Geneva association, nearly a generation passed before PR was introduced for elections to the grand council of Geneva. By that time electoral reforms had been introduced in other cantons.

Tessin (or Ticino) was one of the cantons in which the most acute difficulties arose through the misrepresentation of parties on the cantonal grand council. In this canton, unlike many others, there was no great division between communities on account of race, language or religion, since the population was overwhelmingly Italian and Catholic, and since immigrants also were mostly Italian and Catholic. However, the Liberal Radicals who competed for power with the Conservatives, became, like the liberals and nationalists in neighbouring Italy during the *risorgimento*, increasingly anti-clerical in outlook. After seizing power by force in 1839, the Liberal Radicals remained in power until 1875. The canton was bitterly divided during the Sonderbund period from 1843 to 1848, and violence erupted again in 1855.

In 1875 the Conservatives gained power, and the Liberals, after their defeat, contested the validity of the elections on the grounds that since the seats had last been distributed between constituencies in 1830, shifts in population had given rise to discrepancies in representation to such an extent that they amounted to a violation of the constitution, which declared that all Swiss citizens were equal before the law. Their appeal under the federal constitution was upheld, and the constitution of the canton was accordingly amended in 1876 to provide for a redistribution of seats in thirty-eight constituencies.

However, in subsequent elections the Liberal Radicals were again substantially under-represented. In 1889 violence broke out, members of the government were imprisoned by insurgents and one of them was killed. Order was restored by the federal government, which then proposed that elections should be held by a system of proportional representation. It was eventually agreed by both sides that a constituent assembly should be elected by PR on the basis of a revised distribution of seats, but the Liberals later changed their minds and boycotted the elections, so that the constituent assembly, when elected, consisted entirely of Conservatives. The assembly proceeded to submit a constitutional amendment in favour of proportional representation to a referendum, and this was carried by a very small margin. It was exclusively the Conservatives who were finally responsible for this reform.

There were similar troubles in other cantons, including Geneva and Zurich, which demonstrated the extent to which the composition and decisions of the grand councils could be at variance with the opinions of the electorate. The example of Tessin in adopting PR was followed by some of the other cantons. Its adoption by Neuchâtel in 1891 was particularly significant, since here it was adopted spontaneously, and not as a result of a breakdown in government. In Geneva, the grand council finally recommended a system of PR which was approved by the electorate in a referendum in 1892. By 1916 proportional representation had been introduced in other cantons including Zug, Solothurn, Basle Town, Schwyz, Lucerne, St Gallen and Zurich.

In the cantons where majority elections were held using the 'block vote', the disparity between votes and seats tended to be all the greater where there were only a small number of constituencies into which the electorate were divided. Where the constituencies were more numerous, minorities, under majority voting systems, had a better chance of representation, provided their strength was sufficiently concentrated in at least some constituencies. This was the situation in the confederation as a whole, since there were forty-nine constituencies for elections to the national council, and the various language, religious and ethnic communities were each able to secure majorities in at least some constituencies. It is not surprising, therefore, that agitation for electoral reform should have been directed at first at cantonal rather than federal elections, and that after PR had been adopted in Tessin nearly thirty years passed before it was introduced for national council elections.

The party system in Switzerland was complicated by the fact that most of the parties tended to be organised on a cantonal basis, and their outlook and policies might vary appreciably from one canton to another. The principal party from 1896 onwards were the (liberal) Radical Democrats (in German, the Freisinnige-demokratische Partei, or free-thinking democrats), who always had a majority of seats up to and during the First World War. They represented the Protestant left, and sought to strengthen the federal organs of government. The main opposition were the Catholic Conservatives, who, on the contrary, sought to safeguard the autonomy of the individual cantons. The Catholics always had at least 20 per cent of the seats until 1911. There were three other parties which regularly had some representation in the national council. The strongest of these in 1896 were the Liberal Conservatives, otherwise known as the Liberal Democrats, but their share of the vote diminished in the first decade of the twentieth century, while the Social Democrat Party, which were formed in 1888 and gained their first seat in 1893, were steadily growing in strength. The remaining party were the Democrats, a union of cantonal parties of the centre, which never had more than a handful of seats.

Under the 'block vote' majority system of voting for the national council there was some disparity between votes and seats before the First World War, but not so great a disparity as to excite much hostile criticism of the electoral system. The Radical Democrats always had a majority of seats, but in most elections before 1917 they also had a majority of votes, so this could not be regarded as a great injustice. The greatest disparity was in 1905, when they had 62·3 per cent of the seats for 49·7 per cent of the votes. The Catholic Conservatives and the Liberal Conservatives also sometimes gained a greater share of seats than of votes, and had therefore little to complain about; while the Democrats usually had a share of seats which was almost the same as their share of votes.

It was only the Social Democrats who were consistently at a disadvantage. In 1908 and 1911 their share of the votes had increased to 17·7 per cent and 20·1 per cent respectively, but their share of the seats was only 4·2 and 9·1 per cent. In 1914 there was a reasonably close correspondence between votes and seats, but in 1917 the disparities, more pronounced than ever before, were as indicated in Table 13.1. The Radical Democrats had, as usual, a substantially greater share of seats than of votes, while the Catholic Conservatives, with not much more than half the number of votes gained by the Social Democrats, had nearly twice as many seats.

Table 13.1 *Swiss national council election, 1917*

	Percentage of votes	Percentage of seats
Radical Democrats	41·0	55·6
Social Democrats	30·9	11·6
Catholic Conservatives	16·5	22·2
Liberal Conservatives	4·9	6·3
Democrats	3·3	2·1

In 1891 a constitutional amendment had made it possible to amend the constitution itself by means of a popular initiative, that is to say, a proposal initiated by the electors and submitted to a referendum. So far, the constitution had neither prescribed nor prohibited particular electoral systems, but attempts were now made to have a proportional system inserted in the constitution and made compulsory. The Catholics in general, and those in small Catholic cantons in particular, tended to be in favour of this proposal, and so were the Social Democrats, but the Radical Democrats, who for so long had benefited from the majority system, were opposed to the suggested reform, and advised their adherents to vote against it. In a referendum in 1900 the proposal for PR was defeated by 59 per cent of the votes to 41 per cent, and by eleven and a half of the cantons to ten and a half. In a second referendum in 1910 a similar proposal was defeated by 52 per cent of the votes to 48 per cent, although twelve of the cantons were now in favour and only ten against. Finally, after the election of 1917, the demands for electoral reform were renewed, and when a proposal for the adoption of a system of PR was submitted to a referendum in October 1918 it was approved by 57 per cent of the votes to 43 per cent, and by nineteen and a half out of the twenty-two cantons.

Article 73 of the constitution was now amended to provide that elections for the national council should be by proportional representation, and that for this purpose each canton or half-canton should form an electoral district. Since there were nineteen cantons and six half-cantons this meant that there were to be twenty-five electoral districts, within each of which proportionality was to be achieved, and short of a further amendment of the constitution this ruled out the possibility that proportionality might be established at the national level.

As regards the size of the national council, the number of seats had been increased from 111 in 1848 to 189 in 1917, to correspond with the increase in population. Article 72 of the constitution provided that there should continue to be, as there had been since 1848, one deputy on the national council for every 20,000 of population, and one additional deputy if the remaining population in a district exceeded half that number. As population increased, it was necessary either to accept an increase in the number of deputies, or to increase the number of persons represented by each, or both. In 1931 the number of the population represented by each deputy was increased to 22,000, and in 1950 to 24,000. The number of deputies rose to 196, and on the basis of the population figures for 1960 it could have risen to 226. To prevent any further substantial increase in the number of deputies the constitution was amended in 1962 to fix the number permanently at 200, which was the traditional number of members of the grand councils of certain cantons. The cantons and half-cantons which in 1975 fell into the category of those entitled to only one deputy were five in number, and in each of these a single member was returned by a majority vote. In such constituencies voting by PR was not, of course, possible. There were now nine constituencies which had fewer than five seats each, and collectively had fourteen, and in these only a limited degree of proportionality was possible.

The system of election which was introduced in 1919 was a list system by which seats were distributed to the parties in each canton in accordance with the D'Hondt/Hagenbach-Bischoff method. Each list might contain only as many candidates as there were seats in the canton. An elector was entitled to cast as many votes for individual candidates as there were seats in the constituency. He might do so by voting for an entire party list, in which case the list received as many votes as there were candidates. He might also strike out the name of a candidate on the party list, and he might *cumulate* up to two personal votes on candidates whom he particularly wished to support. The elector might also delete a name from the list and substitute one from another list (*panachage*), in which case the votes which were counted for the party were only those for candidates who appeared on its own list, while the vote for a candidate taken from another list counted for the party from whom the name was taken. Two (cumulated) votes might be cast for candidates introduced from other lists. If a cumulated vote was cast for a candidate, either by the party in the list of candidates whom it nominated, or by the elector himself, two votes were counted for the party as well as two votes for the candidate.

For the allocation of seats to parties *apparentement* was permitted, that is, the combination of parties for the purpose of the election. It has been estimated that *apparentement* has normally made a difference to an election result in only about one case in three in which combinations were formed, and that it has altered the allocation of only about five or six seats out of two hundred; but this was nevertheless of some advantage to small parties.

Hardly any changes have been made in the electoral system since it was adopted in 1919. In 1939 it was provided by an amendment to the electoral law that no candidate could stand in more than one canton, nor appear in more than one list. In 1942 a popular initiative sought to weaken the control of parties over the election of individual candidates by declaring that cumulative voting should not be permitted in an official list of the candidates nominated, but this proposal was defeated in the referendum.

In the Swiss electoral system there is no 'exclusion clause' requiring that a party should receive a minimum number of votes before it is entitled to a proportional share of the seats. The 'exclusion clause' is, however, used in some cantons for the purpose of cantonal elections.

The greatest constitutional and electoral change since 1919 has been the extension of the parliamentary suffrage to women, and Switzerland was the last of the Western democracies to adopt this reform. There were many communes where women were entitled to vote in communal affairs, but when proposals were made for the extension of the suffrage to women at the federal level these were on several occasions unsuccessful. In 1959 a referendum was held on the proposition that women should be entitled to vote and stand for election in federal assembly elections, and this was supported by majorities in the main parties in the assembly itself. However, those entitled to vote in the referendum were composed of the same exclusively male electorate as that which was entitled to vote in national council elections, and they massively rejected the proposition by 95 per cent of the votes to 5 per cent. Nevertheless, the climate of opinion was changing, and during the next few years women's suffrage was introduced in the mainly or largely French-speaking cantons of Geneva, Neuchâtel, Vaud, Basle City and Basle Province.

In 1970 the national council unanimously adopted a proposal for the amendment of the constitution to extend the suffrage to women, and when a referendum was held once more in February 1971 this was approved by some 66 per cent of the votes to 34 per cent. Women's suffrage was adopted in the same year for cantonal elections in several cantons where it did not already exist.

In a country with such a varied local history it was natural that there should be numerous separate parties. On the whole, however, there was no great change in the strength of individual parties when proportional representation was first introduced, and the structure of parties which emerged from the first PR election in 1919 has remained remarkably stable ever since. The principal change in 1919 was that the Social Democrats emerged as a party of equal standing in the national council with the two main parties of the prewar era, the Radical Democrats and the Catholic Conservatives. Already in 1917, under the system of majority voting, the Social Democrats had gained more votes than the Catholic Conservatives, and their share of the votes had been only 10 per cent less than the share of the still-dominant Radical Democrats. Now they had as many *seats* as the Catholic Conservatives, and their share of *seats* was only 10 per cent less than that of the Radical Democrats.

Throughout the period since 1919 these three parties have dominated the national council. The Social Democrats and the Radical Democrats have always been almost equal in strength, with the balance varying only slightly in favour of one or the other. From 1925 onwards the Catholics always had slightly fewer seats than the other two parties, but the margin of difference was always very small, and never as much as 4 per cent of the total number of seats. Only one other party consistently had a substantial representation on the National Council, and this was the party of Farmers, Traders and Citizens, which in 1971 changed their name to the Swiss People's Party. Between 1919 and 1931 their share of seats was always over 15 per cent, and although their representation declined somewhat thereafter it never fell below 10 per cent.

From 1922 the Communist Party were always, except in 1943, represented in the National Council, but never had more than a handful of seats. Apart from the Communists, there were a few small parties which regularly derived their support from certain limited geographical areas. Other parties have had a more ephemeral or more recent existence, including the National Action and Republican parties, both of them highly nationalistic and opposed to immigration and the purchase of land by foreigners. These two parties between them gained eleven seats in 1971, but lost five of them in 1975.

The system of proportional representation has been imperfect for a number of reasons: because it is determined at the local level in twenty-five constituencies and not in the nation as a whole; because there are differences in the extent to which support for different parties is concentrated or diffused; and because some parties have had *apparentement* arrangements against others. On the whole the system has benefited the major parties, which have normally gained a greater share of seats than of votes. This has always been the case for the Radical Democrats and the Catholics. The share of seats obtained by the Social Democrats was almost always slightly less than their share of votes before 1955, but greater than their share of votes from 1963 onwards. For the small parties, conversely, their share of seats was seldom as great as their share of votes. In spite of the deficiencies in the system, there was only one year in which there were marked divergences between the shares of votes and seats. This was in 1939, when the election was strongly contested by numerous small parties, which all gained a much greater share of votes than of seats. The beneficiaries of the consequent disproportion in the distribution of seats were the Catholics and the Radical Democrats.

After the adoption of PR for the national council elections, it was adopted also for cantonal elections by most cantons which had not already done so, until, by 1969, the only cantons which still held elections by majority systems were the Appenzell half-cantons, the Unterwalden half-cantons, and the cantons of Grisons, Schaffhausen and Uri.

At the federal level the democratic principle was, as already noted, carried so far in the 1848 constitution as to provide that the government or executive of seven members should be elected individually by the two chambers of the federal assembly. These elections tended in time to embody the principle of proportional representation, but this took much longer to achieve and did not function without friction. Although the Social Democrats were always one of the strongest parties from 1922 onwards, and always thereafter stronger than the Catholics, they gained a seat on the federal council (the executive) for the first time only in 1943. In 1953 they claimed two seats on the council on the grounds that in the previous national council election they had received more votes than any other party, but the non-socialist parties rejected this claim, and so the Social Democrats refused to accept any seat on the federal council.

In 1959 four vacancies occurred on the federal council through resignations, and the Catholic Conservatives now agreed with the Social Democrats that the seats on the federal council should be distributed on the basis of two each for the Catholic Conservatives, Radical Democrats and Social Democrats, and one for the party of Farmers, Traders and Citizens. This agreement was strongly but unsuccessfully opposed by the Radical Democrats, who, like the Catholic Conservatives, previously had three seats on the federal council. After every subsequent general election seats on the federal council were allocated in accordance with the terms of this agreement.

The functioning of the Swiss constitution has been criticised on the grounds that it has resulted in 'immobility' in Swiss politics, and that the assembly has failed to exercise control over the executive. As regards 'immobility', the complaint is about the almost unchanging representation of the four main parties in the national council since 1919, and the inability of any single party to 'break through' and gain the power to implement a particular political programme. As regards parliamentary control, the federal council is not, under the constitution, accountable to the assembly, which elects it for a whole term of four years, and in practice almost always re-elects the same members until they resign. Moreover, the constitution prohibits any member of the federal council from serving simultaneously as a member of either chamber of the assembly.

Dissatisfaction with the functioning of the constitution led in 1966 to the appointment by the federal council of a working party to make recommendations for constitutional revision, but although there was support for a popularly elected single-chamber parliament instead of the existing two chambers, there was little support for the abandonment of PR in favour of a majority system of election. A modification of the electoral system which it was proposed should accompany the abolition of the council of states was the adoption of the 'personalised' system of PR on the West German model, combining majority elections in single-member constituencies with a list system of PR in the cantons. Since, however, the proposed constitutional changes were not implemented, the occasion for alterations in the electoral system did not arise.

REFERENCES: CHAPTER 13

For Switzerland, much information on the earlier electoral reform movement is contained in the publications of the Association Réformiste de Genève and the Société Suisse pour la Représentation Proportionnelle, to which the Swiss philosopher Ernest Naville was a prolific contributor. *The Federal Constitution of Switzerland* by Christopher Hughes gives the text of the constitution, including provisions relating to federal elections, with annotations indicating the changes which had been introduced since the constitution was adopted in 1848. Comments on the working of the electoral system are to be found in G. A. Codding, *The Federal Government of Switzerland*; Christopher Hughes, *The Parliament of Switzerland*; and Jean-François Aubert, *Traité de droit constitutionnel Suisse*. The earlier election results under the 1848 constitution are detailed in *Die Schweizerische Bundesversammlung, 1848–1920* by E. Grüner and others. The first introduction of proportional representation in a Swiss canton is described in J. J. Galland, *La démocratie Tessinoise et la représentation proportionnelle*. The contemporary electoral system for the national assembly is explained in detail in *Die Nationalratswahlung*, published by the Swiss parliament.

The Great Powers on the Continent

14

Italy

When Italy in 1860 achieved her national independence, and almost (apart from Venezia and the city of Rome) gained her natural frontiers, the constitution inherited by the new nation was that of the kingdom of Piedmont, which had been granted by Charles Albert in 1848. This constitution was the only survivor of those which had been conceded by several of the rulers of the Italian states during the revolutionary risings of 1848 and 1849, but which were abrogated when those risings were crushed with the aid of Austrian troops. The example and inspiration given by Charles Albert when he declared war on Austria in March 1848 eventually placed the movement for national liberation under the leadership of the House of Savoy, and this leadership survived both the defeat of Piedmont at the Battle of Novara and the abdication of Charles Albert immediately afterwards. The armed strength of Piedmont was sufficient, in spite of this defeat, to preserve the new constitution. This *Statuto*, granted to Piedmont in 1848, provided for a parliament with two chambers – a senate nominated for life by the king, and an elected chamber of deputies – which were together to provide a 'representative monarchical form of government'.

After the Austrians had in 1859 been defeated with French aid at Magenta and Solferino, the states which had been under the rule of Austria, or of foreign princes, or of the papacy, each sought union with Piedmont and representation in its parliament. The accession of the formerly separate states to the new nation was confirmed by plebiscites; the first national parliament was opened by King Victor Emmanuel of Savoy on 20 January 1861; and an Act of Parliament declared him to be King of Italy.

The Piedmontese constitution of 1848 was adopted for the kingdom of Italy in 1861, and so was the system of election which had been used for the Piedmontese parliament. This was a male franchise based on a minimum age of 25, on literacy, and on a property qualification which at that time gave the suffrage to less than 2 per cent of the population. Election was in single-member constituencies, and required an absolute majority of votes and the support of at least one-third of the electorate in a first ballot, or, if necessary, a second ballot in which only those contestants could take part who were leading in the first ballot.

In 1882 the age limit was reduced from 25 to 21, the means-test requirements were relaxed, and the franchise was extended on the basis of educational attainments. The number of electors increased from just over 2 per cent of the population in 1880 to just over 7 per cent in 1882, and those qualified by educational attainments rather than the means test increased from 20 per cent to 65 per cent of the total electorate. In 1894, during a period when repressive measures were being taken against labour organisations regarded as subversive, educational tests were more stringently applied, with the result that the electorate was reduced from 9·4 to 6·7 per cent of the population. In 1912 the suffrage was granted to all males aged 30 or over, without regard to property or literacy, and also to males aged between 21 and 30 who satisfied a means test or had performed military service. By this reform, falling not far short of universal manhood suffrage, the electorate was increased from less than 3 million to nearly 8½ million.

The narrow basis of the franchise during the first fifty years of the new kingdom of Italy made it easier for political leaders, and particularly the government, to manipulate elections. Local administration by prefects appointed by the government gave the minister of the interior wide powers of patronage by means of appointments to offices of many kinds; and in parliament bribery and preferment were extensively employed to secure the support of elected representatives.

A change in the electoral system was introduced in 1882, at the same time as the extension of the franchise in that year. Instead of single-member constituencies, multi-member constituencies were established, each returning deputies varying in number from two to five. Voting was for party lists, without the possibility of voting for candidates on more than one list (that is to say, *panachage* was not permitted). In constituencies where there were not more than four seats to be filled electors could vote for as many candidates as there were seats, and this was an example of the 'block vote' system. Where five deputies were to be elected each elector could cast only four votes, which was an example of the operation of the 'limited vote'. At a first ballot, votes from an absolute majority of voters and of one-eighth of the electorate were required for the return of a candidate; at a second ballot the leading candidates at the first ballot were permitted to stand again, up to a number limited to twice the number of vacant seats, and those with most votes were elected. This electoral system was used for three elections between 1882 and 1890, but did not have the desired effect of strengthening the party system.

In 1892 there was a return to single-member constituencies with second ballots. For election at a first ballot it was still necessary to gain votes from half the voters, but the 'quorum' of the electorate whose support was required was reduced from one-third to one-sixth; and from 1900 the absolute majority which was required was of valid votes only. These changes greatly reduced the number of second ballots which had to be held. This system remained in force until universal male suffrage was introduced and the electoral system reformed in 1912.

There were many factors other than the methods of election which had an influence on the party system, and indeed on the attitudes of the people towards the whole system of parliamentary democracy introduced in 1861. Those which were most important, and which survived in some form into the period after the Second World War, were the alienation of much of the population from the system of government itself; the continued existence of strong local feelings against tendencies for the centralisation of government; religious questions involving the authority of the church; and social questions arising from the great inequalities of wealth both between classes of society and between geographical areas. These circumstances cannot be wholly separated from each other, and on the contrary were often closely related.

Alienation from the prevailing system of government was something to which most of the Italian people had become accustomed during centuries of foreign domination and rule by foreign princes. One unifying force in the *risorgimento* had been rebellion against Austrian occupation. The unification of Italy itself had been a secondary objective, and in the wars of 1848 and 1849 had not been sought even by Charles Albert of Piedmont, who had limited his ambition to the creation of a kingdom of north Italy. It was Cavour who was the principal architect of a united Italy, prevailing against his ally Napoleon III, who wished to establish a federation of four Italian states which would remain separate. Although unification was completed by the annexation of Rome in 1870, the resistance to centralised control weakened support for the new regime. There were great regional differences in culture and economy within Italy, most pronounced between north and south but evident in other regions as well; and there was little confidence in local representation in the national parliament.

The narrow franchise meant that most of the population regarded parliament and the activities of deputies as being in no way related to their own affairs. Deputies had the reputation (which still survives) of being concerned only with their own material interests and careers. Parliamentary democracy affected only the small middle-class element in the towns, and not the illiterate peasantry who formed the bulk of the population. The bourgeois liberals and parliamentarians who achieved constitutional government were also largely anti-clerical, an attitude which, until the eve of the First World War, served to alienate the church and its most faithful adherents from all participation in parliamentary activities and elections. The members of the trade union and labour movements, which gained strength from the 1870s onwards, found themselves for their part virtually excluded by the franchise and by hostile legislation from political activity in parliament. This strengthened their tendency to be revolutionary and 'anti-system' in outlook.

A natural consequence of the alienation of much of the people from the system of government was the resort to conspiracy and acts of violence. In the eighteenth century an earlier phase of conspiratorial activity was to be found in the spread to Italy of freemasonry, which was anti-Catholic in attitude; and towards the end of the century the movement became permeated by French revolutionary influence. This led, during the Napoleonic wars, to the formation of societies of Carbonari, which were anti-Austrian, hostile to Napoleon and patriotically Italian. These flourished after the Napoleonic wars also, and contributed to revolts in Naples and Piedmont in 1821 which were crushed by Austrian troops. Conspiratorial activity continued later among the followers of Mazzini, who aimed to establish a republican form of government. After the unification of Italy and the attainment of independence, secret society activity continued to flourish through the organisation of the notorious Mafia in Sicily and the Camorra in Naples. In the twentieth century, manifestations of conspiratorial activities and resort to violence continued in the Communist and Fascist parties, and most recently in various organisations of the extreme left and extreme right.

Religious issues assumed a special importance in Italy, both because Rome was the centre of the universal Catholic Church, and because the church had exercised temporal power in the Papal States stretching from Rome to the Adriatic coast and to the River Po. The church had been hostile not only to liberal and democratic reforms but also to any movement for the unification of Italy which threatened to absorb its own territories. In the course of the 1850s the passing of measures against convents and monasteries in Piedmont alienated the church from the movement for Italian independence led by the House of Savoy, as well as from the principles of parliamentary democracy practised in Piedmont. It was only by force of arms that the Papal States were annexed to the United Italian nation in 1860, and Rome itself in 1870.

For most of the period until the First World War the church refused to sanction the participation of its adherents in the political affairs of the nation. In 1874 a pronouncement of the pope, referred to as the *non expedit*, required that Catholics should not take part in elections for the chamber of deputies by casting votes or standing as candidates, and this prohibition remained formally in force until 1919. It was only under the conciliatory policies of the Liberal Giovanni Giolitti from 1904 onwards that the policy of non-participation was relaxed. Giolitti secured the support of Catholics against the socialists and extreme anti-clericals, and after the adoption of universal male suffrage in 1912 he negotiated an electoral agreement with Count Gentiloni and his Clerical Party which secured for the Giolitti Liberals a substantial majority in the chamber of deputies, and about 6 per cent of the votes and seats for the Catholics themselves. In 1919, after the adoption of proportional representation, the Catholic Popular Party secured 20 per cent of the votes and seats in the chamber; but as its long history of non-participation showed, the church had no firm commitment to parliamentary democracy, and offered little resistance to its overthrow by the Fascists after the March on Rome in October 1922.

Equally, there was no effective social democratic party on the centre-left of the political spectrum which might have come to the defence of the parliamentary regime. This, too, is explained by the nature of political developments in earlier decades. For the entire period between the attainment of national unity and independence and the First World War, political power had been in the hands of the Liberals who represented the small middle-class element in the population, and who in social and economic affairs were conservative or downright reactionary. Compared with other leading nations, Italy was a country of widespread poverty, and the disparity of wealth between the north and the south tended to increase rather than diminish. Revenue for the state was raised through onerous indirect taxes on necessities. It was only in the decade or two before the First World War that industrialisation and economic growth began to accelerate.

The slow process of industrialisation was accompanied by a slow spread of socialist doctrine and organisation, particularly in north Italy. A Socialist Party was formed in about 1892, and in spite of harsh repressive measures in the 1890s the movement expanded and a number of Socialist deputies were elected, increasing from twelve in 1895 to thirty-three in 1900. The Socialists advocated, among other things, universal manhood suffrage, but did not abandon revolutionary aims directed towards the overthrow of the parliamentary system in favour of the dictatorship of the proletariat; and in the chamber they played a purely negative role in obstructing business as much as possible. Although, therefore, the Socialists had succeeded in establishing themselves within the parliamentary system, this could not be counted upon to strengthen the parliamentary regime. The Socialist Party did not offer a practical alternative to the parties of the right which had hitherto invariably held power.

In these circumstances there did not develop in Italy a party system upon which responsible government could effectively be based – certainly not a two-party system of government and opposition, and not even a system of changing coalitions, but only factions organised behind leading politicians. In 1876 a long period of office of what was 'the right' came to an end – these had been the successors of Cavour, who had aimed chiefly at the consolidation of national unity under a strong central government. There followed a period of office for liberals of 'the left', led by Depretis, who, in an appeal for support to the deputies in the chamber, urged them to 'transform' themselves from advocates of local or particular interests into supporters of the government of the nation. The phrase *transformismo* came to mean, however, the abandonment of principles and policies in favour of power and office, and has commonly been used in this sense to describe the behaviour regarded as typical of Italian deputies. In the absence of effective and coherent parties, political leaders such as Depretis, Crispi and Giolitti maintained themselves in power through the manipulation of elections and the bribery or appointment to office of elected deputies.

The demand for universal manhood suffrage was based on the democratic ideals which had been proclaimed by Garibaldi. The demand became insistent with the rise of the labour and socialist movements, and from 1895 onwards Bills for universal suffrage were repeatedly introduced in the chamber. In 1910 there was introduced a Bill which, while abolishing property qualifications, still proposed a literacy test, the effect of which would have been to disqualify more than one-third of the adult male population. Giolitti, however, succeeded against right-wing opposition in pushing through a Bill for almost universal manhood suffrage. This gave the franchise to all men over 30, and also to all men over 21 who satisfied certain property or educational qualifications or had performed military service. As a result, the electorate was increased from 8·3 per cent of the population in 1909 to 23·2 per cent in 1912. It was not only the industrial workers of the north who were enfranchised, but also the greater part of the peasantry and rural labourers, who accounted for some 55 per cent of the population. In August 1919 the establishment of universal manhood suffrage was completed when it was extended to all men over 21 and also to those under 21 who had served in the armed forces during the war. A Bill for women's suffrage was defeated in the senate.

In 1912, when the suffrage was extended, the electoral system was left almost unchanged. It was still based on single-member constituencies, with an absolute majority required in the first ballot, and a second ballot held between the leading candidates if necessary. The only change was that the necessary quorum of votes for a successful candidate in the first ballot was diminished from one-sixth to one-tenth, which further reduced the number of second ballots which it was necessary to hold.

In 1918 Vittorio Orlando, who became prime minister after the Italian defeat at Caporetto, proposed the extension of the suffrage which was later implemented, and also a system of proportional representation. This was desired by the Liberals, who now feared serious losses under the majority system, and it was acceptable also to the Socialists, who in the election of 1913 had gained only fifty-two seats instead of the eighty-nine to which they would have been entitled under a PR system. The Catholic Popular Party, newly formed in 1919, was on the whole favourably disposed towards liberal reforms and had no special bias against a more accurately representative system of election. In Italy, therefore, as in several other countries after the First World War, PR was introduced with little opposition. Orlando resigned in June 1919, over the refusal of the Allies at the peace conference to award Fiume and Dalmatia to Italy, but his successor, Francesco Nitti, gave an undertaking on his assumption of office that the introduction of PR would be the principal item in his domestic policy. An Act implementing this was passed in August 1919, and the suffrage was extended at the same time.

The electoral system was now based on the D'Hondt method, the seats being allocated to party lists at the level of constituencies only. Electors were entitled to vote for as many individual candidates as there were seats in the constituency, and *panachage* was permitted. The votes for the individual candidates were aggregated to determine the number of votes for the party lists in which they were included. In the election of 1919 there were fifty-four constituencies, varying in size from five to twenty seats; and in that of 1921 there were forty constituencies, varying from one to twenty-eight seats.

In the election of 1919 the Liberals suffered heavy losses, chiefly to the advantage of the Italian Socialist Party and the new Catholic Popular Party. The increased strength of the Socialists, who gained 30 per cent of the seats, was attributable not only to electoral reform but also to greatly increased support from the electorate; while the Catholic Popular Party, putting forward candidates for the first time in 1919, gained about 20 per cent of the seats. Although the Liberals were still the strongest single group in the chamber of deputies, the whole political structure of parliament had now been altered. The Liberals, although the largest party, were greatly divided among themselves, and whereas, before, there had scarcely existed a definable party system, there were now three organised parties of comparable strength. However, the other two parties refused to form a coalition either with the Liberals or with each other, and in these circumstances parliamentary government broke down. Meanwhile the economic life of the country collapsed into something approaching anarchy. There was an epidemic of strikes in 1919, factories were occupied by revolutionary workers and came to a standstill, and wages remained unpaid. Peasants seized land, especially in the south. Disturbances were aggravated by the activities of Mussolini's armed bands of Fascists, who offered themselves as counter-revolutionary defenders of the nation against Communist domination.

The veteran Giolitti, who had returned to power, called a general election in May 1921, hoping to secure a majority of Liberals over all other parties, but in this he was disappointed. The Liberals secured some 41 per cent of the seats, which was only slightly more than they had gained in 1919, but the Socialist Party's seats declined from 31 to 23 per cent of the total, partly because of splits within the party. The Catholic Popular Party's share of the seats remained almost unchanged, while the Fascists, who had been unrepresented in the chamber in 1919, gained only 38 out of the 535 seats in 1921.

Disturbances and virtual anarchy continued, and after the March on Rome in October 1922 Mussolini, in spite of the very small representation of his party in parliament, was invited to form a government in an attempt to avert civil war. Mussolini depended on the support of the Liberals, from whom he succeeded in gaining a vote of confidence and the grant of emergency powers. With the aim of securing strong and stable government Mussolini introduced in November 1923 an amendment of the electoral law which was intended to ensure the return of a single party with a substantial majority in the chamber of deputies. This law provided a 'bonus' of seats to the party which, in the country as a whole, had a relative majority of votes. Some two-thirds of all seats (356 out of 535) were to be allocated to this party in fifteen multi-member constituencies. The other seats were to be allocated proportionately to the other parties, under a quota system, using the Hare quota and the method of the largest remainder.

This Act was passed with the aid of intimidation and the corruption of deputies. In the election which followed in April 1924, the Fascists, including many Liberals standing with Fascist Party support, gained 64·5 per cent of the votes. They would thus have gained some two-thirds of the seats in any case under a proportional system. After the election there ensued a period in which democratic liberties were systematically suppressed. Finally, in January 1938, the chamber of deputies was abolished and replaced by the chamber of Fascists and corporations.

Until the First World War the Catholic Church and its adherents had little reason to favour a democratic parliamentary regime through which, for generations, legislation had been passed which was contrary to the interests of the church. After the war, many Catholics were complacent about the extinction of political liberties by the Fascists, who did at least appear to offer protection against Communist advances. However, in 1927 the Catholic Popular Party itself became a victim of Fascist repression when it was proscribed by the government, and its secretary-general, Alcide de Gasperi, went into exile abroad. In 1929, also, the government severely restricted the activities of the Catholic Action movement. These events opened the possibility of co-operation against the dictatorship between Catholics and disaffected Liberals, in spite of the long history of mutual hostility between them.

Mussolini realised, nevertheless, that the Fascist regime required the support of the masses of practising Catholics in the population, and to this end arrived at an accommodation with the Vatican which defined the respective spheres of authority of the church and the state. Under the Lateran Pact of 1929 the church renounced all claims to the former Papal States, and recognised the legitimacy of the Italian state. In return, the pope was declared to be in sovereign possession of the Vatican City, and to have jurisdiction over certain churches and other buildings in Rome; Catholicism was declared to be the sole religion of the Italian nation; the church calendar was adopted for public holidays; the state agreed to provide religious instruction in schools; Catholic marriages were to have legal status; and the clergy were to be exempt from military service.

During the Second World War the most effective resistance to the Fascist dictatorship came from the Communists. As a party familiar with the techniques of conspiracy and clandestine organisation, and trained for methods of violence, this was the only movement able effectively to oppose force with force. The persistence and achievements of the resistance movement, in which the Communists played a decisive part, gave the party a new popularity and prestige, and gained for it after the war the role of one of the leading parties in contention for power.

Italian military defeats, the Allied invasion and the advance northwards of the theatre of war led to the resignation of Mussolini in July 1943, and the formation of a government by Marshal Badoglio. The chamber of Fascists and corporations was at once dissolved, and new elections were proposed for a revived chamber of deputies. Representatives of the anti-Fascist parties were taken into the government, and by a decree of April 1945 a consultative assembly was established. The first responsibility of a provisional government formed by the Catholic Party leader, Alcide de Gasperi, was to arrange for the election of a constituent assembly, which would have the task of drafting a new constitution.

A decree of 10 March 1946, for the election of the constituent assembly, extended the suffrage for the first time to women, and included all men and women over the age of 21 (the age limit was reduced to 18 in 1975). The electoral system was PR based on party lists in multi-member constituencies, whose number of seats (except in Aosta, which had only one seat) varied from seven to thirty-six. Each party list might contain as many names as there were seats to be filled; electors were entitled to cast a vote for a party list and personal votes for up to three candidates; allocation of seats to lists was by means of a quota system, the divisor used to determine the necessary number of votes being the number of seats *plus one* in constituencies with twenty seats or less, and the number of seats *plus two* in constituencies which had more than twenty seats. Remaining seats were to be allocated to parties at the national level, for which purpose parties contesting at least six constituencies were entitled to submit lists containing at least twelve names. For the allocation of the remaining seats to the remaining votes the simple quota was used, and if any seats still remained these were allocated to the parties (and thereafter the constituencies) with the largest remainders. The allocation of constituency seats to individuals on party lists was determined by the number of votes each candidate had gained, but the allocation of remaining seats on a national basis was determined by the order of names on the party lists.

In the elections for the constituent assembly the Christian Democrats emerged as much the strongest single party, with 37 per cent of the seats, nearly twice as many as either the Socialists or the Communists. The Liberals, who had lost heavily in the period immediately after the First World War, lost heavily again, and ceased to be a major political force. The monarchy was abolished as a result of a referendum held on the same day as the elections for the constituent assembly, but the Republicans, who had traditions going back to Mazzini, continued to be the only party other than the Christian Democrats, Socialists, Communists and Liberals which consistently returned some members to parliament in every subsequent election.

For thirty years after the elections of 1946 the party structure remained in several respects remarkably stable. The Christian Democrat Party, which continued consistently to be the strongest, achieved an absolute majority of seats in 1948, but otherwise always depended on other parties for the formation of a coalition government. Until 1963, government was by means of an alliance of centre-right parties, including Christian Democrats, Social Democrats, Liberals and Republicans.

After the adoption of the new constitution, which did not prescribe the method of election, the electoral system adopted in 1946 was much the same as that which had been used for the constituent assembly itself. Apart from one single-member constituency the nation was divided into thirty-one multi-member constituencies, with seats ranging in number from five to thirty-seven. The same party-list system with personal voting for individual candidates was maintained, but when the number of seats in a constituency exceeded fifteen the number of personal votes which might be cast for individuals was increased from three to four. Remaining seats could be allocated at the national level only to parties which had contested at least ten constituencies. In the distribution of remaining seats those parties were excluded which had failed to gain at least one constituency seat, and this resulted in the reduction of seats gained by 'splinter' groups from nineteen in 1946 to five in 1948. For the calculation of the quota of votes required for election the divisor in the constituencies was now the number of seats which had to be allocated *plus three*. This had the effect of reducing the number of seats which had to be allocated at the national level from eighty in 1946 to twenty-one in 1948.

The variety of issues over which differences between parties might arise, including those affecting the church, social legislation, local government and regional policy, made it difficult to hold together any coalition of parties, and frequent Cabinet reshuffles were necessary. In view of the instability of government there was a growing body of opinion that a bonus of seats should be awarded to the largest party, so that it could count upon the support of a reliable majority in the chamber. With this end in view, the Christian Democrat Party succeeded in securing the passage of the electoral law of March 1953, which provided that any party or combination of parties which obtained a majority of all votes cast should be allocated 380 of the 590 seats (nearly two-thirds of the total); but if no party or combination of parties gained a majority of the votes the electoral procedure of 1948 would apply. This measure differed only in detail and not in principle from the Fascist measure which was adopted in 1923, and was for this reason widely discredited and opposed.

In the following election of July 1953, the combined votes of government parties reached only 49·2 per cent of the total, and thus narrowly failed to achieve the level which would have gained them the right to two-thirds of the seats. A period of continued government instability followed, but in response to the unfavourable public reaction to the change in the electoral system the electoral law was amended once again in May 1956, and a return was made, with some modifications, to the system previously in force. One change made in response to the demands of the smaller parties was that the divisor used for calculating the quota of votes necessary for election was reduced from seats *plus three* to seats *plus two*. This meant that there would be more remaining seats to be allocated. The number of remaining seats in fact increased from twenty-one and thirty-eight in 1948 and 1953, to sixty-seven, sixty-two and sixty in the elections of 1958, 1963 and 1968 respectively. However, to be eligible for a share of the remaining seats, a party now had to have received at least 300,000 votes in the country as a whole, and to have gained a seat in at least one constituency.

The difficulty of maintaining a centre-right coalition in power, the growing strength of the left wing of the Christian Democrat Party, and the need to offer a programme of reform to counteract the growing strength of the Communist Party, all led to increasing advocacy of a centre-left coalition, commonly called the *apertura a sinistra*, or opening to the left. This achieved fulfilment in a government formed by Aldo Moro in 1966, with the support of the Italian Socialist Party under Pietro Nenni. It was followed by the union of the Socialist and Social Democrat parties in a United Socialist Party.

However, by the time of the 1972 election the United Socialist Party had split up once again. This election is a good example of the detailed working of the electoral system. In 1968 the left-wing Party of

Proletarian Unity had over 1,414,000 votes and gained twenty-three seats. In 1972 they had 648,000 votes, which was still well above the minimum of 300,000 required for the allocation of remaining seats, but since their votes were widely dispersed they did not succeed in satisfying the other requirement, that they should have gained a seat in at least one constituency. They were not therefore eligible for the allocation of *any* seats in 1972.

From 1966 until October 1974 there was a succession of centre-left governments, but the coalitions between the parties were fragile, and each of the parties which at one time or another formed a coalition with the Christian Democrats subsequently withdrew their support on one or more of the many issues which became the subject of disagreement. For some months both in 1968 and in 1972 the Christian Democrats alone formed minority governments, depending for survival on the forbearance of the other parties in the chamber.

During the summer of 1974 there was a considerable debate within each of the parties over the proposal of the Communist Enrico Berlinguer that in the national interest there should be collaboration of the anti-Fascist parties, including the Christian Democrats and the Communists. This possible arrangement was termed the 'historic compromise', and proposed the revival of the earlier co-operation of the two parties in the provisional administration at the end of the Second World War. This proposal came to occupy the forefront of political controversy, dividing all the parties except those on the extreme right or the extreme left, which were unequivocally hostile to the idea. The main question now was whether it was possible for the Communist Party, dedicated as it was to the overthrow of capitalism and capitalist institutions, to co-operate with any sincerity within the regime which it sought ultimately to destroy.

In the general election of 1976, which was only the second to be held prematurely since the end of the Second World War, the Communist Party increased their share of the votes, but still, with only 36 per cent of the seats, did not succeed in their ambition of becoming the strongest single party. The Christian Democrats still had 42 per cent of the seats, and it was the smaller parties which chiefly incurred the losses. There was much debate about the role of the electoral system in the crisis of government which had arisen. In particular, it was proposed that a majority system, preferably with a second ballot, should be substituted for PR, in the hope that this would provide the opportunity for effective collaboration between parties which supported the parliamentary system.

However, historical experience of majority elections and the second ballot in Italy itself before 1919 was not such as to fortify such expectations. Such a system had done little to secure popular support for the parliamentary system, or to strengthen particular parties within parliament. Later, the system of election by PR may have contributed to an excessive number of parties in the Italian parliament, and certainly the socialist parties in particular were prone to disintegration, but on the other hand there was a countervailing tendency, of which the election of 1976 is an example, for votes to 'polarise' between the Christian Democrats on the one hand and the Communist Party on the other. In the general election of June 1979, however, there was less polarisation, and at the expense of both the Christian Democrats and the Communists votes were gained by smaller parties, including the Liberals, Social Democrats and Republicans. There have been forces pulling in opposite directions, and in the context of the debate over the 'historic compromise' polarisation is counteracted by strong differences within each party, and among their supporters, about proposals for collaboration with other parties having widely divergent aims. In a situation of such complexity it is unlikely that a single solution, whether a particular electoral system or anything else, could prove by itself to be a panacea capable of creating a stable political regime.

REFERENCES: CHAPTER 14

A history of the electoral system is contained in a contribution by Giovanni Schepis to the *Enciclopedia del Diritto*, entitled 'Storia dei sistemi elettorali in Italia'. This is confined mainly to the technical changes in the electoral system and gives little attention to the manner in which it operated in practice. That is, on the contrary, the main theme of D. Fisichella in a chapter entitled 'The Italian experience' in *Adversary Politics and Electoral Reform*. References to the working of the electoral system are made by A. S. White in *The Evolution of Modern Italy*, and by Dante Germino and Stefano Passigli in *The Government and Politics of Contemporary Italy*. It is difficult to keep abreast with developments in the current political crisis in Italy, but reference may be made to articles by M. Clark and R. E. M. Irving in *Parliamentary Affairs*, 'The Italian political crisis and the general election' (1972), and 'The Italian general election of June, 1976' (1977).

15

The Federal German Republic

The nature of the electoral system has in recent decades raised issues of as great magnitude for Germany as it has for probably any other country, yet before the advent to power of the National Socialists there had been relatively little contention about electoral systems. No change of any consequence in the electoral mechanism was ever made between the establishment of the German Empire in 1871 and the Weimar Republic of 1918. Since 1949, again, there have not been any fundamental changes but only a strengthening of certain provisions of the electoral law. The durability of the electoral system in Germany during these periods has been in marked contrast with the experience in France, where governments and parties in power were addicted to the amendment or revision of existing electoral laws.

Unlike the experience in most other countries, the question of the suffrage for the German parliament was settled at a fairly early date, universal male suffrage with direct, equal and secret elections having been introduced for the parliament of the North German Confederation in 1867, and for the imperial parliament in 1871. (The vote was extended equally to women in 1918.)

The stability of the electoral system is the more remarkable since there was in Germany a proliferation of parties which in other countries often led to demands for electoral reform, the purpose of which would be to limit the number of parties which could gain representation in parliament, and thus make it easier to form governments with adequate party support. In Germany the pressure for electoral reform before 1914 was not important. The main reason for this was that governments were not constitutionally responsible to parliament, and there was therefore no urgent need for parliament to provide a stable majority for a government in office. Under the imperial constitution of 1871 sovereignty and executive power lay with the Bundesrat, or federal council, an autocratic body nominated by the component states of the German nation. This was a large and unwieldy body, and great power accrued in practice to the emperor, as technically president of the federal council. The emperor was also commander-in-chief of the armed forces, he nominated the chancellor, and neither he nor the chancellor was responsible to parliament for the exercise of his functions of government. It was not until after the Second World War that responsible parliamentary government was effectively established, and since then the nature of the electoral system has become of more central importance.

Before the First World War, the attempts of liberals in Germany to achieve both German unification and constitutional reforms in favour of parliamentary government and democratic freedoms had generally been a failure, set back by waves of reaction, and achieving success only in some periods in some of the states. Bismarck, after his military and diplomatic successes, outbid the liberals for popular support by proposing universal, direct and equal manhood suffrage for the North German Confederation in 1867 and for the electoral law of the imperial parliament in 1871. The electoral system now established was one of single-member constituencies with two ballots if necessary. An absolute majority was required in the first ballot, and in the second ballot, if needed, there was a straight contest between the two leading candidates in the first. This was the system which had existed in most German states in the past, and for the imperial parliament it survived until 1918.

For election purposes, the states were divided into single-member constituencies containing approximately 100,000 inhabitants or 20,000 electors. These boundaries remained unaltered until 1918, and in view of variations in the increase of population in different localities, and the urbanisation which accompanied industrial growth, increasing discrepancies arose in the size of different constituencies. Among the interests which benefited were the Conservatives and the Poles, whose support lay principally in the more slowly growing rural constituencies which were increasingly over-represented. Those who suffered most were the Social Democrats, whose support was greatest in the increasingly under-represented towns.

Before 1914 a multi-party system arose, with normally about four major parties. Twelve parties were represented in the first Reichstag, and the number varied around a dozen or more up to the First World War. There were several reasons for the multiplication of parties, but possibly the most important was the absence of responsible parliamentary government. There was no pressure on parties to combine or coalesce in order to sustain a government in power, and little sense among politicians that they had responsibility for controlling the affairs of the nation. All parties tended to act like opposition parties, or to fly into opposition on slender grounds. This is a defect which was inherited by the Weimar

Republic. Another reason for the large number of parties was that in single-member constituencies locally concentrated minorities were able to achieve considerable representation, including the Poles in East Germany, the Danes in Schleswig-Holstein and the French in Alsace-Lorraine.

One effect of the second ballot is to improve the chances of smaller parties, unable to obtain a majority on their own, but likely to secure, in a second ballot, the support of sympathisers from other parties which have been even less successful. However, the extent to which this happened in Germany before 1914 was not so significant as to account for the number of parties which existed at that time. In the first two decades or so after the foundation of the empire there was a high proportion of uncontested elections; where there were contests there were very commonly only two candidates; and the number of second ballots which had to be held was quite small. Commonly there were many two-party contests between different parties in the various regions.

Later, the number of candidates and of second ballots increased, and where this happened it was often to the disadvantage of the Social Democrats, who were less able than middle-class anti-socialist parties to rely on other similarly disposed parties for mutual support. In 1907 an alliance of Liberals and Conservatives won so many seats on the second ballot that they gained 47 per cent of the seats in the Reichstag with only 29 per cent of the first-ballot votes. At other times, however, even after the number of second-ballot contests had increased from the 1890s onwards, there were so many candidates who won on the second ballot after gaining a relative majority on the first that the substitution of relative majority elections for the two-ballot system would probably have made no fundamental difference to the party system in the Reichstag.

It is not surprising that one of the main objects of the Social Democrats came to be electoral reform. One change which was advocated jointly by the Social Democrats and some other parties was a readjustment of the electoral boundaries, which had ceased to correspond with the distribution of the population; but from the time of the party's conference at Erfurt in 1891 they also advocated proportional representation, of which the principal supporter in the party was Walter Liebknecht. However, neither of these reforms was achieved before the First World War.

After Kaiser Wilhelm II abdicated on 9 November 1918, the chancellor handed over his functions to Fritz Ebert, now leader of the Social Democrat Party. Ebert invited Hugo Preuss, a professor of constitutional law and now a secretary in the Ministry of the Interior, to draft a constitution for the new republic, and plans were prepared for the election of a national constituent assembly. For the elections to that assembly it was required by the Social Democratic Party, in conformity with their policy since 1891, that a system of PR should be introduced. A rigid list system was adopted for thirty-seven large constituencies, and the D'Hondt method was applied to achieve proportionality at the constituency level only. The suffrage was extended equally to all men and women aged 20 or over. *Apparentement* was permitted at the constituency level, as a result of which about half the lists in the subsequent election were allied with others, but it was exclusively the non-socialist parties which availed themselves of this facility. Nineteen parties took part in the election and ten succeeded in gaining representation. The Social Democrats and the Independent Socialists failed to gain an absolute majority.

In the constitution which was adopted, a significant feature was the subsequently fatal division of responsibility for government between the president of the republic and the Reichstag. The powers of the president were considerable, and included that of nominating and dismissing the chancellor. The constitution simultaneously provided that the chancellor should be responsible to the Reichstag, which could not, however, replace him by one of their own nominees if it decided not to support the government. The chancellor therefore had two masters, which was perhaps the most important single factor which led to the collapse of the government under the Weimar Republic. It led to irresponsible behaviour of the parties; this disrupted the business of legislation and of government, which justified the increasing use of presidential decrees, which in turn diminished the role and authority of parliament still further.

The electoral law established under the Weimar Republic was a new type of proportional representation. In the election of the constituent assembly about 1⅓ million votes had been 'wasted' on unsuccessful parties and failed to influence the balance between the parties represented in the Reichstag. Under the constitution of 1919, which required that elections should be by PR, an electoral law of 1920 provided for the adoption of the 'automatic' system. Using a system of rigid lists, one deputy was to be elected for every 60,000 votes which a party gained at constituency level. Surplus or 'remaining' votes for parties were to be aggregated at a second level of 'constituency unions', and again one seat was allocated for every 60,000 votes gained by a party. Finally, an allocation of seats on the same basis was to take place at the national level, to candidates on special lists prepared by the parties, and an additional seat was to be allocated for any 'remaining' votes in excess of 30,000.

The purpose was to avoid the 'wastage' of votes which had earlier occurred, and a corollary of this method was that the number of members of the Reichstag was not fixed, but varied with the size of the electorate, the turn-out at particular elections and the distribution of 'remaining' votes. However, the regulations also required that only parties which had gained at least one seat in the first two stages of the election might share in the distribution of seats at the national level. Contrary to expectations, the number of 'wasted' votes remained high, and even higher in 1924 and 1928 than it had been in 1919. This was the result of the fragmentation of the parties contesting the election, many of which failed to gain any seats at the first two stages of the election. The number of parties which submitted lists increased from nineteen in 1919 to forty-two in 1932. The highest number of parties which succeeded in gaining at least one seat was fifteen in 1928 and 1930.

The immense difficulties which confronted the German government after 1918 were aggravated by two important circumstances: first, the system of parliamentary government was a novelty without traditions which might have been built upon; and secondly, Germany inherited the social structure of an autocratic regime, reflected in the army, the bureaucracy, industry, commerce and the educational institutions, which were largely hostile to parliamentary democracy.

The record of government and parliament from 1918 to 1933 was one of repeated collapses of coalitions and governments, commonly after renewed acts of hostility on the part of the victorious powers, or under the impact of economic disaster. During the period of recovery between 1924 and 1928 the parties which supported parliament and democracy did not fare so badly, but between 1928 and 1930 the vote for the National Socialists increased eightfold, and by 1932 it doubled again. This was not much at the expense of the Social Democrats, whose vote did not fall to a correspondingly great degree, nor of the Centre Party or the Communists, whose votes actually increased. The National Socialists obtained their votes by absorbing those of the Nationalists and other small parties on the right. In November 1932 the National Socialist vote fell, while Communist and other parties' votes increased, but Hitler's appointment as chancellor on 30 January 1933, followed by the Reichstag fire, preceded the election of March 1933. When the National Socialists still failed to gain an absolute majority of votes, the Nationalist vote enabled the National Socialists to secure support in the Reichstag for the granting of plenary powers to Hitler as chancellor, and he then proceeded to refashion the constitution of the German state in the manner he had outlined in *Mein Kampf*.

The proliferation of parties during the Weimar Republic was not the result of PR, since this proliferation had already existed before. PR may have encouraged the continued existence and representation of parties which had already been formed, but even this is doubtful in view of the experience of the Federal German Republic since the Second World War. It was rather the polarisation of the parties, and the extremism of the parties at either pole, which prevented the achievement of stable majorities for governments under the Weimar Republic.

A relative majority system might have delayed the rise of the National Socialist Party, but would not necessarily have prevented it. Right-wing radicalism was not an insignificant movement, but had a widespread appeal which was manifested in a variety of forms until it was finally consolidated into the National Socialist Party. It had local strongholds of support, not only in Bavaria but also in many other regions, and under a relative majority system the concentration of support in particular localities would have made it possible for these movements to gain representation, and ultimately, perhaps, a landslide victory which was not possible under a PR system.

Towards the end of the Second World War the future of Germany was determined partly by the agreements of the Allied Powers at the Teheran, Yalta and Potsdam conferences. One agreement which was adhered to, and which lasted beyond the original intention, was the demarcation between the Soviet and the Western zones in Germany. It had also been agreed that political institutions should be re-established on a democratic basis, but before the Potsdam Conference preparations had already been made for the assumption of power by the Communist Party in the Soviet zone, and also plans for the formation of an 'anti-Fascist' bloc of parties in the West, designed also to come under Communist influence. The reaction to the danger of Communist power in the West was such as to provide at least one common bond between the parties of the Federal German Republic which had an enduring influence on the party system.

In the West, the reconstruction of democratic forms of government was methodically begun at the local and then at the Land level. Thereafter, the military governors of the Western zones invited the ministers – president of the states, or *Länder*, to convene a constituent assembly and draft a constitution for the republic. The eleven state assemblies elected delegates who formed a parliamentary council, which in turn appointed a committee to draw up the constitution. As compared with Weimar, a principal change was that the president was now reduced to little more than a formal head of state, without the powers he had enjoyed under the Weimar Republic. The office of chancellor now depended on majority support in the Reichstag, and to prevent any 'vacuum' in government through irresponsible opposition in the Reichstag there was adopted the device of the 'constructive vote of no confidence', which provided that a vote of no confidence in the chancellor could take effect only if a successor were simultaneously nominated by a majority of the members of the Reichstag. With this proviso, a system of responsible parliamentary government was now established, which did not effectively exist under the Weimar Republic.

In spite of the Weimar experience, the electoral system which was established was one of proportional representation. The form which it took was, however, different, and influenced by a desire to achieve a compromise between different proposals. The conservative parties, that is to say, the Christian Democrats and their Bavarian allies, the Christian Social Union, were from the outset, and always consistently thereafter, in favour of a relative majority system on the British model. The Social Democrats and Liberals, or Free Democratic Party, favoured a system of proportional representation. In 1949 the compromise took the form of providing for the election of about 60 per cent of the members of the Reichstag by relative majority in single-member constituencies, and the remaining 40 per cent as additional members under a rigid list system, to achieve proportional representation in each of the Länder. For this purpose the D'Hondt method of election was applied, but no party was entitled to share in the allocation of additional seats unless they had gained at least one seat in a single-member constituency, or at least 5 per cent of the votes in one of the Länder. Each elector was entitled to cast one vote only, which served as a vote both for a candidate in a single-member constituency, and for the party list of the party to which the candidate belonged.

In 1953 certain amendments were introduced, partly improving and partly reducing the proportional element in the system. Only half the members were now to be elected in single-member constituencies, instead of 60 per cent, and the other half were to be elected by means of party lists to achieve proportionality. This reduced the possibility that the degree of *dis*proportionality arising from elections in single-member constituencies would be too great to be compensated by the election of other members under a PR system of election. On the other hand the exclusion clauses were now made more severe, by requiring that the allocation of additional seats should be confined to parties which had either gained one seat or had 5 per cent of the votes, not in one of the Länder, but in the nation as a whole. A further change, which increased the choice available to electors, was that each elector was now able to exercise two votes, one for a single candidate and the second for a party list, which need not be the same list as that of the party which the single candidate supported.

Finally, in 1956, further amendments were introduced which once again affected proportionality in opposite ways. Proportionality between votes and seats was now to be established at the level of the nation as a whole, and party seats were then to be distributed to parties in each of the Länder. On the other hand, the exclusion clauses were once again made more severe, since the allocation of additional seats from party lists was now restricted to parties which had gained 5 per cent of the votes at the national level, or *three* seats in single-member constituencies.

During the immediate postwar period the four-power Allied Control Council agreed that four political parties should be permitted to resume political activities, and prepare the way for the restoration of a democratic regime. These were the Social Democratic Party, the Centre Party, which now became an alliance between the Christian Democratic Union and the Christian Social Union, the Communist Party and the Free Democratic Party. The strongest parties surviving from the Weimar era were the Christian Democrats and the Social Democrats. In the election of 1949 the Christian Democrats proved to be the stronger, and until 1956 formed a government with the support of the Free Democrats. From 1957 until 1961 the alliance of the Christian Democrats with the Christian Social Union had an absolute majority in the Reichstag, but thereafter lost some seats and had to depend once more on the support of the Free Democrats between 1961 and 1965. In 1966 a 'Grand Coalition' was formed between the Christian Democrats, the Christian Social Union and the Social Democrats, which lasted until 1969.

Thus, for twenty years after 1949 the Christian Democrats were never out of office. It was remarkable that the middle-class and mainly conservative parties were able to combine with such permanent cohesion and strength after the experience of the Weimar period, when parties were fragmented and engaged in internecine conflicts. One explanation is that by the end of the war there had been a social revolution which had swept away most of the remnants of the earlier autocratic regimes; but it was also largely a personal achievement of Chancellor Adenauer, who succeeded in building up an inter-confessional conservative party out of those which had previously been divided on grounds of religion, sectional economic interest and local loyalties.

The Social Democrats suffered an eclipse from which they did not begin to recover until after the party's conference at Bad Godesberg in 1959, when a programme was adopted which, discarding some Marxist elements from their earlier programme, accepted the role of Germany in the Western economy and in Western defence, the continuance of a market economy in place of pure socialism, and an appeal to the entire electorate instead of to the working classes alone. A revival in the electoral support for the Social Democrats had the result that in 1966 they achieved office for the first time since the war, though only in collaboration with the Christian Democrats and the Christian Social Union. In 1969 they were the dominant partners in a coalition with the Free Democrats. In 1972, for the first time, they won an absolute majority of seats in the single-member constituencies, though not in the nation as a whole. They continued to rely on the support of the Free Democrats after that election, and after the election of 1976.

There has thus been a remarkable continuity and stability of government in Western Germany since the Second World War. Contrary to some expectations, the PR system which was adopted did not lead to a fragmentation of parties and difficulties in assembling support for government coalitions. On the contrary, the number of parties which secured representation in the Bundestag declined continuously from eleven in 1949 to three from 1961 onwards. (For this purpose the Christian Democrats and the Christian Social Union are classified as one, since they acted in alliance and did not compete with each other in elections. The Christian Social Union was confined to Bavaria, and the Christian Democrats did not intervene there.)

Nor did PR open the door to extremist parties, as it is alleged to have done under the Weimar Republic. One reason for the lack of success of such parties was the exclusion clause in the electoral regulations, which in effect prevented all but the three major parties from being represented in the Bundestag from 1961 onwards.

The exclusion clause undoubtedly contributed to a reduction in the number of parties which succeeded in gaining representation, but only at the expense of reducing the degree of proportionality between votes and seats in the nation as a whole. An unsatisfactory aspect of the system has been the large number of seats which can be affected by a small margin of votes on one side of the barrier or the other. In 1953 the Party of Exiles and Refugees from East Germany had 5·9 per cent of the votes and twenty-seven seats in the Bundestag. As a result of measures to relocate these communities and alleviate their unemployment, the vote of the party fell to 4·6 per cent, that is, below the exclusion barrier of 5 per cent, and they ceased to have any representation in the Bundestag at all.

The electoral system adopted in 1949 is commonly described as a 'personalised' system of proportional representation, because an elector's first vote (until 1953 his only vote) was for a person in a single-member constituency. The role and functions of political parties are also, however, recognised in the basic law, and they are regulated by a federal law which came into force in 1967. These functions include the nomination of candidates for federal, state and local elections, and one regulation requires that the organisation of parties must be democratic. However, the law does not prescribe how democratic procedures are to be observed, and methods of nomination may vary from state to state and from one party to another.

For the smaller parties, the chance of securing seats in single-member constituencies is slight. In six elections from 1957 onwards the Free Democrats gained in each election a minimum of thirty seats and a maximum of sixty-seven, but in only one of these elections was any of these seats in a single-member constituency, and that was only one seat in 1957. The Christian Democrats, on the other hand, always gained more single-member seats than party-list seats until 1969. In that year the Social Democrats gained more single-member seats than party-list seats for the first time.

When any party, but especially a small party, wishes to ensure the election of a candidate of particular importance, they will place his name at the top of the party list; but in the major parties, at least, such candidates are usually nominated for single-member constituencies as well. Otherwise, the candidate's prospects may be endangered by the very success of the party. If the size and the distribution of the votes for a party in a particular state are such that they win most or all of the seats in single-member constituencies, they may be entitled, on a proportional basis, to very few party-list seats, or to none at all. In such a case a prominent candidate, even though placed at or near the head of a list, may fail to gain election in any seat. That is what happened in certain Landtag elections in North Rhine-Westphalia in 1966.

The two votes which an elector can exercise make it possible for him to vote for a candidate of one party and for the party list of another. This can be of importance in promoting an alliance between two parties. After an alliance was established between the Free Democrats and the Social Democrats, a supporter of the Free Democrats, realising that his candidate had very little chance in the single-member constituency, would vote in the constituency for the Social Democrat, but for the Free Democrat party list. A Social Democrat elector, knowing that his party had never gained as many votes as the alliance between the Christian Democrats and the Christian Social Union, might consider that the best chance his party had of forming a government was in alliance with the Free Democrats. He would therefore give his party-list vote (but not his constituency vote) to the Free Democrats, hoping to ensure that the Free Democrats would surmount the exclusion barrier and thus gain at least twenty-six seats in the Bundestag. He might also wish to support the coalition on its merits, as moderating the policy of the Social Democrats and averting measures advocated by more left-wing socialists. It appears that for this variety of reasons much of the voting in the 1972 election took place in these ways.

From 1949 until 1957, and again from 1961 until 1965, the Christian Democrat Party formed coalition governments which almost always included the Free Democrats. This dependence on the Free Democrats was a constant source of irritation for Chancellor Adenauer and the Christian Democrat Party, and when in 1961 and 1962 the Free Democrats appeared to be making excessive demands in return for their support of the government the Christian Democrats threatened that they would seek to form a temporary alliance with the Social Democrats, the purpose of which would be to change the electoral system from PR to a relative majority system. The representation of the Free Democrats was already precarious under the existing system, and it seemed most unlikely that they could survive if a majority system were adopted. The Christian Democrats had always favoured the relative majority system on its merits, and it was at that time also to their particular advantage as the largest party.

The suggestion of a partnership in a coalition government had attractions at that time for the Social Democrats, who had been out of power since 1949. After the general election of 1965, the 'Grand Coalition' of the Social Democrats and Christian Social Union was at last formed, and in a statement of the policy of the new government Chancellor Kiesinger declared that one item of agreement was the adoption of a new electoral system, to enable elections after 1969 to create a clear majority for a single party. This system was moreover to be incorporated into the basic law.

After the formation of the 'Grand Coalition' in 1966, the minister of the interior, Paul Lücke, set up a committee on electoral law reform. The committee, which included F. A. Hermens, a leading opponent of PR, recommended that the Bundestag should consist of 500 members, all to be elected by relative majority votes in single-member constituencies. It also recommended that the requisite electoral law should be passed in time for the next election in 1969.

The proposal was not, however, accepted by the Social Democrat Party, in spite of their initial agreement to electoral reform at the time when the 'Grand Coalition' was formed. On general grounds, it was a hazard for the Social Democrats at the time to agree to the adoption of a majority system, since in every previous election they had gained fewer votes than the alliance of the Christian Democrats and the Christian Social Union. At the time of the debate it was predicted by the Institute of Applied Social Science that the plurality system would be greatly to the disadvantage of the Social Democrat Party. While the system could produce clear winners it could also produce clear losers, and on the basis of a sociological study of the electorate it seemed that in a straight fight the Social Democrats would lose. The party were calculated to have the definite support of the working class to the extent of about 30 per cent of the electorate, while the Christian Democrats and the Christian Social Union could count on the support of about two-thirds of the Catholics, the middle-class and the self-employed, amounting to about 40 per cent of the electorate. A plurality system would tend to produce a decisive result for a leading party, and would be appropriate for achieving an alternation in power when the two leading parties were nearly equal in strength; but it would be to the grave disadvantage of a smaller second party, such as the Social Democrats then appeared to be. The advocates of the relative majority system, on the other hand, stressed the 'dynamic' effects it would have which, over a period of time, would change the voting habits of the electorate and the structure of the parties.

It is not clear why Willi Brandt and other leaders of the Social Democratic Party changed their minds about electoral reform. The Free Democrats had, of course, been entirely opposed to such a change in the electoral system. It may have been partly out of recognition for the election on 5 March 1969 of Gustav Heinemann, the Social Democrat candidate, as president of the republic, with the support of the Free Democrats, that the Social Democrats decided not to support a reform which could have extinguished the Free Democrats as a party represented in the Bundestag. It is possible that their decision was influenced by their poor results in recent Land elections which, if repeated at the federal level in elections by relative majority, would have led to a considerable loss of seats. They were perhaps guided by the expert advice given by the sociologists. At all events, it was decided at the Nuremberg Conference of the party held on 17–21 March 1969 that the passage of the electoral reform proposal was no longer feasible during the current Bundestag; and since electoral reform had been a point of agreement when the 'Grand Coalition' was formed, Paul Lücke, the minister of the interior, resigned.

The proposals of the Christian Democrats and the Christian Social Union for electoral reform in 1968 had the effect of alienating the Free Democrats from those parties, and paved the way for the coalition between the Social Democrats and the Free Democrats which was formed after the success of the Social Democrats in the election of 1969. After the prediction of losses by the Social Democrats under a relative majority system, it is ironical that, having rejected this reform, they should in 1969, for the first time, have gained more seats in single-member constituencies than the Christian Democrats and the Christian Social Union. However, in view of the variable pattern of voting between candidates and party lists, to which reference has previously been made, it does not follow that a similar result would have been achieved if the electoral system had been different.

The Free Democrats, in contrast to the Social Democrats, had performed poorly in the 1969 election, but the new coalition with the Social Democrats was cemented and renewed before the election of 1972. This time the Free Democrats performed very much better, since the coalition now had strong backing from Free Democrat electors. This was part of a wider popular support for the Social Democrats as their policies in the course of the 1960s had become more 'social democratic' and less 'socialist'.

In the election of 1976, however, the Social Democrats and the Free Democrats both lost a good deal of support, though they continued to form a government. The losses of the Free Democrats were partly due to the fact that there was much less 'splitting' of votes between single candidates and party lists than there had been in 1972, and the reason for this may have been that with Helmut Schmidt as chancellor there was less need for moderate supporters of the Social Democrats to guard against the left wing of the party by voting for the Free Democrats. In such circumstances it became uncertain whether the Free Democrats could continue to surmount the exclusion clause in elections, and continue to be represented in parliament.

REFERENCES: CHAPTER 15

A definitive history of the electoral system in Germany is contained in *Wahlen in Deutschland: Theorie-Geschichte-Dokumente, 1848–1970,* by Bernard Vogel, Dieter Nohlen and Rainer-Olaf Schultze. Developments since the Second World War are described by Tony Burkett in *Parties and Elections in West Germany,* while the operation of the modern electoral system is outlined in a booklet by Richard Holme, *A Democracy Which Works.* A recent example of the working of the electoral system is studied by R. E. M. Irving and W. E. Paterson in an article on 'The West German election of 1976' in *Parliamentary Affairs,* 1977. The debate on proposals to revert to a majority instead of a proportional system of election is discussed by David P. Conradt in 'Electoral law politics in West Germany', *Political Studies,* 1970.

16

France

The French revolution spread throughout Europe the notion that political sovereignty lies with the people, and that liberty consists in the opportunity to exercise that sovereignty. France was much less successful, however, in indicating by precept or example the practical methods by which these principles might be implemented. The fact that since 1789 there have been five republics, two monarchies, two empires and about fifteen constitutions (depending on what magnitude of change is regarded as a new constitution) is an indication of the numerous changes which took place.

Between 1848, when universal manhood suffrage was adopted for assembly elections, and 1958, when the Fifth Republic was established, these changes included fourteen major changes of the electoral law. The electoral system was rarely based on proportional representation, and indeed it was only between 1945 and 1951 that a true form of PR was adopted. There were, however, many other changes in the electoral system, though France has never adopted the one which has prevailed in Britain since 1885, that is to say, the relative majority system in single-member constituencies.

Elections for the national assembly from 1789 to 1817 were indirect, but in 1817 direct elections were established, and also an electoral system based on multi-member constituencies. Under this system, an absolute majority was required for election in the first two out of three possible ballots, and also a number of votes equal to at least a quarter of the registered electorate. In 1820 the system was changed to single-member constituencies, and for election in either of the first two ballots votes equivalent to one-third of the registered electorate were now required. From 1831 onwards the system of single-member constituencies was continued, but candidates could now, and for more than half a century thereafter, stand for election in more than one constituency (though of course taking a seat in only one of them). It was in this period that deputies began to organise themselves into party groups, and that socialist ideas spread, culminating in the revolution of February 1848, the end of the July monarchy and the accession of the House of Orleans.

Many different electoral systems have existed since 1848, but the second-ballot system in single-member constituencies, with an absolute majority required in the first ballot, existed in all but the following periods:

1848−52 and 1871−3 multi-member constituencies, with a relative majority sufficing for election, but a second ballot required if a sufficient number of candidates did not achieve a stipulated number of votes;

1873−5 and 1885−9 multi-member constituencies, with an absolute majority required at a first ballot, but a relative majority sufficing at a second ballot;

1919−27 and 1951−8 mixed majority and proportional systems;

1945−51 a proportional system.

From 1789 onwards elections were based on a means-tested suffrage. Universal manhood suffrage was introduced in 1848, but it was not until after the establishment of the Third Republic in 1870 that elections were able to function freely and fairly. Between 1815 and 1848 the assembly had frequently been dissolved by the monarch if members were recalcitrant in opposition to government policy, and elections were highly corrupt. Under the Second Empire, from 1852 to 1869, elections were systematically manipulated by the government to secure the return of a compliant body of members. Even after 1870 means were sometimes found by one faction or another to manipulate the electoral system to their own advantage. Also, although the commonest election system was the absolute majority in a first ballot in a single-member constituency, it was at first unusual for more than two candidates to stand for election in a constituency, and only one ballot was commonly needed. Since most constituency elections were won at the first ballot the system was much the same in practice, though not in form, as the relative majority or 'first past the post' system. Later in the nineteenth century and before the First World War the number of second ballots varied considerably, but in 1927 they reached 70 per cent of all constituency elections, and remained at a high level thereafter.

One of the prominent features of the electoral systems in France was the addiction of French governments to what is commonly referred to as 'electoral engineering'. A government in power has on many occasions passed an electoral law with a bias introduced in its own favour, in the hope, which was however often disappointed, that the out-going representatives might be returned to office. From the period since 1848 some examples of this may be selected.

After the 1848 revolution electoral systems based on multi-member constituencies were adopted, but when Napoleon III gained power in 1851 he introduced in their place, in 1852, the system of single-member constituencies, and elections based on an absolute majority in a first ballot. A significant feature of the particular system adopted was that candidatures at the second ballot were open to any candidate, and not confined to those who had participated in the first. This made it easier for the government to manipulate the results of an election by introducing a candidate of its own at the second stage. Elections were so extensively manipulated during the period of the Second Empire that free elections could hardly be said to have existed at that time.

After the war of 1870 and the establishment of the Third Republic the electoral system reverted to the law of 1849 which provided for elections in multi-member constituencies. In the election of 1871 the members returned were mainly Conservatives and Monarchists. At that time, however, and until 1889, it was possible for candidates to stand in more than one constituency (though to occupy only one seat), so that in July 1871 numerous by-elections had to be held for seats remaining unfilled, and in these it was mainly Republicans who were successful. The Conservatives and Monarchists still had a majority after the by-elections, but their failure in these was due to disagreements within the parties and their division into Legitimists, Orleanists and Bonapartists, who were less successful in forming electoral agreements than the Republicans. Through an electoral law of 1875 the Conservative majority restored single-member constituencies, in the hope that this would enable local magnates and the clergy to exert greater influence on the electorate; and the second-ballot system, reintroduced in 1873, was retained. The disunity of the Conservatives was such, however, that at the second ballot the Republicans obtained 70 per cent of the seats with 58 per cent of the votes, so that the attempt to manipulate the electoral system to the advantage of the Conservatives proved to be a failure.

Meanwhile Marshal McMahon had been elected president by a Conservative majority, but in 1877 he caused outrage by dissolving the assembly, and in the ensuing election in the same year the Republicans were returned with a substantial majority of both votes and seats. In spite of their successive victories in single-member constituencies the Republicans considered that multi-member constituencies were to their greater advantage. After a further Republican victory in 1881 a Bill was at last passed in 1885, restoring multi-member constituencies with second ballots. The election of 1885 was the only one held under this new Electoral Act, and the first ballot falsified the expectations of the Republicans, since with 56 per cent of the votes they gained only 127 seats as against 177 for the Conservatives. It was only through superior organisation at the second ballot that they succeeded in the end in gaining a substantial overall majority.

During the period from 1885 to 1889 the Republicans were discredited by scandals, and General Boulanger entered the field as an advocate of reform. He became an exponent of a particular type of electoral manipulation in that he himself stood as a candidate in several constituencies, so as to propagate his cause as widely as possible, at the cost of making it necessary to hold numerous by-elections. In 1889 multiple candidatures were prohibited, and the electoral system was changed back to single-member constituencies and two ballots. At this time members of the assembly had largely changed their views about the merits of the various electoral systems, single-member constituencies now being favoured by the Republicans, and multi-member constituencies by the Conservatives. The election of 1889 inflicted another decisive defeat upon the Conservatives, and from this time onwards the Republican form of government came to be generally accepted, and support for the monarchist cause dwindled. During the period up to 1914 it was the Radicals who gained most seats under the then existing electoral system, and both Conservatives and Socialists now increasingly advocated proportional representation.

The electoral law of 1919 was a compromise between the Radicals and the Socialists, and was an attempt to combine the merits of proportional representation with those of the majority system. Under this law elections were held in multi-member constituencies, and electors were given as many votes as there were seats to be filled. *Panachage* was permitted, but not cumulative voting. Seats in each constituency were allocated to parties and candidates in three stages. (1) Any candidate supported by an absolute majority of voters was elected. (2) A Hare quota was calculated by dividing the number of voters by the number of seats to be filled. For each party list the average vote for candidates was calculated by dividing the number of votes for the list by the number of candidates. Each party obtained as many seats as the number of times the constituency quota was contained in the party's average of votes per candidate. (3) If any seats remained vacant, they *all* went to the party with the highest average of votes per candidate. At the second and third stages of the election seats were allocated to those individual candidates on the party lists who had most votes.

This electoral system was intended to promote the establishment of a party in parliament with a majority of seats, or at least with a strong enough support to be able effectively to maintain a government in power, but it had certain defects. It was highly unproportional, especially in the third stage of allocation of seats to parties. Also it could result in the election of some candidates who had fewer votes than others not elected, since a list might have a high average of votes per candidate through attracting many votes for one or two popular candidates, and this might gain seats for other party candidates with relatively few votes, and fewer than some candidates in less successful parties.

Having largely surrendered their demand for PR, the Socialists suffered a disadvantage from the system they had helped to introduce, gaining only 11 per cent of the seats for 23 per cent of the votes. In 1924, however, the Alliance of the Left (Cartel des Gauches) gained 47 per cent of the seats for 38 per cent of the votes. In 1927 the Radicals persuaded the Socialists to support the reintroduction of single-member constituencies and two ballots, but once again the results were miscalculated. In 1928 it was the right and the right-centre who were better organised, and they gained sixty-seven of the seats which the left might have won if the electoral system had not been changed.

It was next the turn of the right to seek to manipulate the electoral system by establishing a relative majority system on British lines (one of the few occasions on which this was seriously considered), but a Bill to achieve this was rejected by the senate. Under the same electoral system as in 1928 it was the Socialists who were better organised in 1932, and they gained a majority through a shift of Radical voters to the left. Finally there was a victory for the left-wing Popular Front in the election of 1936, the last of the elections of the Third Republic.

Unlike most of the countries in Western Europe, France did not, either before or soon after the First World War, establish a system of proportional representation, and it was only in 1945 that a true form of PR was introduced for the first time. The municipal elections of that year showed that the Socialist and Communist parties were now much stronger than they had been before the war, and much stronger also than any party of the centre or right. There had for a long time been a demand within the Socialist and Communist parties and in the labour movement generally for the establishment of PR, on grounds of both principles and expediency. The provisional government formed at the end of the war sought to encourage the creation of a few large, stable and well-disciplined parties which would act responsibly and sustain an effective government in power, but also to achieve a fair and accurate representation of political opinion in parliament, which would be a source of strength to any government which reflected that opinion, and confer 'legitimacy' on the new regime. This last consideration provided an inducement for parties of the centre and right as well as of the left to accept a proportional system for the election of a constituent assembly.

The electoral law of 1945 provided for a rigid party-list system of PR. The distribution of seats took place at the constituency level only, most of the constituencies being individual departments, and it took place in two stages in accordance with the D'Hondt/Hagenbach-Bischoff system. The Hare quota was used at the first stage of the count, and the D'Hondt divisor method at the second. This system favoured the larger parties, which were the parties of the left, and it was particularly favourable to those parties in the smaller constituencies.

In April 1946 the Socialists proposed that in addition to the seats won in the constituencies each eligible party should be entitled to the allocation of additional seats on the basis of proportionality at the national level. This was to be achieved by the application of the D'Hondt/ Hagenbach-Bischoff method (with Hare quota) to the votes and seats of the parties in the nation as a whole. However, the proposed electoral system was defeated in a referendum in May 1946. It was a provision in the proposals which confined candidatures to party nominees, offering no choice between individual candidates, which aroused most opposition from the centre and the right.

The Radicals and parties on the left now agreed on a new formula which was accepted. Electors were still permitted to vote for only one list (that is, no *panachage* was permitted), but they could vote for candidates on the list in order of preference. However, the preferences were not to be taken into account unless half the electors in the constituency had varied the order on the list, and this was so seldom the case that electors had virtually no influence on the order of the candidates on the lists. The attempt to achieve proportionality at the national as well as the constituency level was abandoned. Only one election was held under this system, that of 1 November 1946, when a reasonably good correspondence between votes and seats was achieved.

In 1947 General de Gaulle formed a party of his supporters, the Rassemblement du Peuple Francais, and politicians of the centre became alarmed at the prospect of advances being made by this party on the right and the Communists on the left, both regarded as hostile to the parliamentary system of government. An electoral system was therefore devised to operate to the disadvantage of these two parties. This involved, in effect, the application of two separate electoral systems, one for the Paris region where the Gaullists and Communists were strong, and one for the provinces where they were weaker. In the Paris region there was applied one of the electoral systems which favours the smallest parties to the greatest extent, which was the Hare quota system with remaining seats allocated on the basis of the 'largest remainders'. For the provinces, the proportional system previously in existence was partly retained, but subject to certain far-reaching modifications. First it was provided that if any party list, or any alliance of party lists, succeeded in gaining an absolute majority of votes in a constituency, then the list or alliance should be awarded *all* the seats in that constituency. Secondly, the right to form alliances was restricted to 'national' parties, which were defined as those which submitted lists in at least thirty constituencies. Thirdly, each list must contain as many candidates as there were seats to be filled in the constituency. Fourthly, if no party or alliance had an absolute majority of votes in a constituency, then the seats were to be allocated to party lists and alliances by application of the D'Hondt system; and the allocation of seats to lists within an alliance was also to be by the D'Hondt system.

This electoral system gave a great advantage to those parties which formed alliances, or in other words to those parties of the centre who had collaborated to devise it, and which intended to collaborate in the formation of alliances. It was easier for an alliance than for a single party to achieve an absolute majority of votes in a constituency and thus gain all the seats; and even where there was no absolute majority the D'Hondt system gave an advantage to larger parties and alliances.

In the elections of June 1951, the results in the Paris area were reasonably proportional, which meant that the strength of the Gaullists and Communists in that area gave neither of those parties an advantage over the rest. In the provinces, however, the electoral system discriminated against the Communists and the Gaullists, and how it did so may be demonstrated by certain examples (cited by Cotteret and Emeri) in Tables 16.1 and 16.2.

Table 16.1   *Election in Ariège, June 1951*

	Percentage of votes	Number of seats
Allied lists		
Socialists	30·0	2
Radical Socialists	25·0	1
MRP	8·6	—
Total	63·6	3
Separate lists		
Communists	30·0	—
Gaullists	6·4	—

In Table 16.1 the allied lists gained together an absolute majority of votes, and were therefore allocated all the seats. By application of the D'Hondt method to the parties within the alliance, the Socialists were allocated two of the seats, and the Radical Socialists were allocated one. Although the Communists had about as many votes as the Socialists and more than the Radical Socialists, they obtained no seat.

To show how the system worked when there was no absolute majority for a list or an alliance, an example is provided in Table 16.2 from Bouchés-du-Rhône, in a constituency where four seats were to be allocated. By application of the D'Hondt system, two seats were allocated to the allied lists, and two to the Communists. Within the allied lists, the D'Hondt system allocated one seat to the Socialists and one to the Radical Socialists. Thus the Radical Socialists gained a seat with fewer votes than the Gaullists, who gained none.

There were many other anomalous results in this election, which

Table 16.2   *Election in Bouchés-du-Rhône, June 1951*

	Number of votes	Number of seats
Allied lists		
Socialists	31,819	1
Radical Socialists	17,617	1
MRP	13,533	—
Total	62,969	2
Separate lists		
Communists	47,235	2
Gaullists	18,985	—

worked out according to the plans of the centre parties but could hardly be regarded as other than fraudulent. If the 1946 electoral system had been retained, and if the voting pattern had been the same as in 1951, the Communists would have gained 169 seats and the Gaullists 133, but instead they gained only 97 and 107 respectively. Only in one constituency did a single party list gain an absolute majority of votes, and therefore receive all the seats, but alliances (of centre parties) achieved this result in thirty-nine constituencies. Parties of the centre gained 51 per cent of the votes, but 62·5 per cent of the seats.

Although the electoral system was designed to protect parliament from 'anti-system' parties, its manifest unfairness had the effect of reducing confidence in parliament and the politicians, and even the beneficiaries of the system became alarmed at the results. Further electoral reform was therefore in the air, but it was not achieved before the government, as a result of successive defeats in parliament, exercised its right to dissolve parliament and hold another general election. For this election the same electoral system had to be used again. This time it was the *Poujadistes* who succeeded in exploiting the system to the greatest extent, by fielding notionally separate parties of shopkeepers, peasants and consumers respectively, spreading the net to catch as many votes as possible, and filling party lists with straw candidates to ensure that the parties would be represented in at least thirty constituencies to gain recognition as 'national' parties entitled to form alliances among themselves. The lists then formed alliances in about half the constituencies.

General de Gaulle had hitherto taken an unfavourable view of majority electoral systems in single-member constituencies. He did not consider that in the interwar period they had provided the clear-cut results of which they were supposed to be capable. In 1950 he declared in a press conference that the only types of election which were 'frank and honest' were those achieved by means of party lists, and all the other types were fakes or swindles (*truquages*). Yet when he was returned to power in 1958 the electoral system which he established by a decree in October of that year was the same as that which was established by Louis-Napoleon after his *coup d'état* in December 1851; and for the next ten years this system served de Gaulle's purpose very well. This was the two-ballot system in single-member constituencies. A modification introduced by de Gaulle, in order to discourage frivolous candidatures, was that candidates who failed to secure 5 per cent of the votes were disqualified from standing at a second ballot, forfeited their deposit, and had to reimburse certain election expenses to the state. No new candidates were permitted at the second ballot.

At the election of 1958, under the new electoral system, only 9 per cent of the seats were filled at the first ballot, which was much fewer than in any election during the Third Republic. The most striking result was that the Gaullists, with 20 per cent of the votes, gained more than 40 per cent of the seats, while the Communists, with 19 per cent of the votes, gained only 2 per cent of the seats. This was the consequence of votes being transferred at the second ballot, which left the Communists isolated without support. In 1962, after de Gaulle had won a referendum on the issue that the president of the Republic should be elected directly by the people, the Gaullists won an even greater victory in the election of that year, with the Communists again the chief party to suffer. The trend in favour of the Gaullists continued in the elections of 1967 and 1968. In 1968 the Communists gained 20 per cent of the votes but only 7 per cent of the seats, while the Gaullists achieved 70 per cent of the seats with only 44 per cent of the votes.

The advantage for the Gaullists under this electoral system lay in the close collaboration which now existed between the parties which supported de Gaulle, so that collectively they benefited much more than other parties at the second ballot. It was the operation of the system in practice, rather than the nature of the regulations, which was significantly to the advantage of the Gaullists. The allied parties commonly agreed upon a single candidate to represent them in each constituency.

However, by 1973, other new alliances and alignments were also emerging, particularly an electoral agreement, for the first time since 1934, between the Socialists and the Communists. The representation of the Gaullists and their supporters fell from over 72 per cent of the seats in 1968 to less than 55 per cent in 1973. The Communists, with 14·9 per cent of the votes, succeeded in obtaining exactly the same share of the seats, and the left-wing alliance as a whole gained about 36 per cent of the seats from 46 per cent of the votes. Events were beginning to suggest that the Gaullists might not continue to enjoy the main benefits of the existing electoral system, nor remain much longer in office.

In 1966 Etienne Weill-Raynal, a member of the executive committee of the Socialist Party, had put forward proposals for proportional representation based on single-member constituencies, with the allocation of additional seats to achieve proportionality at the national level. This was different from the PR system which had existed between 1945 and 1951, when party lists were submitted and proportionality determined at the constituency level only. Weill-Raynal pointed out that his proposals were similar to those made by Léon Blum as early as 1926, and they were in the main adopted by a convention of the Socialist Party which was held at Suresnes in March 1972.

It was proposed that to compensate for disproportionality arising out of elections by relative majority in single-member constituencies, proportionality should be achieved successively at the levels of the regions and the nation as a whole. There were to be 321 single-member constituency seats, 152 additional regional seats, and 70 additional national seats, the additional seats to be allocated to parties by means of a quota and the method of the largest remainder. The additional seats were to be allocated to constituencies in accordance with the percentage share of the total vote which each party had gained in its constituencies. Since departments and constituencies varied considerably in size, it was provided that small constituencies should be assured of a minimum number of constituency seats. Since, on the other hand, large departments would then be liable to have relatively fewer seats in terms of population, it was also provided that there should be a limit on the number of additional seats which each department might be awarded. These provisions were a departure from true proportionality, and so also was another provision that to share in the allocation of additional seats a party must have gained at least 5 per cent of the national vote.

At least as early as 1966 the Communist Party had also adopted PR as part of their own party programme, and as an element in any joint programme which parties of the left might agree to support. This did in fact become part of the common programme when the electoral agreement was formed between the Socialists and the Communists for the election of 1973.

The left were not, however, the only advocates of PR. This had traditionally been a policy of the radical Mouvement Républicain Populaire until the establishment of the Fifth Republic. In 1957 Valéry Giscard d'Estaing had supported a Bill to establish PR on the lines of the German system, and in October 1972 a union of parties of the centre approved a report by Senator Barrachin which recommended the adoption of such a system. The parties of the centre had a common interest in preventing the unduly inflated representation which the majority system was liable to give to major parties, including those of the extreme right or the extreme left. The Communist Party, for their part, appeared to have surrendered, for the time being at least, their more remote prospects of achieving the totality of power, and had opted instead for a better prospect of achieving a share of it. For the attainment of electoral reform, however, it was necessary first that the left or centre should be able, under the existing electoral system, to achieve a victory over the Gaullists and their allies, and this they did not succeed in doing in 1973 or 1978.

France is a conspicuous example of a country in which the possibilities of 'electoral engineering' have been fully realised, and in which the electoral system has been especially prone to manipulation by parties in power. This has sometimes been done in the supposed interest of safe-guarding the parliamentary system against anti-democratic or 'anti-system' parties, but the constant manipulation of the electoral system has itself been liable to bring discredit upon parliament as a body which purports to be representative.

There is little evidence on the other hand that it is the electoral system which has mainly determined the nature of the party and political system. During the period between 1831 and 1881 the two-ballot system worked very much as if it were a one-ballot system, with only a small minority of results decided at a second ballot, so that for half a century it functioned in the manner of a relative majority system. But there was no tendency then for a two-party system to emerge. When universal manhood suffrage increased the electorate from a quarter of a million to 8 million voters there was no party in existence which could at that time cope with the task of organisation which the new mass electorate required. After the establishment of the Third Republic the various conservative and republican parties were much divided among themselves, and it was only about the turn of the century that mass party organisation began to emerge.

Moreover there was a strong element of localism in French politics which had a long tradition behind it and which even in the twentieth century remained an abiding characteristic. The concentration of power, wealth and administration in Paris had been, and continued to be, counteracted by particularism in the provinces. Parties still tended to be groups of deputies in the assembly rather than cohesive national organisa-tions. There was much mobility of membership between parties as deputies decided their alignment on constantly changing issues of current politics.

Since in France there is no 'stable' two-party system which might be sacrificed by electoral reform, the case is all the stronger for establishing a 'stable' electoral system. The most stable system is likely to be one which is manifestly fair and achieves a high degree of correspondence between votes and seats. There appears in recent years to have been growing support from several political parties for an electoral system of this kind.

REFERENCES: CHAPTER 16

Successive changes in the French electoral system are fully described by Peter Campbell in *French Electoral Systems and Elections since 1789*, and particular attention is given to the French experience by Jean-Marie Cotteret and Claude Emeri in *Les systèmes électoraux*. Developments during the last twenty years or so are examined by J. R. Fears in *Political Parties and Elections in the French Fifth Republic*. Recent movements in favour of proportional representation in France were discussed by Etienne Weill-Raynal in the *Revue politique et parlementaire*, in articles entitled 'La représentation nationale proportionnelle avec scrutin individuel' (1966), and 'La réforme electorale, enjeu des prochaines élections?' (1973).

PART SIX
The United Kingdom and Ireland

17

The United Kingdom

In the United Kingdom, unlike all other countries in Western Europe apart from the Swiss Republic, the constitutional balance of power between Crown and parliament had already by the beginning of the nineteenth century been settled decisively in favour of parliament. However, the French revolution and the Napoleonic wars and their aftermath were periods in which far-reaching economic changes were taking place in Britain, and these were accompanied by social upheaval and political unrest. At this time existing political institutions came under criticism and attack, and although there was little support for sweeping and radical measures there was a mounting demand for parliamentary reform. It was in response to this popular demand that a Whig government introduced the Reform Bill which was passed in 1832.

What this Act chiefly accomplished was to remove some notorious abuses and anomalies by abolishing a number of 'rotten boroughs' in which members of parliament were nominated by some landed magnate, and a start was made at the same time with several other parliamentary reforms. Of the changes made in the 'age of reform' between 1832 and 1885 there were four of particular importance: an extension of the franchise by stages in 1832, 1867 and 1884; the registration from 1832 onwards of those who were entitled to vote; changes in the designation of constituencies and the distribution of seats, to correspond more closely with the distribution of population; and measures to check the corruption in elections which tended to nullify the representative character of parliament. It took more than fifty years to complete the transformation of parliament from a body which was largely under the control of aristocrats and wealthy landowners into one which represented most of the adult male population. It is in the light of these changes that one should consider the nature and effects of the electoral system which was used.

In many respects, the legislation of 1883 to 1885 marked a turning-point in the electoral history of the United Kingdom. After this, representation was placed on a much fairer basis, and the outcome of elections was much more a reflection of the will of the electorate, and much less the result of influence and manipulation by the powerful few. The boroughs and the southern counties were no longer grossly over-represented; the urban and industrial areas were no longer grossly under-represented; corruption in elections was at last brought under control; and the influence of landed magnates on the election of members was greatly reduced. Until this time the electoral system, in the sense of how seats were allocated to votes, was of relatively minor importance, since the votes themselves could scarcely be regarded as a true expression of the opinions of the electorate.

The first extension of the franchise in 1832 increased the electorate by 49 per cent in both boroughs and counties. In the counties the chief qualification continued to be the possession of a 40-shilling freehold, but as a concession to the landed interest the franchise was extended also to certain categories of copyholders, leaseholders and tenants. In the boroughs, the qualifications for the franchise had varied considerably from one borough to another. Ancient franchises were continued (except in the case of freemen, only for the lifetime of those who possessed them), but a new franchise applicable to all boroughs was introduced in the form of a £10 household franchise, that is, a voting right for all those who occupied a building to the value of £10 per annum.

In 1867 the suffrage was extended to citizens in boroughs who were householders, regardless of the value of the house, and this for the first time enfranchised the working classes in the boroughs, but while the electorate was increased by 88 per cent overall, it was increased by 134 per cent in the boroughs and only 45 per cent in the counties.

In 1884 there was at last introduced a uniform qualification in the form of the household suffrage, which removed the great anomalies which had often existed on either side of a boundary between borough and county. This measure increased the electorate by 162 per cent in the counties, 11 per cent in the boroughs and 67 per cent overall. The increases in the electorate which resulted from each successive extension of the franchise were as indicated by the figures in Table 17.1.

Table 17.1 *UK electorate as a percentage of the population, 1831–86*

1831	1·8%
1833	2·7%
1869	6·4%
1886	12·1%

The representation introduced in Simon de Montfort's parliament in 1265 was based on two-member constituencies in counties and boroughs, and in England in 1831 the two-member constituencies were still almost universal. There were some exceptions, since four members each were returned by London, Yorkshire and the borough of Weymouth and Morecombe Regis, and only one member each from the boroughs of Abingdon, Banbury, Bewdley, Higham Ferrers and Monmouth; but these seventeen seats accounted for less than 4 per cent of those in England, and all the rest were from two-member constituencies. It was quite otherwise in the countries of the 'Celtic fringe'. In Ireland, all the boroughs except Dublin and Cork had each since 1800 been represented by one member only, making thirty-two single-member seats out of one hundred. In Wales, all counties and boroughs alike had throughout the eighteenth century been represented by only one member each. In Scotland, not only had each constituency been represented by only one member since 1707, but some shires did not even have one, since three pairs of shires each shared one member between them, alternating from one shire to the other in successive elections. However, in the United Kingdom as a whole in 1831 single-member constituencies accounted for only 107 out of 758 seats, or little more than 16 per cent of all seats. Elections were by relative majority, and in the multi-member constituencies this was the 'block vote' system.

In the redistribution of 1831 the number of single-member constituencies in Ireland and Wales was slightly reduced, but those in England were increased by fifty-one, and those in Scotland were also increased. However, single-member constituencies, now 145 in number in the United Kingdom, still accounted for only 22 per cent of the total number of seats. On the other hand some *county* constituencies with large populations were allocated more than two seats in multi-member constituencies – Yorkshire received two more seats, and between 1832 and 1885 there were seven counties with three seats each, including Berkshire, Buckinghamshire, Cambridgeshire, Dorsetshire, Herefordshire, Hertfordshire and Oxfordshire.

In the redistribution of 1867–8 there was a net addition of twenty-six single-member constituencies in the United Kingdom, but this still did not greatly alter the balance in favour of such seats – they still accounted for little more than a quarter of the total number of 660 seats at that time. In the same redistribution, the number of three-member constituencies was increased by allocating one additional seat each to the heavily populated *cities* of Birmingham, Leeds, Liverpool, Manchester and Glasgow.

It was only in 1885 that a great and decisive change was made in favour of single-member constituencies. After the redistribution of that year there survived (apart from the universities) only twenty-four constituencies which had two members each, and none which had more than two members. (Only twelve of these twenty-four constituencies continued to have two members between 1918 and 1948.) With the exception of these two-member constituencies, all counties and boroughs were in 1885 split up into as many divisions as they had been allotted seats, and each division returned one member of parliament.

The conservative (Whig and Tory) sentiment had hitherto been in favour of representation of communities and interests rather than a numerically determined fraction of the population, yet in 1885 it was the Conservatives who favoured single-member constituencies as a system from which they could hope to secure greater representation for minorities than was likely under the 'block vote' system in two-member or multi-member constituencies. The great extension of the suffrage in 1884 had made it seem urgent to secure some safeguard against the mass vote of the working class; the best safeguard appeared to the Tories at the time to be the adoption of numerous single-member constituencies; and it was on the understanding that redistribution would be based on such constituencies that the Tories in the House of Lords had withdrawn their opposition to the Reform Bill of 1884.

The preference for single-member constituencies in order that minorities might be better represented was well founded in view of the existing majority system of election. The majority system had itself, however, come under critcism. In 1831 a Tory member, W. M. Praed, protested that, while parliament had been trying to reconstruct the framework of representative government, that particular part of its machinery which regulated how the opinions of all classes of the community might be fairly represented in parliament had passed wholly unnoticed in the parliamentary debates. He proposed that in the seven counties which were to have three members each an elector should have only two votes. Lord Althorp opposed Praed's amendment on the grounds that past evidence did not suggest that minorities were inadequately represented in parliaments which had majority systems of election. Nevertheless, proposals in favour of the limited vote were later renewed by Lord John Russell in 1854 and 1860. He sought to counter-balance an extension of the franchise by this system of election so as to ensure representation for minorities in the three-member constituencies.

When the household suffrage was adopted for the boroughs in 1867, the limited vote system was introduced for all constituencies which had more than two members. This meant that in the five cities and seven counties which had three-member constituencies electors would be entitled to cast not more than two votes each; and in London, which had four seats, they could not cast more than three. But all these consti-tuencies together accounted for only 40 out of the 660 seats in parliament in 1868.

The limited vote did not, moreover, *guarantee* representation for a minority, or even for a majority, since the result depended on how many candidates stood on behalf of a party or group, and how the votes were distributed between them. A party could promote their own interest by accurately assessing the maximum number of candidates they should nominate, and by organising the votes of their supporters in such a way as to secure for each candidate the minimum number of votes necessary for his election. The Liberal Party 'caucus' in Birmingham were most successful in organising their elections in this manner, and no Conservative was elected from Birmingham between 1867 and 1885.

So far as electoral results are concerned, a scrutiny of the voting in the three-member constituencies other than Birmingham does not suggest that party organisation was often effective, or even consistently used to influence elections. In most of the three-member elections seats were fairly divided between the parties and manipulation was not much in evidence. Nevertheless, by 1885 the limited vote had a poor reputation, largely as a result of the Birmingham experience, and it now had few supporters. At this time there was more debate on proposals for pro-portional representation which had been the subject of much discussion after the publication, in 1859, of Thomas Hare's treatise on *The Election of Representatives, Parliamentary and Municipal,* and the whole-hearted support given to his proposals by John Stuart Mill, who said that they were 'among the very greatest improvements yet made in the theory and practice of government'.

To safeguard the representation of minorities Lord John Russell had proposed a redistribution of constituency seats and the limited vote, but Hare proposed the abolition of all constituency boundaries, and the use of the single transferable vote for the election of all members of parliament in a single constituency. The proposal of a single national constituency was one aspect of the proposal of the single transferable vote which came under the strongest attack from its critics, including Walter Bagehot, who regarded this as its fundamental defect, regardless of other details. However, as the idea of the single constituency was soon discarded, it is other criticisms by Bagehot which have had more enduring influence. Of these the most fundamental was that representa-tion was only one of the functions of parliament, and that in Bagehot's view a more important function, indeed the most important of all, was the choice of a government and its maintenance in power. Bagehot himself was undogmatic in his opinion that in this respect the existing system was satisfactory – he said that the best government was that which people thought was the best, and 'tried by this rule, the House of Commons does its appointing business well. It chooses rulers as we wish rulers to be chosen. If it did not, in a speaking and writing age, we should soon know.'

For both Hare and Mill the chief aim of the electoral system was that voters should be able to elect not merely mediocre party 'hacks', but members of the educated and intellectual 'elite' (a term which Mill used freely, but not of course in its modern pejorative sense); and their chief fear was that through the extension of the franchise irresistible power should pass to the uneducated masses and lead to disastrous class legislation. They saw the single transferable vote as a means of ensuring the representation of minorities, but the one minority whose representation they thought was vital was the minority of the educated elite. Hare would have been content to leave the franchise as it was at the time, which would have restricted the electorate to about one-sixth of the adult male population. Mill, on the other hand, favoured the extension of the franchise, but feared the consequences of working-class votes. He found a solution to this dilemma in Hare's electoral system, since it provided a vital safeguard for the educated minority, whose influence in parliament he expected to be greater than its numbers.

Both Mill and Hare took a highly unfavourable view of the role and influence of political parties, and for this reason the single transferable vote had for them a particular attraction in being a personal and not a party system of voting. Mill believed that electors should not vote for a candidate because of his party membership, or even the particular views which he held, but because of his superior capacity for making independent judgements based on knowledge and wisdom. Nevertheless, Mill foresaw the possibility that even with the single transferable vote electors might seek the election of members who would act in their own particular interest, and in parliament a majority of such members might exercise their power in an oppressive manner. He therefore advocated a system of plural voting in which extra votes would be given to electors with educational qualifications and attainments.

Bagehot agreed with Mill on the need for a governing elite, but for him, in the 'deferential society' which existed in England, this object was already attained, since electors habitually voted for their social superiors. Bagehot also took an opposite view about parties. Assuming that the main function of parliament was maintaining a government in power, he said 'we at once perceive that party is of its essence. There never was an election without a party . . . The House of Commons lies in a state of perpetual potential choice: at any moment it can choose a ruler and dismiss a ruler. And therefore party is inherent in it, it is bone of its bone, and breath of its breath.'

When Mill agreed to stand as a candidate for Westminster in the general election of 1865, he stood as an independent, and refused to commit himself to support any party or local interest, or any policies except those which he had himself publicly advocated. In parliament he proposed an amendment to the Reform Bill of 1867 which would have introduced STV, but withdrew it in the interest of ensuring that the Bill as a whole should be passed.

When the next Reform Bill was debated the movement in favour of STV was revived, and in 1884 the Proportional Representation Society was established under the chairmanship of Sir John Lubbock. However, in the face of the reluctance of the Tories in the House of Lords to accept the extension of the franchise, an understanding was reached between the Liberal and Tory leaders that seats should be redistributed in such a way as to separate the urban from the rural parts of county constituencies, so that rural Tory votes should not be swamped by urban Liberals. As already related, the means of achieving this involved the division of existing constituencies, and resulted in single-member representation in all except twenty-four of the constituencies. This excluded the possibility of the single transferable vote in multi-member constituencies, and in consequence Sir Robert Courtney, who was a strong supporter of STV, resigned from the Liberal government. For the next twenty years the movement for a reform of the electoral system made little headway.

After the turn of the century the advocacy of electoral reform was revived, partly through public interest in the adoption of PR in Belgium and subsequently in some other countries. A Royal Commission on Electoral Systems, appointed in 1909, submitted a report which rejected PR, including the single transferable vote, but recommended the adoption of the alternative vote. At this time, however, parliament and the nation were preoccupied with the constitutional crisis between the Commons and the Lords, and the Royal Commission's report was not even debated in the House of Commons. Neither its evidence nor its conclusions appear to have had much influence on public opinion.

During the First World War there was an accumulation of problems which made it necessary to consider some electoral changes, not only women's suffrage but also votes for servicemen, the state of the electoral register, and the unresolved issue of proportional representation. In August 1916, when Asquith was still prime minister, the speaker of the House of Commons, J. W. Lowther, agreed to convene a conference of members of both houses of parliament to make recommendations on electoral reforms. Among its numerous recommendations was one unanimously in favour of the single transferable vote system of election in all boroughs which elected three or more members, and the alternative vote system in single-member constituencies.

A Bill based on the recommendations of the speaker's conference was introduced, but Lloyd George, who was now prime minister, insisted that a decision not only on women's suffrage but also, in spite of the unanimous recommendation of the speaker's conference, on the electoral system, should be left to a free vote in the House of Commons. It seems that the leaders of both the Liberal and Conservative parties were at this time hostile to the conference's proposals on this subject. In view of the unanimous recommendation of the all-party conference some members of parliament, including F. E. Smith on the Conservative side and Ramsay Macdonald and Philip Snowden among Labour members, criticised the decision to leave the choice of electoral system to a free vote, and controversy on this point weakened confidence in the speaker's conferences as a means of achieving agreement on such issues.

In the Commons, at the committee stage of the Bill, the single transferable vote was rejected, and the alternative vote was accepted by a majority of one vote. The Lords subsequently rejected the alternative vote in favour of STV, and finally a compromise was reached when it was agreed to instruct the boundary commissioners to prepare a limited scheme which would apply STV for the election of 100 members. When the scheme was prepared it was opposed by practically every member who would have been personally affected by it, and this contributed largely to its rejection.

In succeeding years a campaign for the single transferable vote was continued, but in 1920 a Bill for its adoption was rejected in the Commons by 211 votes to 112. On this occasion more than 80 per cent of the Independent Liberals and Labour members voted in favour, and more than 80 per cent of the Conservatives against, but more than one-third of the Coalition Liberals were also against the measure. The Liberals had always been divided on the issue, and it was only in the general election of 1922 that proportional representation became for the first time part of the official policy of the Independent Liberal Party.

In May 1924, during the minority Labour government, a Bill for proportional representation was put forward by the Liberals, but Labour backbenchers resented a suggestion that Liberal support for the government might be reconsidered if they did not support this measure. Labour members refused to accept a recommendation by their own government that they should facilitate the passing of the Bill, and it was rejected by a majority of nearly two to one. On this occasion nearly three-quarters of the Labour vote was against the Bill, as well as 95 per cent of the Conservative vote. It seems that it was from about the time of the 1923 election that a majority of Labour members turned against proportional representation. Success at the polls, and the prospect of outright victory under the existing electoral system, were powerful reasons for changing their minds.

The next serious attempt to achieve electoral reform was made during the next minority Labour government of 1929 to 1931. Once again an objective of the Liberals was to secure electoral reform in return for their support of the Labour government, and once again there was resentment on the Labour side at having to pay this price for Liberal support. However, an all-party conference was convened, with the former speaker, Lowther, now Viscount Ullswater, as chairman, not the current speaker, Captain Fitzroy, but still commonly referred to as a speaker's conference. This conference found it impossible to reconcile divergent aims and opinions, and it ended without making any agreed recommendations.

The Ullswater Conference having terminated in the summer of 1930, the Liberals through Lloyd George still offered to maintain the government in power in return for a measure of electoral reform. However, the government would propose only the alternative vote and would not support PR, although the National Liberal Federation had just declared in favour of PR and had rejected the alternative vote even as a second-best solution. A Bill which included the alternative vote was passed in the Commons, only to be drastically altered by amendments in the Lords. Before any further consideration of the measure had taken place in the Commons the government had fallen, and that was the end of the Bill.

During the Second World War an accumulation of problems which affected the organisation of elections resulted in the establishment in 1943 of another speaker's conference. In the conference, proportional representation was rejected by 25 votes to 4, and the alternative vote by 20 votes to 5.

In 1945 the Labour Party received 62 per cent of the seats in parliament with 48 per cent of the votes, whereas in 1931, with 30 per cent of the votes, they had received fewer than 9 per cent of the seats. Their confidence that the electoral system would eventually operate to their advantage now proved to be justified. On other electoral matters measures were taken by the Labour government which aroused some controversy. During the recent speaker's conference it had been agreed that while a spouse should no longer be permitted to exercise an additional vote by virtue of any business vote for which her husband was qualified, neither the business vote itself nor the university vote should be abolished. Nevertheless, in the Representation of the People Bill of 1948, plural voting was abolished, and both the business vote and the university vote were swept aside. These and other alleged breaches of interparty agreements raised again, as in 1918, the question whether the speaker's conferences could be relied upon to resolve disagreements between parties on matters relating to electoral reform.

In 1948 single-member constituencies, which had become the norm since 1885, at last became the sole type of constituency. The problem of redistribution of constituencies had also become urgent in view of past population changes, and in 1944 the solution was to establish permanent boundary commissions. At first the commissions were under instruction to review the constituency boundaries every three to seven years, but in time it was felt that frequent changes in constituencies caused confusion, prevented continuity of representation and made it necessary both to rearrange party political organisations at constituency level, and to alter the local administration of elections. By an Act of 1958 the maximum time-limit between reviews of boundaries was extended to fifteen years, but this raised other difficulties. Shifts in population, especially out of city centres into suburban or largely rural areas, worked at this time to the disadvantage of the Conservatives, and the longer the delay between each redistribution the greater was their disadvantage likely to be.

In 1884–5 the Conservatives had favoured single-member constituencies for the sake of fairer representation under the relative majority system, but over the years since 1884 there were many occasions on which considerable discrepancies had appeared in the election results between the votes obtained by the parties and the seats they had won. In many elections, both before the First World War and in the interwar period, so many seats were uncontested that it is difficult to assess what the electoral support for each party was. Since the Second World War, however, when uncontested seats have been negligible in number, there have clearly been great discrepancies between votes and seats. The most conspicuous anomalies arose in 1974, when in the two elections of that year the Liberals obtained 19·3 and 18·3 per cent of the votes but only 2·2 and 2·0 per cent respectively of the seats.

In view of the obvious discrepancies between votes and seats, greater emphasis has been placed by supporters of the existing electoral system on the fact that single-member constituencies make possible an intimate and valuable relationship between a member and his constituents, since it makes the member responsible for finding remedies for their grievances and protecting their interests whatever their views or political affiliations may be. There is little doubt that for members themselves this is a salutary function, though it may make excessive demands on their time and energy. Whether the monopoly enjoyed in this respect by a single member in each constituency is equally to the advantage of the constituents themselves is more open to question. Also, the view of a member as essentially a servant of his constituents is at variance with the view, expounded much earlier by Edmund Burke, that he should be essentially a servant of the nation as a whole, regardless of local interests. On an empirical level, it may be questioned whether the aggregate results achieved by members through their action on behalf of individual constituents can bear comparison with the results they achieve by the way they vote in parliament, and whether the benefits of the personal relationship can justify the misrepresentation in parliament of the views of the electorate.

However, the chief argument in favour of the relative majority system has been that while anomalies in representation may be deplored the system performs the vital function of returning a party with a solid majority of seats in parliament, and therefore promotes strong and stable government. Against this it may be pointed out that on no occasion after 1906 has any party, other than a coalition, secured a majority of the *votes* which were cast, and on many occasions solid party majorities did not emerge. The minority Labour governments of the interwar years are cases in point. Since the Second World War, in five general elections out of eleven (1950, 1951, 1964 and February and October 1974) the governing party held fewer than 51 per cent of the seats in parliament, and on one occasion (February 1974) fewer than 48 per cent. On two occasions (1951 and February 1974) the party which formed the government had more seats but fewer votes than the main opposition party. On two occasions (February and October 1974) the governing party had fewer than 40 per cent of the votes cast.

Apart from the failure of the electoral system to achieve its intended purpose, it has recently been maintained that the two-party system, with each party alternating in power, has led in recent years in the United Kingdom to 'adversary politics' which threaten the stability and continuity of government. Consensus on major issues of policy no longer exists, governments tend increasingly to reverse the policies of their predecessors, and policies and reforms requiring long periods for their fulfilment are neglected in favour of short-term expedients.

In spite of earlier unsuccessful attempts to introduce a reform of the electoral system, a speaker's conference had once more been appointed in 1965 to consider, among other things, the 'methods of election, with particular reference to preferential voting'. In 1968 the conference recommended by 19 votes to 1 against any change in the existing system. In 1975, concern over the more recent working of the electoral system led to the convening by the Hansard Society of a Commission on Electoral Reform, whose report advocated the adoption of an 'additional member system', or else the single transferable vote. This report was followed by the formation of the National Committee for Electoral Reform under the chairmanship of Lord Harlech. Pressure groups favouring electoral reform were also established within each of the main political parties. The proposal of the 'additional member system' was intended to combine the merits of personal relationships in single-member constituencies with those of proportional representation of parties.

Britain's membership of the European Community has raised questions of electoral systems in a different form. For elections to the European assembly, after the first direct elections in 1979, it has been agreed in the assembly that a common system of election should be adopted by all member nations for subsequent elections. If this is accomplished, it does not seem likely that the simple majority system which, among the EEC nations, is used only in the United Kingdom, will be the one which will be adopted. The introduction of a different system for the European assembly could eventually reinforce demands for the adoption of a different system in the United Kingdom itself.

REFERENCES: CHAPTER 17

A standard work on electoral reforms in Britain in the nineteenth century is Charles

Seymour, *Electoral Reform in England and Wales*. The extent and significance of the earlier changes are examined by Norman Gash in *Politics in the Age of Peel*. The reforms proposed and those achieved after the return of a Liberal government in 1906 are the subject of *Electoral Reform in War and Peace, 1906–1918*, by Martin Pugh. For developments after the First World War the authority is David Butler, in *The Electoral System in Britain, 1918–1951*. The consequences of the electoral system are discussed by Peter Pulzer in *Political Representation and Elections in Britain*. For information on the structure of constituencies and election results before the Reform Acts one may consult Henry Stooke Smith's *The Parliaments of England from 1715 to 1847*; and for the period after 1832 the series of *British Parliamentary Election Results*, edited by F. W. S. Craig.

18

The Republic of Ireland

During the Napoleonic wars an organisation called the United Irish Society sought to achieve a politically separate and Catholic Ireland, and in 1798 there was an ill-organised rebellion against the British government, which was easily put down. This led to the suppression of the Irish parliament by the Act of Union in 1800, which provided that Irish constituencies should return 100 members to the House of Commons in the UK parliament.

Irish nationalism, having first made an impact in the rebellion of 1798, was thereafter regarded by the ruling classes in Britain with as much revulsion as revolutionary socialism, but for most of the nineteenth century nationalist movements were ineffectual, and even the revolutionary year of 1848 produced only a feeble demonstration. There was no effective organisation until the Fenian Brotherhood, alternatively known as the Irish Republican Brotherhood, was established in 1867. This movement had resort to conspiracy and violence, and benefited from the training in arms of those of its members who had previously served in the British armed forces. In 1867 the Brotherhood provided the first of the martyrs to the cause of Irish nationalism whose fate turned sentiments of patriotism into passion and fanaticism; and the influence of the Brotherhood was eventually decisive in the events of 1916–22.

The Irish Party in the House of Commons made its presence felt under the leadership of Charles Parnell from 1877 to 1890, but Home Rule Bills were defeated in 1886 and 1893, and after 1900 the party was less forceful under the leadership of John Redmond. In 1905 Arthur Griffith was mainly responsible for the foundation of the Sinn Fein ('Ourselves Alone') Party, which sought home rule for Ireland but was not at first republican, and favoured a loose association with England under the monarchy. However, a Home Rule Bill of 1914 failed to complete its progress before the outbreak of the First World War, which caused the settlement of the issue to be postponed.

The Easter Rebellion of 1916, organised by the Irish Republican Brotherhood, owed its failure partly to the seizure by the British navy of a consignment of arms on its way from Germany, and partly to differences among the movements which supported the rising. However, the execution of the leaders fanned the flames of rebellion, whose success resulted at last in the passing of the Government of Ireland Act of 1920, the 'Treaty' of 1921, and the adoption of an Irish constitution by an Irish parliament in 1922.

The historical background of the nationalist movement and of the rebellion had enduring consequences for Irish politics and parliamentary affairs after independence was obtained. There had been two opposing tendencies in the nationalist movement, one which sought to achieve constitutionally the establishment of an independent Irish parliament, and another which, as a result of frustrations experienced in the UK parliament, resorted to extra-parliamentary action and to violence. After partition, and the establishment of a separate parliament and administration in the north, the tendency to violence survived.

Events during the rebellion itself also had an enduring effect on the subsequent course of Irish politics. After the Easter Rising the Sinn Fein Party accepted the aims of the republicans and assumed the leadership of the nationalist movement, with de Valera elected president in July 1917, and with armed support from the Irish Volunteers who had been formed in 1913. The Irish Parliamentary Party was extinguished in the UK general election of 1918, and in that election the Sinn Fein Party swept the board in southern Ireland. The elected Sinn Fein members met as a separate parliament in January 1919, forming the first Dáil Éireann, or Parliament of Ireland, and they 'unilaterally' established an independent Irish government.

Hostilities between the Irish 'rebels' and the British forces followed. The Government of Ireland Act of 1920 established separate parliaments in southern and northern Ireland, and in the general election held under that Act in May 1921 all seats in the south were uncontested and gained by the Sinn Fein Party. A month later hostilities were suspended, negotiations were begun between Irish representatives and the British government, and on 6 December 1921 the 'Treaty' was signed. This provided that southern Ireland should have the status of a dominion under the British Crown (to which members of the Irish parliament would be bound by oath), reserving certain defence and port facilities for the British government.

This caused a split in the Sinn Fein into 'pro-Treaty' and 'anti-Treaty' parties, the first accepting and the second rejecting allegiance to the British Crown and membership of the British Commonwealth. The pro-Treaty party formed the Cumann na nGaedheal (Irish Association) in 1923, and in 1933 joined with a Centre Party and a right-wing Army

Comrades Association to form the Fine Gael (United Ireland) Party. Opponents of the Treaty, led by de Valera, formed the Fianna Fáil (Soldiers of Destiny) Party in 1926. Although in 1933 a Fianna Fáil government abolished the oath by members of the Irish parliament to the British Crown, and although in 1949 a Fine Gael government established the Irish Republic and took southern Ireland out of the British Commonwealth, so that the original causes of dispute hardly continued to exist, these two parties have ever since maintained their rivalry, and continued to be the main contenders for power in the Irish parliament.

One provision of the 1920 Government of Ireland Act which caused little discussion and virtually no opposition in southern Ireland was that elections to the parliaments in both the north and the south should be 'according to the principles of proportional representation, each elector having one transferable vote'. The acceptance of PR in southern Ireland is largely attributable to a visit paid to Dublin in 1911 by Lord Courtney of Penwith, president of the British Proportional Representation Society. He advocated PR as an aid to the solution of the home rule problem, since it would ensure representation of the Protestant minority. Arthur Griffith, founder of the Sinn Fein Party, accepted this both in principle and as a means of conciliating the Protestants. The Proportional Representation Society of Ireland was formed, with Griffith as one of its founder members, and by 1914 the society had gained considerable support, from nationalists and members of the Protestant community alike. Supporters also included James Connolly, the socialist and trade union leader. As a result of pressure from these quarters an element of proportional representation was included in the abortive Home Rule Bill of 1914.

In the truce between the British forces and the Sinn Fein after the general election of 1921, Arthur Griffith was chairman of the Irish delegates who negotiated the 'Treaty'. During the negotiations Griffith gave an assurance to southern Unionists that to ensure their fair share of representation in the Dáil the system of election would be PR by the single transferable vote, and PR was in fact prescribed in the 1922 constitution of the Irish Free State. The electoral system was not one of the provisions of the settlement over which there was any dispute in the 'troubles' which followed between the southern Irish supporters and opponents of the 'Treaty'.

In assessing the working of the electoral system in southern Ireland it is necessary to regard the elections for the first three Dáils as special cases. The first, in 1918, was elected by the 'first past the post' system under the UK Representation of the People Act of 1918. The second was elected in May 1921 under the Government of Ireland Act of 1920, which prescribed PR by the single transferable vote, but in the south not one of the 124 seats was contested, and in each of them a Sinn Fein candidate was returned unopposed. In the 'Pact Election' of May 1922 it was agreed that to avoid the threat of violence the parliamentary factions for and against the 'Treaty' should put up numbers of candidates in the same proportion as their membership of the previous Dáil.

Other candidates also stood for election, however, and since most of these supported the 'Treaty' de Valera and his followers complained that they had been deceived, and refused to take their seats in the Dáil. The 'anti-Treaty' followers of de Valera stood for election as Republicans in the 1923 election, but again their elected candidates refused to take their seats. It was only after de Valera formed the Fianna Fáil Party in 1926, and after the subsequent general election in 1927, that the de Valera party took their seats in the Dáil for the first time since 1922.

Unlike the experience in other countries which have adopted PR, the party system which has prevailed in southern Ireland was created almost entirely after the adoption of PR, and was not inherited from the past. There have been several parties other than the two main contenders, but none strong enough to make an effective challenge for power.

The party system after independence reflected the absence of any effective socialist movement, partly because of the absence of any large labour force in industry, and partly because of the prevalence of a rural community of peasant proprietors influenced by a socially conservative priesthood. The Labour Party have frequently succeeded in gaining more than 10 per cent of the seats, but they have had limited support even from the working-class section of the community, and have never come within sight of power except as a junior member of an alliance with one of the major parties.

A Farmers' Party returned several members between 1922 and 1932, and as many as 15 members out of 153 in 1923, but they never gained as many as 10 per cent of the seats in the Dáil. The party's cohesion and effectiveness were diminished by the diversity of farming interests in different parts of the country.

The Clann na Poblachta, or Republican Party, contested elections between 1948 and 1965, gaining ten seats in 1948 but very few thereafter. Their main achievement was to help Fine Gael in 1948 to form a coalition government for the first time in the history of the independent Irish state, and to end in this way the monopoly of power which Fianna Fáil had exercised for the previous seventeen years. However, a campaign by Clann na Poblachta for an end to partition had no success, their social policies ran into opposition from the Catholic Church, and support for the party rapidly diminished.

The Clann na Talmhan (Party of the Land) represented chiefly small farmers in the west, and gained 14 seats out of 138 in 1943, but only a dwindling number thereafter until their last member was elected in 1961.

From 1923 until the eve of the general election of 1977 there were seventeen general elections. The average duration of a parliament was therefore some three years and two months. However, two distinct periods can be distinguished in which the frequency of elections varied. Between 1923 and 1944 the Dáil was prematurely dissolved within less than two years of its election on four occasions (1927, 1933, 1938 and 1944) because of the lack of an effective government majority. During this period the average duration of a parliament was two years and seven months. After 1944 no parliament was dissolved within two years, and the average duration of a parliament was three years and eight months.

The increasing stability of government which this suggests was achieved in spite of fears that PR might lead to an increasing proliferation of parties. On the contrary, the political scene was dominated throughout the period by the two main political parties which became Fine Gael and Fianna Fáil, and if one adds the seats of the Labour Party, as the third of the three main parties, the share of these three together in the fifty years after 1927 averaged just over 90 per cent of the seats, and from 1965 onwards did not fall below 97·8 per cent.

Nevertheless it has frequently not been possible for a single party to form a government supported by an absolute majority of votes in the Dáil. Only seven of the eighteen general elections from 1923 onwards produced results which made the formation of a majority government possible. In February 1932 Fianna Fáil for the first time gained more seats than the 'pro-Treaty' party (at that time Cumann na nGaedheal), but had only a minority of all seats, and de Valera had to rely on Labour Party support. He soon sought a dissolution of parliament, and in the January 1933 election he gained a bare majority. In July 1937 Fianna Fáil won exactly half the seats, parliament was again prematurely dissolved, and in June 1938 the party once again obtained an absolute majority of seats. In 1943 Fianna Fáil gained just under half the seats, once more parliament was prematurely dissolved, and yet again an absolute majority was gained by the party in the subsequent election of May 1944.

These difficulties in gaining a majority explain why de Valera came to form an unfavourable opinion of the STV system of election. Yet the party obtained under that system an absolute majority of seats not only on the three occasions mentioned but also subsequently in the general elections of 1957, 1965 (if the speaker is not counted), 1969 and 1977 – indeed, in four out of the last six general elections.

As regards the experience of coalitions, Cumann na nGaedheal formed a government in September 1927 which did not have an outright majority but was maintained in power through a formal agreement with the Farmers' Party. Although the Farmers were not represented in the government this could be regarded as a sort of coalition. Fine Gael in 1948 formed a coalition with all parties other than Fianna Fáil, in 1954 with Labour and Clann na Talmhan, and in 1973 with Labour.

Single-party minority governments account for the remainder of the period since 1927, but from 1944 until the general election of 1977 only one parliament lasted for less than three years. Thus, in spite of the PR system of election which is commonly expected to lead to a fragmentation of parties, there has emerged in Ireland a party structure which has normally been dominated by two main parties, with a third party contending for influence but not within sight of power on its own account. A few other parties have been mostly of a transitory importance. The confrontation between the two main parties originated in differences over constitutional issues. So bitter and divisive was the hostility between the 'pro-Treaty' and the 'anti-Treaty' factions that the two political parties which expressed these differences continued to occupy the arena of conflict long after the constitutional issues which had divided them were largely resolved. The party system in Ireland was based on recent historical traditions rather than on social and economic differences within the community.

In all general elections the results tended to favour the large parties by giving them a more than proportionate share of the seats in parliament. The Fianna Fáil Party invariably gained a greater share of seats than of votes; and so did the Cumann na nGaedheal or Fine Gael Party, except in 1938, 1965 and 1977. The Labour Party on the other hand usually had a smaller share of seats than of votes. The results in favour of the largest parties are what one would expect under this electoral system when voting takes place in numerous separate constituencies. A small party can, however, obtain favourable overall results if their support is heavily concentrated in certain localities and if the party concentrate their efforts in those localities. In 1951, Clann na Talmhan put up only seven candidates in selected constituencies, and six were elected, although on a strictly proportional basis in the nation as a whole the party should have obtained only four seats. On the other hand, parties may dissipate their strength by putting up too many candidates where they have little chance, and little prospect of picking up later preference votes. Clann na Poblachta had high hopes of becoming another major party in 1948, and put up ninety-two candidates, compared with one hundred and eighteen for Fianna Fáil and eighty-two for Fine Gael, but only ten of their candidates were elected, instead of the twenty to which the party would have been entitled on a strictly proportional basis at national level. Similarly, Sinn Fein put up nineteen candidates in 1957, but only four were elected, instead of the eight which would have been their proportional entitlement.

As a rule, the fewer the number of seats there are in each constituency the greater is likely to be the advantage in favour of the larger parties, and successive changes which were made in the electoral system had the effect of substantially reducing the size of constituencies in the republic.

Under the first Irish Electoral Act of 1923, and modifications made by means of subsequent Acts, changes in the size-distribution of constituencies were as indicated in Table 18.1.

Table 18.1 *Size distribution of constituencies in Ireland*

Electoral Act	Number of elections	Number of constituencies of each size (number of seats)						Number of constituencies
		nine	eight	seven	five	four	three	
1923	5	1	3	5	9	4	8	30
1935	4			3	8	8	15	34
1947	4				9	9	22	40
1961	2				9	12	17	38
1969	2				2	14	26	42
1974	1				6	10	26	42

(There were no constituencies of six seats under any of the Acts.)

It is commonly held that to provide an acceptable degree of proportionality between votes and seats under STV the number of seats in each constituency should not as a rule be less than five. As Table 18.1 indicates, the whole tendency from 1923 to 1969 was for the number of constituencies having less than five seats to be increased. Before 1935 nearly three-quarters of the members of the Dáil were elected from constituencies having five seats or more, but from 1947 the number of these amounted to less than one-third and in 1969 and 1973 only 7 per cent.

One might have expected that because the average size of the constituencies was reduced the bias of the electoral system in favour of large parties would have increased. However, the advantages gained by one of the two main parties in some constituencies of a given size were usually offset by losses they incurred to their rival in other constituencies of the same size, so that neither party gained at the expense of the others from the reduction in the size of the constituencies.

Since 1969 there has been considerable interest in the extent to which the size of a constituency may be an advantage or a disadvantage to a party, depending on its share of the votes in that constituency. After changes in the number and distribution of constituencies of different sizes it was sometimes suspected that there had in some way been a 'gerrymandering' of constituencies by the government party responsible for electoral legislation, which was, from 1935 to 1969, the Fianna Fáil Party. However, Garret FitzGerald (foreign minister in the Fine Gael government of 1973 to 1977, and leader of Fine Gael from 1977), in describing how the pattern of votes in constituencies of different sizes might give a 'bonus' of seats to a particular party, stated that 'this feature of the STV multi-seat electoral system first became apparent in the 1969 redistribution in the Republic of Ireland'. (This was in his foreword to J. Knight and N. Baxter-Moore, *Republic of Ireland: the General Elections of 1969 and 1973*, p. 8.) There is no evidence that the size-distribution of constituencies before 1969 operated to any significant degree in favour of the Fianna Fáil Party.

In the general election of 1969, however, under the Electoral Act of that year, nearly two-thirds of the constituencies proved to be of the optimum size for the Fianna Fáil Party, and it was believed by the Fine Gael Party that this had been deliberately contrived. The number of five-member constituencies, which discriminated less against the smaller parties, was reduced from nine to two. The number of three-member constituencies was increased from seventeen to twenty-six, and these were located mainly in the western provinces of Connacht and Munster and the western counties of Ulster, where Fianna Fáil generally had about 50 per cent of the votes, and could therefore expect to win two out of the three seats in each of these constituencies. The four-member constituencies were concentrated mainly in Leinster, in the east, where the Fine Gael Party were strongest and could have expected to win two out of three seats in three-member constituencies, but where, if there were four-member constituencies, Fianna Fáil, with a smaller share of the votes, could still hope to gain half the seats.

In Dublin City and County, and in Dun Laoghaire, where Fine Gael usually had their strongest support, there were designated only two three-member constituencies and eight four-member constituencies, and in the 1969 election Fianna Fáil gained half the seats in seven out of these eight four-member constituencies. Here, and in the country as a whole, the party's changes in the size distribution of constituencies appear to have been very much to their own advantage, and they gained an absolute majority of seats in the Dáil. Moreover, with a smaller share of the votes than in 1965 they gained a larger share of the seats (their shares of votes and seats were respectively 47·7 and 50·3 per cent in 1965, but 45·7 and 51·7 per cent in 1969).

Nevertheless, when the 1973 general election was held under the same Electoral Act, and with the same size-distribution of constituencies, the results were entirely different. This time the Fine Gael and Labour parties formed an electoral pact under which the supporters of each were successfully persuaded to allocate their later preference votes to candidates of the other party, and thus present a united front in opposition to Fianna Fáil. The result of this was that although the share of first-preference votes which was given to Fine Gael and Labour showed a decline from a combined total of 51·1 per cent in 1969 to 48·8 per cent in 1973, the share of the seats which these two parties gained rose from 47·6 per cent to 51·1 per cent, so that the coalition secured an absolute majority in the Dáil.

In 1974, for the first time, the Fine Gael Party had the main responsibility for the passing of a new Electoral Act. Having experienced the consequences of an unfavourable size-distribution of constituencies in 1969, the government was resolved to rectify the situation for the next general election. In the Greater Dublin area the number of seats was increased from thirty-eight to forty-three, and in place of two three-member and eight four-member constituencies there were to be thirteen three-member constituencies and only one with four members. Elsewhere, in areas where the Fianna Fáil Party were stronger (west of Shannon, in Munster, Cavan-Monaghan and north Leinster) the number of three-member constituencies was reduced from twenty-two to eleven, the number of four-member constituencies was increased from four to seven, and four five-member constituencies were created where there was none before.

The results in the 1977 general election did not fulfil expectations that these changes in the size distribution of constituencies would benefit the Fine Gael and Labour coalition. On the contrary, the Fianna Fáil Party won 84 seats out of 144, which was the largest number that any party had ever secured in the history of independent Ireland, and it also secured an absolute majority of first-preference votes. Partly this was due to dissatisfaction with the coalition in the ranks of the Labour Party, whose supporters now gave a smaller proportion of their later-preference votes to candidates of Fine Gael; but it was also due to a decline in the first-preference votes of both these parties, particularly Fine Gael, so that the joint share of total first-preference votes which the two parties gained fell from 48·8 per cent in 1973 to 42·5 per cent in 1977.

In so far as Fianna Fáil resorted to 'electoral engineering' in 1969, and Fine Gael did likewise in 1974, the results of three general elections in 1969, 1973 and 1977 recorded one success and two considerable failures. The failure of 1973 could be attributed to the counter-effect of a successful electoral pact between Fine Gael and Labour; and that of 1977 was mainly due to a switch in the votes of electors from the coalition parties to Fianna Fáil. However, another conclusion to be drawn from this experience is that this form of 'electoral engineering' can badly misfire, and, if prior calculations prove to be wrong, the manipulation of constituencies can penalise a party instead of rewarding it. (The way in which this can happen was demonstrated in Appendix B to Chapter 3.)

If there was a 'gamble' by the Fine Gael Party in the 1977 election, it was a gamble which failed. In the Dublin area, where the size of all constituencies had been reduced by the Fine Gael government to three members each, it was Fianna Fáil which gained two of the three seats in five out of the nine constituencies. This helps to account for the fact that in this election the 'bonus' of seats gained by Fianna Fáil was greater than in any previous election except that of 1943, while Fine Gael secured a smaller share of seats than of votes for only the third time in all elections.

After the 1977 general election it was proposed by the new government that in future the responsibility for constituency revision should be transferred to an independent committee instead of being vested in a minister of the government. If the year 1969 was the first in which the manipulation of constituency sizes was put into effect, 1977 may perhaps be regarded in future as the year in which the hazards and penalties of such manipulation were recognised, and when, by common consent, the possibility of manipulation was removed.

The experience of three elections from 1969 to 1977 does, however, also demonstrate that erratic and disproportionate results are in any case likely to be obtained when constituencies are small in size. The larger the number of seats in a constituency, the more accurately proportional will be the allocation of seats to parties, and the smaller will be the bonuses gained or penalties incurred by parties with different shares of the vote.

The Irish electorate were not given an opportunity to decide upon the electoral system which was adopted in 1920, and again in 1922 and 1923. Since, under the STV system, the mechanism of counting and the means of achieving proportional representation are somewhat complex (Lloyd George professed not to understand them) it is doubtful whether an initial decision by the electorate would have been in its favour. Since, however, the method of casting a vote is simple, and that was all that electors were required to do, and since the results were manifestly fairer to all parties than the relative majority, the new system was before long generally accepted. In 1922, and again in 1923 when an Electoral Bill was debated, there was virtually no discussion of any alternative forms of PR, such as the list systems widely adopted at that time on the Continent. This may have been due to ignorance of this unfamiliar subject.

The first serious criticisms were made in 1930. They came from some supporters of the Fine Gael Party which were then in power, but which lacked an absolute majority in the Dáil and depended on Labour support. De Valera gained office in 1932, and in 1937 introduced proposals for a new constitution which included a provision that elections for the Dáil should not only be based on the principle of proportional representation, as before, but should be conducted by the method of the single transferable vote, which had earlier been used in practice but had not been specifically prescribed in the constitution. The new constitution also provided that after the first three years all future amendments to the constitution (including, therefore, the provisions as to the electoral system) should be subject to approval in a referendum. De Valera argued that this was a safe-guard against changes which might be made in the electoral system to the advantage of any party which might be in power. J. A. Costello, former Fine Gael attorney general, resisted the change, but the Fine Gael Party as a whole were not opposed to it, and in the referendum of 1937 the new constitution was approved by 57 per cent of the voters.

In 1938, de Valera, who had hitherto been in favour of PR, changed his mind and publicly criticised the existing system. This aroused so much controversy and opposition that he took no further action at the time. What had evidently altered his views was the failure of Fianna Fáil to gain absolute majorities in the elections of 1932 and 1937, and the need to hold further elections in 1933 and 1938, when the party did succeed in gaining the majorities desired. However, the Labour Party saw themselves threatened by any change in the electoral system, and Fine Gael, after a period of equivocation, now also became supporters of the existing system.

In 1943 Fianna Fáil again failed to secure a clear majority, and once again resorted to calling a fresh election, at which, in 1944, an absolute majority was obtained. However, in 1948 Fine Gael succeeded in forming a coalition government, and Fianna Fáil did not gain power again until 1957, when they had an overall majority of ten seats. De Valera, exasperated by Fianna Fáil's failure to achieve absolute majorities on several occasions, although they were consistently the largest party, resolved to attempt an amendment of the constitution which would change the electoral system. A Bill for this purpose was debated in the Dáil, the case for and against PR being presented respectively by Costello and de Valera, each of whom had, in the course of time, reversed his views on this subject.

The Bill for a change in the constitution was duly passed by the Fianna Fáil majority in the Dáil, and the necessary referendum was timed to take place on the same day as the election of the president of the republic, for which de Valera was a candidate. On that day de Valera was elected president by 56·3 per cent of the voters, but his proposed constitutional amendment was rejected by 51·8 per cent. One possibly decisive factor in the result was the support given to PR by the Irish Congress of Trade Unions. In Dublin, where the trade unions were strong, there was a particularly marked swing against Fianna Fáil.

A further attempt to change the electoral system from STV to a simple majority system was made by Fianna Fáil in 1968. The occasion for this proposal was a depletion of the population in the western counties through migration, largely to Dublin and Great Britain. The constitution required that each member of the Dáil should represent a population of at least 20,000, that the population represented by each member should be as nearly as possible equal, and that there should be at least three members for each constituency. One of the proposals submitted to a referendum included a provision that representation should take into account the remoteness and the area of constituencies. Another proposal submitted at the same time included a provision for the substitution of simple majority voting in single-member constituencies for the single transferable vote. In the referendum held in October 1968 each of these proposed amendments to the constitution was rejected by 60·8 per cent of the voters.

In the debate on the electoral system in 1958, Costello had argued that during the period of its existence the Irish nation had not had the time to create and foster many of those political traditions which help to maintain public respect for the institutions of the state. Some few traditions had been established, and one of these was to deal fairly with minorities. The nation should hold fast to that tradition, which was embodied in the electoral system. The electors, by their votes in the referenda of 1959 and 1968, showed not only, in the words of Costello, that 'their political education has advanced to such a point that they fully understand the working of the electoral system', but that the system itself was now a tradition of the kind which Costello had described.

REFERENCES: CHAPTER 18

For the political and constitutional background of the electoral system in the Republic of Ireland reference may be made to Nicholas Mansergh, *The Irish Free State: Its Government and Politics*; Basil Chubb, *A Source Book of Irish Government* and *The Government and Politics of Ireland*; and Maurice Manning, *Irish Political Parties: an Introduction*. The working of the STV system was commended by J. F. S. Ross in *The Irish Election System*, but unfavourably reviewed by Cornelius O'Leary in *The Irish Republic and its Experiment with Proportional Representation*. However, in a chapter on 'Ireland: the North and the South' contributed to *Adversary Politics and Electoral Reform* O'Leary indicated that he had changed his mind in favour of the STV system. In two articles in the December 1975 issue of the journal *Political Studies* it is represented that STV elections in Ireland have failed to achieve proportionality. These are by Peter Mair and Michael Laver, 'Proportionality, PR and STV in Ireland' and Michael Gallagher, 'Disproportionality in a proportional system: the Irish experience'.

Conclusions

The great variety of electoral devices, and the very different social, political and constitutional conditions in which they have been applied in each country, make it difficult to arrive at simple conclusions about the working of each system. Nevertheless, a study of the historical experience does reveal some distinctive examples of the reasons why particular electoral devices were proposed or implemented, and what effects they had in practice. In each case it has to be remembered that no single device operates in isolation, and the effects of each depend on its interaction with other parts of the electoral mechanism. An obvious example of this can be found in the working of the quota and/or divisor system which is employed – it may be one which is capable of achieving a high degree of proportionality, but if at the same time an 'exclusion clause' is adopted which prevents smaller parties from gaining representation, then the degree of proportionality which the system actually achieves will be correspondingly reduced.

One factor which may have influenced the adoption or otherwise of a proportional system is the nature of those systems to which a nation had been accustomed in the past. Countries may be more likely to adopt PR if they have already been accustomed to exercising a choice for more than one candidate in multi-member constituencies, or more than once in two or more ballots. The United Kingdom, which never adopted PR (except for university members elected by STV), had never experienced elections of any other kind than the simple majority, and since 1885 these have been held mainly (since 1949 exclusively) in single-member constituencies. Most other countries, before they adopted PR, had been accustomed to elections in multi-member constituencies with second ballots (Belgium, Luxemburg and Switzerland), or single-member constituencies with two or more ballots, if no candidate had an absolute majority in the first (Austria, Germany, Italy, the Netherlands and Norway). France also had periodically sampled different kinds of electoral system. In Sweden and Denmark, however, elections had been by simple majority in single-member constituencies before they adopted PR in 1909 and 1920 respectively. (In Finland there was no period of transition between the Estates system and the adoption of uniform and proportional elections in 1906.)

Looking to the wider social and political context of electoral reform, one may consider the influence of religious, racial and linguistic differences, and rivalries between economic interests and political parties. Wherever any section of the community found itself in an impotent minority, there was liable to be pressure for reform. The Catholics favoured reform, and were instrumental or helpful in securing PR, in Belgium, the Netherlands and certain Swiss cantons. In Southern Ireland the safeguarding of Protestant interests was clearly a principal reason why PR was proposed, and why, in the interest of securing agreement for Irish home rule, it was acceptable also to the Catholic nationalists. In Denmark, the presence of a minority German community in Schleswig-Holstein led to the introduction of the single transferable vote to safeguard minority representation; and the existence of numerous and frequently rebellious nationalities in Austria and Switzerland lent urgency to demands for some system of minority representation in those countries. In Finland, the Swedes supported PR to compensate for the abolition of the Estate of nobles, in which their influence had been predominant.

In recent times, liberal parties have had a special interest in the introduction or preservation of proportional systems, since they have generally been in a minority and in danger of extinction under majority systems. In the nineteenth century, however, they were commonly the leading party, benefiting from the majority system of election, and their attitude to PR varied from time to time and from place to place. As their representation in parliaments tended everywhere to decline, while the strength of the social democrats and socialists increased, they were faced with the prospect of a change from a majority to a minority party. They tended, accordingly, to give increased support to PR, but not always in time to be the chief instrument in securing this reform. It has already been observed that on some occasions it was the Catholics who were responsible for having PR adopted. In Italy and Luxemburg, however, where the liberals had already begun to suffer serious losses under a majority system, they were in favour of PR. In Denmark, the Venstre (Liberal) Party had consistently enjoyed an advantage from the majority electoral system, but when the left wing of that party split off to create the Radical Venstre, which formed coalitions with the Social Democrats, the dissident party favoured electoral reform and PR. There was an opposite situation in Sweden, where the Radical Liberals, under Staaff, were intent on shifting the balance of power to the popularly elected lower chamber in parliament, and regarded electoral reform in favour of PR as little more than a bargaining counter. It was only after the departure of Staaff that the Liberals supported the Conservatives in introducing PR.

The attitude of the social democrats and socialists was equally variable.

Everywhere, inevitably, the party had small beginnings, and as a minority they suffered from the bias of majority systems of election. Wherever electoral reform through PR gained recognition as a practical possibility, the social democrats and socialists tended at first to be in favour of such reform. As the prospect, or achievement, of universal manhood suffrage rendered it increasingly likely that the social democrats would achieve the status of a major or dominant party, it was the bourgeois and non-socialist parties which inclined towards a reform of the electoral system, and the social democrats commonly turned against it. The timing of this change in attitude was seldom such as to prevent the reforms from being carried out, and never succeeded in reversing the adoption of a proportional system. The social democrats, or socialists, favoured PR, and helped to secure its adoption, in the Netherlands, Finland, Italy, Austria, Luxemburg and Germany, while in France the socialists secured the adoption of the proportional element in the hybrid electoral system which existed between 1919 and 1927. In Sweden, on the other hand, the social democrats were at an early date already hostile to PR, but were unsuccessful when they opposed its introduction in 1907.

After the First World War, as the strength of the socialist and social democrat parties everywhere increased, to the point where they became the leading party or one of the leading parties, their support for PR correspondingly diminished. Within these parties, the attitude of members was divided between those who were primarily socialists and those who were primarily democrats, the former tempted by an exclusive enjoyment of power under a majority system of election, and the latter anxious to maintain justice and fairness in parliamentary representation through a proportional electoral system. It was in Austria, Germany and the United Kingdom in particular that the resolving of this dilemma created political and constitutional problems.

In 1966 the Austrian People's Party (formerly the Christian Socialist Party and conservative in their politics) declared their intention to secure a change in the electoral system in favour of majority elections, but before they had done so they succeeded in gaining an absolute majority of seats without reform of the system. At this time the socialists in Austria continued to favour PR, and having gained the largest number of seats in 1970 they joined the liberals in introducing reforms which made the electoral system still more accurately proportional than before. In Germany, also, it was the conservatives, or Christian Democrats, who wished to introduce a majority system in place of PR, but after a period of uncertainty the social democrats rejected this in favour of an alliance with the Free Democrats, who could well have been annihilated as a result of such a change in the electoral system. In the United Kingdom, on the other hand, the Labour Party turned against PR as their prospects of becoming a party of government improved, and from 1923 onwards this created a division between the Labour Party and the Liberals which effectively destroyed the alliance between the two parties.

In other countries, criticisms of the working of the proportional system seldom led to demands for the abandonment of a system of PR altogether, but only for modifications of the manner in which it was applied. Those modifications which were most often sought were changes in the area within which proportionality was to be achieved; or the adoption or rejection of *apparentement* between parties; or 'exclusion clauses' designed to prevent the representation or proliferation of small parties.

As regards the area within which proportionality was to be sought, the significance of the demand for a change was that the fewer the number of such areas the more accurate was the degree of proportionality, and the more favourable this would be to the smaller parties. The most accurate degree of proportionality was obtainable in a system which allocated seats proportionally in the nation as a whole. If, for electoral purposes, the nation were divided into a number of areas or constituencies, and if proportional allocation were to take place solely within each of these, then the allocation would almost certainly be less proportional in the nation as a whole, and the smaller parties would find it more difficult to secure representation. (The existence of numerous constituencies does not in itself mean that the allocation is less proportional or small parties are prejudiced, since proportionality may be more accurately achieved by allocating 'remaining' or 'additional' seats in two-tier or three-tier electoral systems, at an area and/or constituency level and at the national level as well.)

The history of the various countries reveals that the size of constituencies, or of the area in which proportionality is achieved, was rarely manipulated in order to *reduce* the degree of proportionality in any way. The tendency rather was to adopt measures which enlarged the areas within which proportionality was sought, increased its accuracy and improved the chances of smaller parties. In some countries there was no change. In the Netherlands the final allocation of seats has always been made at the national level. In Denmark proportionality has always been sought within each of the three main geographical areas. In Luxemburg the constitution prescribed four constituencies (or provinces) within which proportionality was to be achieved, and this number could not be either reduced or increased without a change in the constitution. In Switzerland, the constituencies for elections to the federal assembly, in each of which proportionality is sought, have all consisted of the individual cantons. In Finland, the Constitution Act of 1906 provided that PR should be secured within each of the constituencies, numbering between twelve and eighteen, and attempts at reform made later on several occasions were not successful in introducing a method of achieving PR at the national level through the allocation of additional seats.

In Norway, a constitutional amendment of 1919, establishing a form of PR, prescribed the number of candidates to be returned from each of twenty constituencies, within each of which proportionality was to be sought, and also prescribed that one-third of the seats in the Storting should be urban, which meant that the towns were over-represented. This last requirement was removed in 1953; and in 1973, although no reduction was made in the number of constituencies, their representation was changed to accord more closely with changes in population. In Sweden, fifty-six constituencies were established in 1907 – 9, within each of which proportionality was to be achieved, but the number was reduced to twenty-eight by the reforms of 1919 – 21. In 1970 a two-tier system was adopted by which forty national seats (changed to thirty-nine in 1976) were added to three hundred and ten constituency seats in order to improve the degree of proportionality at the national level.

In Italy, when PR was introduced in 1919, its application was confined within individual constituencies which numbered fifty-four in 1919 and forty in 1921; but from 1946 the 'remaining' seats left over after a quota had been applied at constituency level were distributed to parties at the level of the nation as a whole.

In two countries there was at one time a reduction in the area of proportional representation, but then a restoration of a larger area at a later date. In Germany, in 1919, when PR was introduced under the Weimar Republic, proportionality was sought at the national level as well as in constituencies and constituency unions. In 1949 proportionality was required within each of the Länder only, but in 1956 at the national level once more. In Austria, in 1920, 15 additional seats were allocated at the national level in addition to 155 seats allocated within 25 constituencies; but in 1923 proportionality was sought within each of four 'constituency unions', and not in the nation as a whole. However, in 1970 the number of constituencies was reduced to nine, corresponding to the Länder represented in the Bundesrat, and the number of 'constituency unions' was reduced to two, one each for upper and lower Austria.

Only in the Republic of Ireland was there a marked and prolonged tendency to reduce the size of constituencies within which PR was sought; and it was only there that an apparently deliberate attempt was made, for a period between 1969 and 1977, to 'gerrymander' the size of constituencies in favour of particular parties.

Since the D'Hondt system is imperfectly proportional and favours the larger parties, some electoral systems have, by way of compensation, permitted *apparentement* in order that smaller parties may share the same advantage by forming electoral alliances. The employment or otherwise of this device has varied considerably between different countries. In Switzerland, since the adoption of PR, it has always been permitted. In Belgium, no provision was made for *apparentement* in 1899, but it was introduced in 1919. In the Netherlands, *apparentement* between different parties was not permitted until 1970. On the other hand, *apparentement* was permitted in Norway until 1949; and in Sweden it was ended in 1952, when the Sainte-Laguë electoral system was introduced as an alternative safeguard for the interests of the smaller parties.

In Austria, *apparentement* was permitted in 1919, but not under the electoral system established in 1923. In Germany, this device was not applicable under the 'automatic' quota system of the Weimar Republic, nor was it included in the electoral systems established from 1949 onwards. For the allocation of seats in the Federal German Republic the Christian Democratic Union and the Christian Social Union were treated under the electoral law as separate parties, although they were political allies in the Bundestag.

Apparentement of separate parties was not permitted in Luxemburg, Denmark or Finland. In France, however, this device played an important part in the electoral system established in 1951 which discriminated against the Gaullists and the Communists.

The electoral systems used in different countries include D'Hondt, Sainte-Laguë, the Danish system, and quota systems with the Hare, Droop, Imperiali or other type of quota, and with 'remainders' allocated in different ways. In some countries the electoral system employs two or more of these devices for the successive allocation of seats to parties, constituencies, electoral areas, or in the nation as a whole, and finally to individual candidates. The working of these systems in each country has been described, but with such a variety of practices it is not easy to summarise their merits and disadvantages. The central problem which has influenced to the greatest extent the devising of the various electoral systems had been whether PR is intended to achieve the most accurate degree of proportionality and give the smallest parties the fairest opportunity to gain representation; or whether, in the real or supposed interest of stable and responsible government, a bias is introduced in favour of the larger or largest parties.

If accurate proportionality, and neutrality between large and small parties, is the object, then theory suggests that either the pure Sainte-Laguë system or the Danish system would be appropriate, if operated at the level of the nation as a whole. Where the object is to include a bias in favour of larger parties, this is achieved most directly by those electoral systems which include some kind of 'exclusion clause', confining the allocation of 'remaining' or 'additional' seats in a second or later stage of the election to those parties which have obtained a minimum number or percentage of seats or votes (or both) in a first stage of the election.

The chief practical objection to this device is the drastic effect it may have. If the exclusion clause is operated at the national level (as in Germany) a trivial number of votes may determine whether a party will be allocated two dozen seats or none at all. If it is operated at a constituency level anomalies are likely to be less serious, but variations in the size or constituencies may make it easier to surmount the barrier in some constituencies than in others; and one party may consequently gain more votes but fewer seats than another, only because it has been unfortunate in the distribution of votes between constituencies.

In other respects, also, anomalies and inconsistencies frequently arise. In the Netherlands, in 1933, a new exclusion clause *raised* the requirement from 75 per cent of the quota for one seat (equivalent at that time to 0·75 per cent of the national vote) to one whole quota; but when the number of members of parliament was increased from 100 to 150 in 1956 this automatically *reduced* the requirement to 0·67 per cent of the national vote. In Denmark, the quota required was *reduced* in 1961 from 60,000 votes (equivalent in 1960 to 2·47 per cent of the national vote) to 2 per cent of the national vote (equivalent then to less than 50,000 votes); but an increase in the population and in the electorate soon meant that 2 per cent again became equivalent to 60,000 votes. A small margin of less than 100 votes could (and did) make the difference between a party receiving four seats or none at all. In some countries, including the Netherlands, Denmark and West Germany, there has been much chopping and changing of the exclusion clauses which have been used.

Moreover, although the intention of these clauses is to exclude small parties and strengthen large ones so that these can form stable governments, the effect is sometimes the opposite of that which is intended. If a major party cannot quite secure an absolute majority of seats, but depend upon a small party for support, then the sudden loss of several seats by that small party because of their failure, by however small a margin, to surmount the exclusion clause barrier, may mean that the major party can no longer form a government. In Germany, for example, the precarious existence of the Free Democratic Party made it doubtful how long the Social Democratic Party could form a government. In Sweden, from 1970 onwards, the ability of the Social Democrats to form a government depended not only on how many seats they themselves gained, but also on whether their potential supporters, the Communists, succeeded in surmounting the barrier of the exclusion clause.

A less brutal, and possibly less invidious, way of discouraging the representation of small parties is to seek proportionality not at the national level but at the level of smaller areas or constituencies. As already observed, the more numerous and the smaller these are, the more difficult it will be, under a proportional system, for smaller parties to secure the election of their candidates. In Switzerland, which is in many aspects of public life a model of proportional representation, there has been a rather low degree of proportionality at the federal level, because proportionality has been sought in federal elections only at the level of each of the twenty-five

cantons or half-cantons. In view of the vigorous assertion of the independent interests of each canton, this has seemed a natural solution. It may be,
therefore, that wherever in a nation there are clearly identifiable regions a
proportional system based on those regions and not on the nation as a
whole may be widely acceptable, and there may be no need to resort to the
exclusion clause to limit the representation of small parties.

Such a solution would, however, discourage those small parties whose
strength is widely diffused through a country, rather than those, such as
parties representing racial or cultural minorities, whose strength may be
heavily concentrated in particular areas. Also, where regions are not clearly
identifiable, such a solution might not be easy to introduce, since the
designation of artificial constituencies or electoral areas could lead to
suspicions of electoral manipulation. However, the history of electoral
systems does not reveal many examples of serious clashes between parties
over the designation of constituencies or electoral areas (except perhaps in
the Irish Republic between 1969 and 1977), and on balance this type of
solution might be the most suitable.

A fundamental choice in the establishment of an electoral system is
whether or not it should, in the first instance, be designed to achieve proportional representation. If one sets on one side the historical experience of
the French, for whom electoral systems have been a series of experiments
or adventures, a contrast is evident between the United Kingdom and all
the other countries of Western Europe.

The majority system in the United Kingdom has been justified on the
grounds that in this country the function of an election is to choose a
government rather than accurately to represent political opinion. However, it would be difficult to maintain that in the countries in which PR
has been adopted it is *not* the function of an election to determine the
choice of a government. The historical experience does confirm that in
most countries having PR systems coalitions are commoner than single-
party governments, and that coalitions are formed more commonly after
general elections than before; and in such cases the election does not
determine the choice of government by 'direct democracy', but only
indirectly through elected representatives. (In Switzerland this has, since
1848, been formalised in the election of the individual members of the
federal council, or executive, by the members of the federal assembly.) Yet
it would, of course, be inappropriate to contrast 'direct democracy' as
being characteristic of the United Kingdom, and 'representative
democracy' as being characteristic of the countries having proportional
representation. So far as legislation is concerned, 'direct democracy'
through popular referenda has been virtually unknown in the United
Kingdom, but frequently practised in some countries having proportional
systems of representation.

Critics of majority elections have, on the other hand, recently raised objections to the two-party system, and the alternation of single parties in government, on the ground that in recent decades the 'adversary politics' this has generated has led to lack of efficiency, stability and consistency in government, with one party's measures being constantly reversed by its successor. It has been argued that this has had an adverse, and even disastrous, effect on social and economic developments.

Another merit claimed for the single-member constituency, and therefore for a non-proportional system of election, is the intimate relationship which this establishes between members and constituents. However, votes in parliament may be assumed to have a greater influence on the social condition of the people than the aggregate of what is achieved by members acting for individual constituents; the manner in which they cast their vote is correspondingly of major importance; and so also is the extent to which these votes represent the opinions of the electorate. The additional member system in the Federal German Republic offers 'personalised proportional representation', combining single-member constituencies with a list system of election. The objection is made that this creates 'two classes' of members of parliament, although German deputies claim that this makes little difference in practice.

Even if majority systems and single-member constituencies are justified, for the reasons stated on their behalf, this does not necessarily *explain* their existence in the United Kingdom. In his recent study of electoral reform in the United Kingdom during the period from 1906 to 1918, when many Western European countries adopted or were on the point of adopting PR, Martin Pugh has described the complex arguments and motives which determined the choice made by members of parliament between the electoral systems whose merits were debated, and how nearly on some occasions the decision might have been in favour of the alternative vote or the single transferable vote.

Finally, there is the question whether an electoral system is, or should be, 'entrenched' in a country's constitution, or in 'basic' or 'fundamental' laws which cannot be changed as easily as ordinary legislation. What significance 'entrenchment' has in practice in this context depends partly on *how* difficult it is to change the constitution, and partly on how the electoral system is defined.

It is common for a constitution to prescribe 'proportional representation' for the electoral system without defining how that is to be measured or achieved. It has usually been interpreted in such a way as to allow departures from true proportionality by limiting the size of constituencies within which proportionality is sought, or by imposing exclusion clauses. In the Irish Republic the constitution prescribes the method by which PR is to be achieved, which in this case is STV, but this has not prevented the manipulation of constituency sizes, which has affected the degree of proportionality achieved.

As regards the practice in different countries, there is of course no written constitution in the United Kingdom, and no constitutional provision for a particular electoral system. Nor is there any such provision in France, which is the only other country among those here considered which does not have a proportional system. In all the other countries except Italy and the Federal German Republic PR was either entrenched in the constitution when it was first adopted or else entrenched at a later date. In Italy, where PR was not entrenched, this opened the way in 1953 to the abortive experiment with the system of 'bonus' seats, giving any party or alliance with over 50 per cent of the votes the right to have two-thirds of the seats in parliament. The experiment was not effective in 1953 and was abandoned in 1956. In the Federal German Republic, also, there is no constitutional impediment to the abandonment of PR, but in spite of the endeavours of the Christian Democrat Party no such change has so far been enacted.

In all the other countries which have proportional electoral systems, this fundamental nature of the electoral system cannot be changed without an amendment of the constitution, or in the basic or fundamental law. In some of those countries a change can be made only by means of a popular referendum. This is the case in Denmark, Switzerland and the Irish Republic. In Austria the constitution provides for the holding of a referendum on constitutional amendments (and in certain circumstances, on ordinary laws) if there is disagreement between the two houses of parliament, or a demand for a referendum by 30 per cent of the members of either house. In Sweden the constitution provides for the holding of consultative referenda only, on constitutional and other issues, but the result need not be (and on occasion has not been) accepted by the legislature.

In France a reform of the electoral system could be introduced without a constitutional referendum; but if it were desired to incorporate the provisions for an electoral system in the constitution this would require the holding of a referendum. In the United Kingdom electoral reform could be achieved by ordinary legislation, but electoral reformers have sensed that there is more support for PR among the electorate than there is among the elected members of parliament, and have therefore proposed that a referendum should be held on whether or not a system of PR should be adopted for the United Kingdom.

Since social and political circumstances have varied greatly in different countries, marked variations have appeared in their electoral systems, providing different solutions to different problems. It would be presumptuous to conclude that there is any one system which is in every circumstance superior to all others, but one can at least gain some guidance from past experience. If one adopts the precept of Walter Bagehot, that the best form of government is that which people regard as the best, one may consult the electorate for an expression of their opinion. If there is a conflict of views about whether there should be a proportional or a majority system, this can first be submitted to a referendum. If the decision is in favour of PR, a system could be devised which would satisfy to some degree the main requirements of an electoral system, but would not satisfy any one of them completely if this were to render wholly unattainable the satisfaction of any of the others. A compromise electoral system might then be offered to the electorate on the following lines.

To satisfy the demand both for single-member constituencies and for fair representation of parties, the system could be based on the model of that which has been adopted for the Federal German Republic, in which the elector can cast one vote for an individual candidate and another for a party.

To satisfy the demand that the seats gained by parties should be as nearly as possible proportional to the votes they receive, the allocation of votes to parties should be by means of a divisor system, perhaps the D'Hondt system, but preferably the pure Sainte-Laguë or the Danish system as being more accurate.

To satisfy the demand that there should not be a proliferation of small and ephemeral parties, proportionality should be sought at a regional level, wherever regions can reasonably be identified, rather than in the nation as a whole. This is preferable to exclusion clauses, unless the barrier is so low that it cannot result in a handful of votes determining the allocation of several seats in parliament. Regions should not be so small that fewer than five members are returned from each, because this creates the danger that the size of constituencies may operate, or be manipulated, in the interests of particular parties.

To satisfy the demand that electors, and not parties, should decide the choice between individual candidates, there should be provision for voting for individual candidates on the party lists. The system of voting should be the single transferable vote, which is probably the fairest way of choosing between candidates as individuals. To ensure that the candidates who are nominated to appear on a party's list are themselves truly representative of the opinions of party members, a postal ballot of party members should be required, or subsidised if held. These 'primary' elections should be 'closed', that is to say, confined to party members, since opponents of a party should not be able to influence their choice of candidates.

The experience of different countries shows that numerous other systems, or combinations of systems, are possible. If there is a demand that the system should be based firmly on voting for persons as well as for parties, it is possible to use the STV system for the election of individual candidates, and the additional member system to ensure the proportional representation of parties, for which purpose the first preference of electors for a candidate could be taken to indicate their vote in favour of the party the candidate supports. Such a vote may, however, be intended primarily for the individual candidate and not for the party he supports. As a further refinement, therefore, it might be desirable to ensure that on this point the ballot expresses without ambiguity what the elector really intends. He could be given the option of a second vote to enable him, in such a case, to cast his vote for another party, or for none.

Selected Bibliography

American Statistical Association and American Economic Association, Joint Committee, 'Report upon the apportionment of representatives', *Quarterly Publication of the American Statistical Association*, vol. 17 (December 1921), pp. 1004–13.

Andrae, Poul, *Andrae and His Invention, the Proportional Representation Method* (Philadelphia: published by the author, 1926).

Association internationale pour le progrès des sciences sociales, *Annales: Congrès d'Amsterdam* (1865), pp. 57–9, 132–50.

Association réformiste pour l'adoption de la représentation proportionnelle, 'Conférence internationale pour la représentation proportionnelle, Anvers, 7, 8 & 9 août, 1885', proceedings reported in *La représentation proportionnelle* (Brussels, 1885), vol. 4, pp. 209–400.

Aubert, Jean-François, *Traité de droit constitutionnel suisse* (Neuchâtel: Editions Ides et Calendes, 1967).

Austrian Federal Press Service, Vienna, *Documentary Background of the General Election in Austria on October 5, 1975* (Austria Documentation, Ce 0035/0001/ 1–5).

Bagehot, Walter, *The English Constitution* (1867; repr. in *Collected Works*, ed. Norman St John-Stevas, vol. V, *Political Essays, The Economist*, 1974).

Barraclough, Geoffrey, *An Introduction to Contemporary History* (Watts, 1964).

Bergh, G. Van den, *Unity in Diversity: A Systematic Critical Analysis of All Electoral Systems* (Batsford, 1956).

Birch, A. H., *Representative and Responsible Government* (Allen & Unwin, 1964).

Birke, Wolfgang, *European Elections by Direct Suffrage* (Leiden: Sijthoff, 1961; repr. 1971).

Black, Duncan, *The Theory of Committees and Elections* (Cambridge University Press, 1963).

Blaustein, Albert B., and Flanz, Gisbert (eds), *Constitutions of the Countries of the World* (Dobbs Ferry, New York: Oceana Publications, in progress).

Board, Joseph B., *The Government and Politics of Sweden* (Boston, Mass.: Houghton Mifflin, 1970).

Braunias, Karl, *Das Parlamentarische Wahlrecht* (Berlin: Walter de Gruyter, 1932).

Brény, H., and Beaufays, J., 'Le rôle et la place de l'apparentement dans les élections législatives belges à la lumière du calcul de la dévolution des sièges selon différents modes', *Res Publica*, vol. 16, pts 3–4 (1974), pp. 205–17.

Bromhead, Peter, *Britain's Developing Constitution* (Allen & Unwin, 1974).

Burkett, Tony, *Parties and Elections in West Germany* (Hurst, 1975).

Burnitz, Gustav, and Varrentrapp, Georg, *Methode bei jeder Art von Wahlen sowohl der Mehrheit als den Minderheiten die ihrer Stärke entsprechende Zahl von Vertretern zu sichern* (Frankfurt-am-Main: Sauerländer's Verlag, 1863).

Butler, David, *The Electoral System in Britain, 1918–1951* (Clarendon Press, 1953).

Campbell, Peter, *French Electoral Systems and Elections since 1789*, 2nd edn (Faber, 1965).

Chubb, Basil, *A Source Book of Irish Government* (Dublin: Institute of Public Administration, 1964).

Chubb, Basil, *The Government and Politics of Ireland* (Oxford University Press, 1971).

Clark, M., and Irving, R. E. M., 'The Italian political crisis and the general election', *Parliamentary Affairs*, vol. 25, no. 3 (1972), pp. 198–223.

Clark, M., and Irving, R. E. M., 'The Italian general election of June, 1976: towards a "historic compromise"?', *Parliamentary Affairs*, vol. 30, no. 1 (1977), pp. 20–31.

Codding, G. A., *The Federal Government of Switzerland* (Boston, Mass.: Houghton Mifflin, 1961).

Cohan, A. S., and McKinlay, R. D., 'The used vote and electoral outcomes: the Irish general election of 1977', *British Journal of Political Science*, vol. 8, pt 4 (1978), pp. 492–8.

Conradt, David P., 'Electoral law politics in West Germany', *Political Studies*, vol. 8, no. 3 (1970), pp. 341–56.

Coppieters, F., *Parliamentary Elections in Belgium* (Institut Belge d'Information et de Documentation, 1974, D 1974/0255/91).

Cotteret, Jean-Marie, and Emeri, Claude, *Les systèmes électoraux* (Paris: Presses Universitaires de France, 1970).

Craig, F. W. S. (ed.), *British Parliamentary Election Results* (Macmillan, *1832–1885*, 1977; *1885–1918*, 1974; *1918–1949*, 1969; *1950–1970*, 1971).

Derry, T. K., *A History of Modern Norway, 1814–1973* (Oxford University Press, 1973).

D'Hondt, Victor, *Question électorale. La représentation proportionnelle des partis, par un électeur* (Brussels: Bruylant, 1878).

D'Hondt, Victor, *Système pratique et raisonné de représentation proportionnelle* (Brussels: Librairie C. Muquardt, 1882).

Dodgson, Charles (Lewis Carroll), *A Discussion of the Various Methods of Procedure in Conducting Elections* (1873; reproduced in Duncan Black, op. cit., pp. 59 ff.).

Dodgson, Charles (Lewis Carroll), *The Principles of Parliamentary Representation* (Harrison, 1884).

Doron, G., and Kronick, R., 'Single transferable vote: an example of a perverse social function', *American Journal of Political Science*, vol. 21, no. 2 (1977), pp. 303–12.

Dreijmanis, John, 'Proportional representation and its effects: the Austrian experience', *Parliamentary Affairs*, vol. 24 (1970–1), pp. 43–52.

Droop, Henry R., *On Methods of Electing Representatives* (Macmillan, 1868).

Droop, Henry R., 'On the political and social effects of different methods of electing representatives', *Papers of the Juridical Society*, vol. 3, pt 12 (1869), pp. 469–507.

Duverger, Maurice, *L'influence des systèmes électoraux sur la vie politique* (Paris: Armand Colin, 1950).

Elder, Neil, 'The Swedish general election of 1976', *Parliamentary Affairs*, vol. 30 (1977), pp. 193–208.

European Parliament, Commission Politique, *Pour l'élection du parlement européen au suffrage universel direct: recueil de documents* (Luxemburg, 1969).

European Parliament, Directorate-General for Research and Documentation,

Electoral Laws of Parliaments of the Member States of the European Communities (Luxemburg, 1977, PE.50.159).

Fears, J. R., *Political Parties and Elections in the French Fifth Republic* (Hurst, 1977).

Fenske, Hans, *Wahlrecht und Parteiensystem: ein Beitrag zur Deutschen Parteingeschichte* (Frankfurt-am-Main: Athenäum Verlag, 1972).

Finer, S. E. (ed.), *Adversary Politics and Electoral Reform* (Anthony Wigram, 1975).

Fusilier, Raymond, 'La représentation proportionnelle en Suède de 1909 à 1952', *Revue internationale d'histoire politique et constitutionnelle* (1954), pp. 257–69.

Gallagher, Michael, 'Disproportionality in a proportional system: the Irish experience', *Political Studies*, vol. 23, no. 4 (1975), pp. 501–13.

Galland, J. J., *La démocratie tessinoise et la représentation proportionnelle* (University of Grenoble, 1909).

Gash, Norman, *Politics in the Age of Peel* (Longman, Green, 1953).

German Federal Republic, Bundesministerium des Innerns, *The Federal Electoral Law in its Version of 1st September, 1975* (Bonn: 1976).

Germino, Dante, and Passigli, Stefano, *The Government and Politics of Contemporary Italy* (New York: Harper & Row, 1968).

Geyerhahn, Siegfried, 'Das Problem der verhältnissmässigen Vertretung: ein Versuch seiner Lösung', in *Wiener Staatswissenschaftliche Studien*, ed. E. Bernatzik and E. von Philippovich, Vol. 3 (1902), Pt 4, pp. 311–60 (Tübingen and Leipzig: Verlag von J. C. B. Mohr/Paul Siebeck).

Gilissen, John, *Le régime représentatif en Belgique depuis 1790* (Brussels: La Renaissance du Livre, 1958).

Goblet D'Alviella, Count (Eugène), *La représentation proportionnelle en Belgique: l'histoire d'une réforme* (Brussels: Weissenbruch, 1900).

Granger, Giles-Gaston, *La mathématique sociale du Marquis de Condorcet* (Paris: Presses Universitaires de France, 1956).

Grüner, E., and Frei, Karl, *Die Schweizerische Bundesversammlung, 1848–1920* (Berne: Francke Verlag, 1966).

Hagenbach-Bischoff, Eduard, *Berechtigung und Ausführbarkeit der Proportionalen Vertretung bei unseren Politischen Wahlen: ein Freies Wort an das Schwizervolk und seine Räthe* (Basle: Benno Schwabe, 1884).

Hagenbach-Bischoff, Eduard, *Die Frage der Einführung einer Proportionalen Vertretung statt des Absoluten Mehrs* (Basle: Georg Verlag, 1888).

Hanham, H. J., *The Nineteenth Century Constitution, 1815–1914: Documents and Commentary* (Cambridge University Press, 1969).

Hansard Society for Parliamentary Government, Commision on Electoral Reform (Chairman: Lord Blake), *Report*, (1976).

Hare, Thomas, *The Election of Representatives, Parliamentary and Municipal* (Longmans, Green, Reader & Dyer, edns of 1859, 1861, 1865 and 1873).

Herlitz, Nils, 'Proportional representation in Sweden', *American Political Science Review*, vol. 19 (1925), pp. 582–92.

Hermens, F. A., *Democracy or Anarchy? A Study of Proportional Representation* (Indiana: University of Notre Dame, 1941).

Hoag, G. C., and Hallett, G. H., *Proportional Representation* (New York: Macmillan, 1926).

Holme, Richard, *A Democracy Which Works* (Parliamentary Democracy Trust,

1978).

Hughes, Christopher, *The Federal Constitution of Switzerland* (Clarendon Press, 1954).

Hughes, Christopher, *The Parliament of Switzerland* (Cassell, 1962).

Humphreys, John, *Proportional Representation* (Methuen, 1911).

Huntington, E. V., 'A new method of apportionment of representatives', *Quarterly Publication of the American Statistical Association.* vol. 17 (1921), pp. 859–70.

Inter-Parliamentary Union, Geneva, *Parliaments of the World: A Reference Compendium* (Macmillan, 1976).

Inter-Parliamentary Union, Geneva, International Centre for Parliamentary Documentation, *Chronicle of Parliamentary Elections* (annual).

Irving, R. E. M., and Paterson, W. E., 'The West German general election of 1976', *Parliamentary Affairs*, vol. 30 (1977), pp. 209–25.

Jenks, William A., *The Austrian Electoral Reform of 1907* (Columbia University Press, 1950; repr. Octagon Books, 1974).

Kastari, Paavo, 'The Finnish constitution and its development', in *Constitution Act and Parliament Act of Finland* (Helsinki: Finnish Ministry of Foreign Affairs, 1967).

Kern, Paul B., 'Universal suffrage without democracy: Thomas Hare and John Stuart Mill', *Review of Politics*, vol. 34, pt 3 (1972), pp. 306–22.

Kitzinger, U. W., 'The Austrian electoral system', *Parliamentary Affairs*, vol. 12 (1958–9), pp. 392–404.

Knight, James, and Baxter-Moore, Nicolas, *Republic of Ireland: The General Elections of 1969 and 1973* (Arthur McDougall Fund, 1973).

Lakeman, Enid, *How Democracies Vote*, 4th edn (Faber, 1974).

Lehmbruch, Gerhard, *Proporzdemokratie* (Tübingen: J. C. B. Mohr/Paul Siebeck, 1967).

Lijphart, Arend, *The Politics of Accommodation: Pluralism and Democracy in the Netherlands*, 2nd edn (University of California Press, 1975).

Lijphart, Arend, 'The Dutch electoral system in comparative perspective', *Netherlands Journal of Sociology*, vol. 14 (1978), pp. 115–33.

Lodge, Juliet, 'Significance of direct elections for the European Parliament's role in the European Community and the drafting of a common electoral law', *Common Market Law Review.* vol. 16, no. 2 (1979), pp. 195–208.

Luxembourg Ministère d'Etat, Service Central de Législation, *Recueil de la législation sur les élections législatives et communales* (1974).

Mackenzie, W. J. M., *Free Elections: An Elementary Textbook* (Allen & Unwin, 1958).

Mackenzie, W. J. M., 'The functions of elections', in *International Encyclopedia of the Social Sciences*, ed. David L. Sills, Vol. 5, (New York: Macmillan Free Press, 1968), pp. 1–6.

Mackie, T. and Rose, R. (eds), *International Almanac of Electoral History* (Macmillan, 1974).

Mackintosh, John P. (ed.), *People and Parliament* (Saxon House, in association with the Hansard Society for Parliamentary Government, 1978).

Mair, Peter, and Laver, Michael, 'Proportionality, PR and STV in Ireland', *Political Studies*, vol. 23, no. 4 (1975), pp. 491–500.

Mair, Peter, and Maguire, Maria, 'The single transferable vote and the Irish general election of 1977', *Economic and Social Review*, Dublin, vol. 9, no. 4 (1978), pp. 319–27.

Manning, Maurice, *Irish Political Parties: An Introduction* (Dublin: Gill & Macmillan, 1972).

Mansergh, Nicholas, *The Irish Free State: Its Government and Politics* (Allen & Unwin, 1934).

Mill, John Stuart, *Considerations on Representative Government* (1861; repr. Oxford University Press, World Classics, 1912).

Miller, Kenneth E., 'The Danish electoral system', *Parliamentary Affairs*, vol. 18 (1964–5), pp. 71–81.

Miller, Kenneth E., *Government and Politics in Denmark* (Boston, Mass.: Houghton Mifflin, 1968).

Molin, Björn, 'Sweden: the first year of the one-chamber Riksdag', *Scandinavian Political Studies*, vol. 7 (1972), pp. 283–6.

Moureau, Léon and Goossens, Charles,'L'évolution des idées concernant la représentation proportionnelle en Belgique', *Revue de droit international et de droit comparé*, vol. 35 (1958), pp. 378–93.

Nanson, E. J., 'Methods of election', Inclosure 4 in No. 27, *Reports from H.M. Representatives in Foreign Countries and in British Colonies Respecting the Application of the Principle of Proportional Representation in Public Elections* (Cd 3501, 1907; paper originally presented to the Royal Society of Victoria, 1882).

Naville, Ernest, *La question électorale en Europe et en Amérique*, 2nd edn (Geneva: Georg, 1871).

Naville, Ernest, *On the Theory and Practice of Representative Elections* (London: Wildy Ridgway, 1872).

Nealon, Ted, *Ireland: A Parliamentary Directory* (Dublin: Institute of Public Administration, 1974).

Netherlands Embassy, London, memorandum: *The Electoral System in the Netherlands* (1976).

Newland, R. A., and Britton, F. S., *How to Conduct an Election by the Single Transferable Vote* (Electoral Reform Society, 1976).

Nguyen Quoc Vinh, 'La réforme du parlement suédois', *Revue du droit et de la science politique*, vol. 39, no. 2 (1973), pp. 395–484.

Nohlen, Dieter, *Wahlsysteme der Welt* (Munich: Piper Verlag, 1978).

Norwegian Ministry of Foreign Affairs, *The Constitution of Norway of 17 May, 1814* (Norway Information, UDA/121/74, 1974).

Norwegian Ministry of Foreign Affairs, *The Norwegian Electoral System (Parliamentary Elections)* (Norway Information, UDA/130/73, 1973).

O'Leary, Cornelius, *The Irish Republic and its Experiment with Proportional Representation* (Indiana: University of Notre Dame, 1961).

Olson, Alison G., *The Radical Duke: Career and Correspondence of Charles Lennox, Third Duke of Richmond* (Oxford University Press, 1961).

Pedersen, Mogens N., 'Preferential voting in Denmark: the voters' influence on the election of Folketing candidates', *Scandinavian Political Studies*, vol. 1 (1966), pp. 167 ff.

Petersson, Olaf, *New Trends in the Swedish Electorate: A Focus on the 1976 Election* (University of Uppsala, 1978).

Pugh, Martin, *Electoral Reform in War and Peace, 1906–1918* (Routledge & Kegan

Paul, 1978).

Pulzer, Peter G. J., *Political Representation and Elections in Britain,* 3rd edn (Allen & Unwin, 1975).

Rae, Douglas W., *The Political Consequences of Electoral Laws,* 2nd edn (Yale University Press, 1967).

Rokkan, Stein, 'Electoral systems', in *International Encyclopedia of the Social Sciences,* ed. David L. Sills, Vol. 5 (New York: Macmillan/Free Press, 1968), pp. 6–19.

Rokkan, Stein, and Meyriat, Jean (eds), *International Guide to Electoral Statistics* (Paris: Mouton, 1969).

Rokkan, Stein, and Torstein, H., 'Norway: the Storting election of September, 1965', *Scandinavian Political Studies,* vol. 1 (1966), pp. 237–45.

Ross, J. F. S., *Elections and Electors* (Eyre & Spottiswoode, 1955).

Ross, J. F. S., *The Irish Election System* (Pall Mall Press, 1959).

Royal Commission on Electoral Systems, *Report* (Cd 5163, 1910); *Evidence* (Cd 5352, 1910).

Rustow, Dankwart A., *The Politics of Compromise: A Study of Parties and Cabinet Government in Sweden* (Princeton University Press, 1955).

Sainte-Laguë, A., 'Calcul des probabilités. La représentation proportionnelle et la méthode des moindres carrés', Académie des Sciences, *Comptes rendus hebdomadaires,* vol. 151 (1910), pp. 377–8.

Schambeck, Herbert, 'Die Entwicklung des oesterreichischen Wahlrecht', *Jahrbuch des Öffentlichen Rechts der Gegenwahrt,* vol. 21 (1972), pp. 247–308.

Schepis, Giovanni, 'Storia dei sistemi elettorali in Italia', in *Enciclopedia del Diritto,* Vol. 14 (Milan: Giuffre), pp. 663–72.

Schmeckebier, Lawrence F., *Congressional Apportionment* (Brookings Institution, Studies in Administration No. 40, 1941).

Schütt, Eberhard, *Wahlsystemsdiskussion und Parlamentarische Demokratie* (Hamburg: Hartmut Lüdke Verlag, 1973).

Senelle, Robert, *The Revision of the Constitution* (Brussels: Ministry of Foreign Affairs, Memos from Belgium Nos 144–6, 1972).

Senelle, Robert, *The Belgian Constitution: Commentary* (Brussels: Ministry of Foreign Affairs, Memo from Belgium No. 166, 1974).

Smith, Henry Stooke, *The Parliaments of England from 1715 to 1847,* 2nd edn, ed. F. W. S. Craig (Political Reference Publications, 1973).

Seymour, Charles, *Electoral Reform in England and Wales* (Oxford University Press, 1915).

Sternberger, Dolf, and Vogel, Bernard (eds), *Die Wahl der Parlamente und Anderer Staatsorgane: ein Handbuch* (Berlin: Walter de Gruyter, Vol. I, Europe, 1969).

Storing, James A., *Norwegian Democracy* (Oslo: University Press, 1963).

Swedish Institute, *The Swedish Political Parties* (Stockholm: 1977).

Swedish Parliament, *Constitutional Documents of Sweden* (Stockholm: 1975).

Swedish Parliament, *Sveriges Riksdag: The Swedish Parliament* (Stockholm: undated, but post-1974).

Swiss Parliament, *Die Nationalratswahlung* (Berne: 1975).

Thomas, Alastair H., *Parliamentary Parties in Denmark, 1945–1972* (University of Strathclyde Survey Research Centre, Occasional Paper No. 13, 1973).

Thompson, Dennis F., *John Stuart Mill and Representative Government* (Princeton

University Press, 1976).

Törnudd, Klaus, *The Electoral System of Finland* (Hugh Evelyn, 1968).

United States House of Representatives, Sub-Committee on Census and Statistics, *The Decennial Population Census and Congressional Apportionment* (Union Calendar No. 628, House Report No. 91–1314, 1970).

Verney, Douglas V., *Parliamentary Reform in Sweden, 1866–1921* (Clarendon Press, 1957).

Vogel, Bernard, Nohlen, Dieter, and Schultze, Rainer-Olaf, *Wahlen in Deutschland: Theorie-Geschichte-Dokumente, 1848–1970* (Berlin: Walter de Gruyter, 1971).

Weill-Raynal, Etienne, 'La représentation nationale proportionnelle avec scrutin individuel', *Revue Politique et Parlementaire*, October 1966, pp. 23–9.

Weill-Raynal, Etienne, 'La réforme electorale, enjeu des prochaines élections?', *Revue Politique et Parlementaire*, vol. 75, no. 839 (1973), pp. 6–22.

White, A. S., *The Evolution of Modern Italy* (Blackwell, 1964).

Addendum

A newly published reference work on contemporary electoral systems in the countries of the European Community is:

Hand, Geoffrey, *et al.*, *European Electoral Systems Handbook* (Butterworth, 1979).

Index